FUNDAMENTALS OF INTERNATIONAL FINANCIAL ACCOUNTING AND REPORTING

FUNDAMENTALS OF
INTERNATIONAL
FINANCIAL
ACCOUNTING AND
REPORTING

Roger Hussey
University of Windsor, Canada

World Scientific

NEW JERSEY · LONDON · SINGAPORE · BEIJING · SHANGHAI · HONG KONG · TAIPEI · CHENNAI

Published by

World Scientific Publishing Co. Pte. Ltd.

5 Toh Tuck Link, Singapore 596224

USA office: 27 Warren Street, Suite 401-402, Hackensack, NJ 07601

UK office: 57 Shelton Street, Covent Garden, London WC2H 9HE

British Library Cataloguing-in-Publication Data
A catalogue record for this book is available from the British Library.

ISBN-13 978-981-4280-23-5
ISBN-10 981-4280-23-2

Typeset by Stallion Press
Email: enquiries@stallionpress.com

Printed in Singapore by B & Jo Enterprise Pte Ltd

Preface

This book, *Fundamentals of International Financial Accounting and Reporting*, is for students who wish to understand International Accounting or, to be more specific, financial statements that are issued by companies in compliance with *International Financial Reporting Standards*.

Over the last decade, we have seen an increasing number of countries and companies adopting the standards issued by the International Accounting Standards Board and abandoning the previous national methods they used to prepare financial statements. In the years ahead, even more companies will be issuing their financial results that have been prepared on the basis of international standards. Students at both the undergraduate and graduate levels need to know the importance and effects of these developments.

At the international level, the terms International Accounting Standards (IASs) and International Financial Reporting Standards (IFRSs) are both used. These standards deal with both financial accounting and reporting issues, and in Chapter 2 we will explain the origin and the use of these terms. There are times when the terms must be used specifically, but in general discussion they can be used interchangeably and we do this in some chapters.

The book focuses on the two main issues underpinning all financial accounting and reporting. One is the identification, or recognition, of economic transactions and events that should appear in a company's financial statements. The other is the methods and principles we use to measure, or place a value on, those transactions and events. The whole basis of being able to understand *International Financial Reporting Standards* is to be able to comprehend these core requirements.

No prior knowledge of accounting is required. Students are introduced in the earlier chapters to the purpose, structure and content of the main financial statements issued by companies. At the same time, those accounting standards that impact directly on these financial statements are explained and illustrated. In subsequent chapters, the remainder of the most important standards are examined. Each chapter has worked examples and excerpts from the Annual Reports of major international companies so that students can benefit from seeing actual company practices.

For undergraduate business students, this book will provide a strong foundation of knowledge on which to progress to advanced accounting for professional examinations. For students of MBAs or other related graduate courses, the book provides an academically robust and practical guide to the world of international accounting.

Acknowledgements

The author of any textbook is acutely aware of the support, assistance and feedback that has been received from colleagues and students over the years. My thanks go to them. I am also grateful to those companies from whom I have used extracts from their Annual Reports and Accounts to illustrate disclosure practices.

My final acknowledgements are to Ms. Yvonne Tan and the staff at World Scientific Publishing for their invaluable support; and to my research assistant, Chuan He, who assisted in the final preparation of the manuscript.

Contents

Guide for Students

The benefit and value of studying International Financial Accounting and Reporting is everywhere. We see its influence daily in the newspapers, on the television, and on the Internet. It affects every aspect of our daily lives: the wages and salaries we enjoy, our pensions, and the availability of goods and services. Companies, enterprises, firms, and other organisations need to make a profit; or, if they are non-profit organisations, to operate within their resources. International accounting measures how they succeed or fail.

In studying this book, *Fundamentals of International Financial Accounting and Reporting*, it would be very helpful if you could obtain the Annual Reports and Accounts of some major companies. Most companies will have websites where you can download them, or you can request for a hard paper copy to be mailed to you. These are very long documents, usually over 100 pages, but you do not have to read them all in one attempt. Use them as reference documents. If, in reading a chapter in this book, you want to know how companies account for a particular item, you can refer to your collection of Annual Reports and Accounts. You can also compare the excerpts we have provided in this book with the examples you have collected.

This book does not require any prior knowledge of accounting. For those of you who have not studied double-entry bookkeeping or do not understand it fully, do not worry. You can master everything we discuss without knowing the basic, and mechanical, techniques of double entry. If you wish to study it or refresh your memory on its main points, you will find that we have included the rules and examples in the Appendices.

It is important that you study and understand each chapter in the sequence it is presented. This is a subject where knowledge is built one stage at a time and you cannot skip chapters. You will find that key definitions are highlighted and the worked examples will help you to comprehend the points being made. You will also find Progress Tests at the end of each chapter. They are there to enhance your understanding and reinforce your knowledge of international accounting and reporting. The answers are given at the end of the book.

Whatever your career aspirations and irrespective of which country you live in, you will find that an appreciation of how businesses operate and how they account for their financial performance and financial position is essential. This book is your key to understanding the complexities of International Financial Accounting and Reporting.

1

Accounting Assumptions and Facts

Learning Objectives

At the end of this chapter you should be able to:

☞ Identify the four main stages of the accounting process
☞ Discuss accounting regulations
☞ Explain the assumptions and qualitative characteristics of financial information
☞ Describe the uses and users of financial statements.

1.1 Introduction

In this chapter we consider the many assumptions that accountants may make when producing the financial statements of an organisation. But before that we need to consider the reasons for doing "Accounting". Even on a personal basis, most of us do some simple form of accounting. We try to ensure that we do not spend more money than we have, we calculate how much money we have in the bank, and decide whether our savings for a vacation or for a special purpose are sufficient. We may also want to decide whether we need a loan and if we can pay it back.

Similarly, the owners and managers of a business will need financial information to make decisions and monitor the activities of managers. The purpose of accounting is to provide that information. The larger the business, the more complex it will be, and there may be various groups of people and individuals who require financial information or are legally entitled to receive it. It is the role of the accountant to meet these information needs. In doing so the accountant will be dealing with facts but will also be compelled to make certain estimates and follow various concepts and assumptions.

In most countries there is some form of regulation that specifies the types of organisations that must produce certain financial information on their activities and who the users are. This regulation may be part of the law of the country but is often in the form of accounting standards issued by a professional accounting body or some organisation specifically established for the purpose within that country.

> **Definition — accounting standards**
>
> Rules and regulations containing legislative and non-legislative pronouncements governing financial accounting and reporting.

Increasingly, countries are adopting International Financial Reporting Standards. These are issued by the International Accounting Standards Board. These standards set out the methods to be used to account for economic transactions and events. This improves the quality of the financial information issued by organisations and allows comparisons to be made on a worldwide basis.

In this chapter we will first discuss the process of accounting and then consider the assumptions that accountants make and those conventions, guidelines and requirements that accounting regulators publish. We will conclude the chapter by discussing the possible uses and users of financial statements. Our main focus is on large organisations in business to make a profit, and we will refer to these as "business entities". Most of our comments, however, may be applied to various types of organisations.

1.2 Definition of Accounting

> **Definition — accounting**
>
> Accounting can be defined as the recognition, measurement, recording and disclosure of economic events and transactions.

There are four main stages in accounting:

Recognising

This is the process of identifying an economic event or transaction such as the purchase or sale of materials, acquisition of machinery, damage to buildings or equipment.

Recognition determines what should be included into the financial records of an organisation and when that should occur. In most instances there are very few problems. The day-to-day operations of a business are easy to recognise. Companies may purchase raw materials, pay the workforce for converting them into finished goods and then sell them. There may be payments for rent, insurance, distribution, administration and many other expenses.

But how do we account for any finished goods that the company has not sold by the end of a financial period? How do we account for the fact that some customers have not paid or have disappeared and will never pay? If there is a major recession, how do we value any investments the company has? If we are trading with foreign companies and the exchange rates of the respective currencies change, what adjustments do we need to make?

For these transactions and events, both accountants and the users of information must be confident that the proper accounting treatment has been used. Users will also wish to be certain that the basis a company has used for the production of financial information is comparable to that produced by other companies and is comparable from one year to the next.

Definition — financial period

The period of time between one balance sheet date for which financial statements are prepared and the next balance sheet date. The period is normally 12 months. In some countries, companies may be encouraged, or required, to publish summary financial statements more frequently, either quarterly or half-yearly.

Measuring

We may have been able to recognise our economic event or transaction, but the next question is whether we can measure it with reliability. Traditionally, accountants have used a method known as historical cost accounting to record the value of items in the accounts. The value of the economic transaction or event at the time that it took place is the value that is used and, with some exceptions, stays at that figure in the records. This method has the great advantage of being very reliable (you know what was paid), but unfortunately, this method has some weaknesses.

Imagine that you had purchased a computer and a house on the same date five years ago. It is definite that the value of your computer will be a lot less now than what you had paid for it as developments in technology will have made it redundant. On the other hand, it is likely that the value of the house will have increased if you have a housing market which is extremely active with many buyers. In both cases, the historic cost is different from the present value of the items and, therefore, of little use for any decisions you wish to make now.

With some transactions and events we may have great difficulty in measuring the value. For example, if you have purchased the right to drill for oil and you have struck lucky, how much is that oil worth? It is obviously worth less whilst it is still in the ground, but how much less? Another example of difficulties in measurement is with brand names. Many of us will purchase clothes or equipment because it has a "brand" name. If that name attracts us to buying the item, then that brand must have value for the company that owns it. But how do we measure that value?

Recording

Economic transactions and events must be recorded if we are to have confidence in our books of account and be able to produce information that is reliable.

Definition — books of account

These are the books in which a business records its accounting transactions. It is now normal practice to maintain these accounting records on a computerised system, even for small businesses.

The usual method for recording transactions is known as double-entry bookkeeping. This method was developed in the fourteenth century, and a book written by Luca Pacioli explaining its use was published in Venice in 1494. The same principles are still used today, whether a manual or computerised system is employed.

You do not need thorough knowledge of bookkeeping to understand the book you are now reading, and we will not be referring to the subject in the main chapters. Some of you may need or wish to understand the basics of double-entry bookkeeping, and an explanation of the main principles is given in the Appendices.

Disclosure

Definition — financial statements

These are the statements summarizing a business entity's economic activities for an interim or annual financial period.

Disclosure is the communication of financial information to those who have a right to receive it or who have an interest in the activities of the entity. In most countries, certain people do have a right to specific financial information. These are usually the shareholders or those who have loaned money, such as banks, to the company.

All businesses, even the smallest ones, will have to prepare some form of accounts to satisfy the tax authorities in the country where the business is situated. The larger the business entity, the more people are likely to be interested in seeing financial information. With companies that have shares or other securities quoted on a stock exchange, there will be a requirement by the exchange to produce financial statements, at least annually, and possibly summary financial statements half-yearly or every three months.

A complete set of annual financial statements comprises:

- A Statement of Financial Position, also known as a balance sheet. This is like a financial snapshot of the business entity at **one point in time** and shows its financial position at the end of a financial period. The Statement of Financial Position will be dated on the very last day of the financial period. The main elements of the Statement of Financial Position are the assets that the company has, the investment by the shareholders and the liabilities of the company.
- A Statement of Comprehensive Income incorporating an Income Statement, also known as a profit and loss account. This shows how well or poorly the entity has performed over a **period of time**. The main elements of the Income Statement will be the revenue that has been received over that period of time and the expenses that have been incurred in generating that revenue.
- A statement of changes in equity, which shows certain transactions that directly affect shareholders.
- A Statement of Cash Flow, which shows from where the entity received cash and how it has used it.
- Notes that explain an entity's accounting policies and important matters relating to the other financial statements. The notes are critical to understanding how a company accounts for economic transactions and events and in this chapter we will use several excerpts from the notes to the accounts of major international companies.

The financial statements issued by companies are general purpose documents. That is, they are intended to meet the needs of several different types of users. In some cases the length of the documents may be explained by the fact that they contain information to meet a wide range of needs.

Even for modest-size businesses, a complete set of annual financial statements will be well over 50 pages and more for larger entities. Usually the financial statements will be included in a document published by the business known as the Annual Report and Accounts. This includes a substantial volume of information and can be over 200 pages in length.

As well as the information required by law, the stock exchange and accounting standards, companies use the Annual Report and Accounts as a promotional document. There are photographs, information on products and services and news of the company's charitable and environmental efforts. If we look at the entire document, a large part of it will be information that is voluntarily provided and is not governed by any regulations.

Many companies have the Annual Report and Accounts on their website. We recommend that you obtain a copy of the published financial statements of a company that interests you. It is best that you look for a company that is listed on a stock exchange. We produce below the Contents page of the Daimler Group Annual Report for 2008:

The above is a long list of material. In this book we will be concentrating on that part of the Annual Report that is concerned with the financial statements. For Daimler, pages 140–215 come under the heading of "Consolidated Financial Statements". In fact, the financial statements themselves take up only a few pages. The vast amount of material is in the Notes to the Financial Statements. As you work through this book you will appreciate that the Notes are very important for understanding the financial statements themselves.

1.3 Accounting Regulations

Many users will be external to the organisation and will want to have confidence that the financial statements are reliable and relevant, and to be able to understand how the financial statements have been drawn up. Unfortunately, there are several problems and issues at every stage of the accounting process.

Many years ago, accountants had considerable flexibility in deciding how to treat various issues and the requirements of the local tax authority frequently established some rules. As business became more complicated there was a need for countries, or the accounting profession or other agencies in a country, to publish guidelines and advice. This ensured that all accountants in that country accounted for economic transactions and events in a similar way. This meant that the users of the financial statements could understand the basis on which the statements had been prepared and would be able to compare the financial results of one entity with another.

The accounting regulations in a country are referred to as Generally Accepted Accounting Principles (GAAP) and consist of any national legislation, accounting standards and stock exchange rules. Accounting standards are usually the most substantial part of GAAP. This interaction between accounting standards and the law is illustrated in the following example from the Annual Report 2008 of the French company, Total. These extracts are taken from the Report by the Independent Auditors:

1) **Opinion on the consolidated financial statements**

We conducted our audit in accordance with the professional standards applicable in France; those standards require that we plan and perform the audit to obtain reasonable assurance about whether the consolidated financial statements are free of material misstatement. An audit includes verifying, by audit sampling and other selective testing procedures, evidence supporting the amounts and disclosures in the consolidated financial statements. An audit also includes assessing the accounting principles used, the significant estimates made by the management, and the overall consolidated financial statements' presentation. We believe that the evidence we have gathered in order to form our opinion is adequate and relevant.

In our opinion, the consolidated financial statements give a true and fair view of the assets, liabilities, financial position and results of the consolidated Group in accordance with the accounting rules and principles applicable under International Financial Reporting Standards, as adopted by the European Union.

2) **Justification of our assessments**

In accordance with the requirements of article L. 823-9 of French Commercial Code (*Code de commerce*) relating to the justification of our assessments, we bring to your attention the following matters:

Some accounting principles applied by TOTAL S.A. involve a significant amount of judgments and estimates principally related to the application of the successful efforts method for the oil and gas activities, the depreciation of long-lived assets, the provisions for dismantlement, removal and environmental costs, the valuation of retirement obligations and the determination of the current and deferred taxation. Detailed information relating to the application of these accounting principles is given in the notes to the consolidated financial statements.

Our procedures relating to the material judgments or estimates made by the management and which can result from the application of these accounting principles enabled us to assess their reasonableness.

These assessments were made as part of our audit of the consolidated financial statements taken as a whole and, therefore, served in forming our audit opinion expressed in the first part of this report.

3) **Specific verification**

We have also verified the information given in the group management report as required by French law.

We have no matters to report regarding its fair presentation and its consistency with the consolidated financial statements.

There are some terms in the above excerpt that you will not understand until you have completed this book. You can appreciate, however, that Total is following International Financial Reporting Standards and complying with French law.

In the next chapter we will explain how the growth of international business revealed that there were many differences amongst the accounting practices when comparing the financial statements drawn up in different countries. This resulted in the establishment in the early 1970s of the International Accounting Standards Committee (IASC), later to become the present International Accounting Standards Board (IASB).

The IASC issued International Accounting Standards (IASs) and the IASB now calls the standards it issues as International Financial Reporting Standards (IFRSs). There are approximately 50 International Accounting Standards and International Financial Reporting Standards currently in force and each standard provides authoritative guidance on the proper method for accounting for specific accounting transactions and events. Periodically, some standards are revised or withdrawn and new standards are issued.

1.4 Basic Accounting Concepts

To carry out their work, accountants have made certain assumptions or developed concepts to deal with economic transactions and events. Over the years, it has been found necessary to formalise these concepts so that accountants use the same basis in preparing financial statements and the users of those statements can better understand the information that is being communicated.

There are many concepts which are also referred to as assumptions, conventions, principles and axioms. Some of these concepts are known as "qualitative characteristics". This refers to the attributes the information should have in order to make it a valuable communication. For example, you would not expect the information to be biased or so incomplete that you misinterpreted it.

At this stage we are going to consider some basic assumptions used by accountants. Most of these are contained in the accounting literature. Some of the assumptions that we are explaining now you will understand more fully as we show you in later chapters how these are applied in practice.

Business entity concept

This assumption means that the accountant is preparing financial statements only for the activities of the business and not for the personal financial activities of the owners. The financial statements will inform us about the financial performance and position of the business but very little about that of the owners. We will be able to obtain information about transactions between the owners and the business (for example, the owners investing money into the business), but we will not have information about the activities of the owners that are not related to the business. For this reason, when you are preparing financial statements, it is useful to think of the business as an "entity" separated completely from the owners. When we examine in detail the requirements of accounting standards in later chapters, you will find that the word "entity" is normally used to describe business.

The consistency concept

This principle has two aspects to it. The first is that there must be a uniformity of treatment for transactions and events of a similar nature. An accountant cannot treat a transaction in one way and then change to another method for a similar transaction. Secondly, an accountant must use the same accounting treatment from one accounting period to another unless there is a very good reason to change. We will consider when a change can be made in a later chapter. The consistency concept reassures the users of the financial statements that accountants do not change their accounting methods to show a more favourable picture of the organisation.

The matching concept

If we want to know the financial performance of an entity for a period, i.e., how much profit or loss it has made, we need to account for the expenses it has incurred in that period and match them with the revenue it has generated. One of the International Accounting Standards that we will discuss in a later chapter is how we identify the amount of revenue an entity has earned in a financial period.

The money measurement concept

This assumes that only the items that are capable of being measured reliably in financial terms are included in the financial records. This usually causes no problems. If a company buys 20 tonnes of steel at $500 per tonne, then $10,000 is entered into the financial records. If a company has 100 employees and pays them each $300 per week, the weekly wage bill is $30,000. What the company is unable to do is to enter into its records how much those employees are "worth". They may be highly skilled and the company may not be able to operate without them, but a money measurement cannot be calculated reliably to account for this.

Another common example is where a successful business has built up a good "reputation". It is known for making excellent products, keeping to delivery times and offering an excellent after-sales service. You will not find a money measurement for these attributes in the records of the company. In Chapter 6 we will explain how the accounting standards permit companies to recognise and measure some items where there are difficulties in measurement.

Historical cost concept

We referred to this concept earlier in the chapter. The principle is that the value of assets is based on their original cost. No adjustments are made for changes in price or value. This concept has the great merit of being extremely reliable. If you wanted to know how much a company had paid for an item of equipment, you would only need to look at the payment.

This method also has some great disadvantages. A company may purchase some land in 1980 for $500,000. It may decide in 2005 to buy an additional piece of land which is identical in all ways to the original purchase but the price is now $650,000. How is the user expected to interpret this information in 2009? The most obvious question the user will ask is "What is the current value of the two pieces of land?"

There have been some attempts to replace historical cost accounting with a different method which better reflects current values, but there are several methods each with their own advantages and disadvantages. These methods make the information more relevant to the user, but the reliability of the information may be uncertain.

In recent years the IASB has tried to introduce alternative methods of valuation and we will consider these in later chapters. These alternatives are sometimes controversial and difficult to operate in changing market conditions. The IASB is constantly trying to improve the methods for different transactions and events, but a definitive solution to cover all eventualities has still not been found.

1.5 Underlying Assumptions

In addition to the above concepts or assumptions, there are two that are fundamental to accounting: the accruals concept and the going concern concept. These are so important that the International Accounting Standards Board has included them in a pronouncement entitled "Framework for the Preparation and Presentation of Financial Statements". This is an old document, also known as the Conceptual Framework, that was published in 1989 and there are proposals to bring it up-to-date. A revised International Accounting Standard 1, issued in 2003, has made some amendments, but further important changes are expected.

In this chapter we will refer to the Conceptual Framework as this is the most comprehensive document. You can think of the Conceptual Framework as a type of theory applied to financial statements. It includes two parts which are specifically concerned with concepts or assumptions. One deals with Underlying Assumptions, which it refers to as the accruals and going concern assumptions. The other part covers "qualitative characteristics" and there is some overlap with the assumptions we have discussed above.

It is important to remember that the Conceptual Framework is not a standard. It is the basis on which standard setters develop their pronouncements. If a company enters into a transaction or there is an event where no standard exists, the company can refer to the Conceptual Framework for guidance.

The accruals assumption

The IASB states that financial statements must be prepared on the accruals basis. It explains that transactions and other events are recognised as they occur and not when cash or any other consideration such as cheques are given or received. These transactions and events must be recorded in the accounting records when they occur and not when payment is made or received.

In some instances the transaction and payment may take place at the same time. You go and have your haircut and you pay for it immediately. You may decide to buy a car in 2009 and the dealer allows you one-year interest-free credit. Using the accruals basis, the dealer must record in the business accounts for 2008 the sale of the car although the cash will not be received until 2009.

To take a personal example to demonstrate the impact of this concept, let us say that you purchased a surfboard for $800. A friend of yours is very keen to buy it and offers you $900. You agree to sell the board on 1 June and that is when your friend takes the board but says he cannot pay you until September. Under the accruals basis, the sale takes place on 1 June and, if you were keeping accounting records, that is when you would record it. Unfortunately, you are now $900 poorer from a cash point of view. That is a problem, but it is a cash problem, and you must resolve that by ensuring that you do collect the money on the agreed date.

The going concern assumption

Financial statements are usually prepared using the assumption that the business is a going concern and will remain so into the foreseeable future. It is assumed that the business does not intend to or need to close down; it is going to continue trading. If there is evidence that this is not the case, for example, the company may have so much debt that it has to close, the accounts will be drawn up on a different basis. This will often entail looking at the "break-up" value of the business, which is likely to be much less than its value if it were a going concern.

1.6 Qualitative Characteristics

In addition to these fundamental assumptions, the Framework for the Preparation and Presentation of Financial Statements refers to the qualitative characteristics of information. These are the attributes that make the information in financial statements useful. There are ten characteristics and we will discuss these briefly and return to them more fully in subsequent chapters.

Understandability

It is essential that the recipients of financial statements should be able to understand them if they are to be useful. However, we are dealing with complex matters, so it is assumed that the recipients have a reasonable knowledge of business, economic and accounting activities and that they are willing to study the information carefully. The level of understanding required is frequently discussed and there is a strong argument that some standards are so complex that even qualified accountants have difficulty understanding them. One response to this criticism is that business activities have now become so complex this means that the standards that regulate these activities will also be complex.

Relevance

If the recipient of the financial statements requires the information to make decisions, such as to buy or sell shares, the information must be relevant to those needs. In other words, the information, will assist the user in arriving at a decision. To ensure the relevance of the information, we need to identify the possible users of the financial statements and the decisions they have to make.

Materiality

If information is likely to influence the decision of the user, then it is assumed to be material and should be included in the financial statements. The assumption is therefore based on the possible omission or misstatement of information and is aimed at ensuring that all relevant information is incorporated. Materiality is judged on the size of the item in the particular circumstances — it is not an absolute amount.

Reliability

Information is considered to be reliable when there are no material errors or biases. The user can therefore depend on the information to represent what it is intended to represent. With financial statements we are not looking for 100% reliability. In constructing the financial statements, accountants will be using the assumptions and concepts discussed in this chapter, but also using estimates because the information is not available at the end of the financial period.

Faithful representation

This characteristic supports that of reliability by emphasising that the information must represent what it claims to represent. This presents some difficulties due to problems in recognising and measuring some transactions and we will consider this issue further towards the end of this chapter.

Substance over form

There is always the possibility that an organisation will enter into a legal agreement that obscures what happened in actual fact. There have been cases where companies have legal agreements that specify a transaction is of a particular type but the reality has been otherwise. Financial statements must be prepared on the economic reality of the transaction and not the legal form.

Neutrality

Financial statements should be free from bias, and information should not be purposely selected or presented in such a way as to mislead the user. You will see that, to some extent, this attribute conflicts with the following one of prudence.

Prudence

Accountants have the reputation of being pessimists and this is due to the caution they exercise when making judgements about uncertainties. When financial statements are prepared, not all of the information will be available and there will be a need to make estimates. Accountants are likely to be cautious in the estimates they make.

Completeness

This characteristic supports the reliability of information. It is, however, impossible to provide detailed information on all the millions of activities that may have taken place in a large business entity. Financial statements are summaries and are considered to be complete within the boundaries of materiality and cost. The advent of the Internet has made more detailed information available for users.

Comparability

Users of financial statements of a particular business entity will wish to compare the progress of that entity over time and also compare it with other entities. It is therefore essential that the preparers of information are consistent in the way that they identify, measure and disclose similar types of transactions and in their approach from year to year. If the preparers decide to change their policy on accounting for a certain transaction, the users must be informed.

If we consider these qualitative characteristics, we can see that there are likely to be problems in applying all of them in each case. One of the greatest problems revolves around relevance and reliability. Usually, for information to be relevant, the user must receive it in time to use it and the information must be up-to-date (in other words, use current values). This timeliness of information is difficult to capture without losing some of the reliability of the information.

For accountants to prepare financial statements takes considerable time and effort. There is always a degree of estimation and uncertainty because not all the information is available at the date of preparing the financial statements. In trying to make information timely, a degree of reliability may be sacrificed. This leads to the question as to how useful is the information to the user in making decisions if there is doubt regarding its reliability. It is the responsibility of the accountant to determine where the balance between the two lies.

There is also a need to balance benefits and costs: the benefit of the information should outweigh the costs of providing it. This is an impossible calculation as it is extremely difficult to assess the benefits to the users, and some people may benefit who were not intended to do so. There is also the additional complication that the costs may be borne by someone other than the users. Standard setters and accountants must attempt to determine how the constraints of the costs incurred are likely to impact on the benefits of the information provided.

Some guidance has been issued by the IASB to resolve some of these issues. It states in International Accounting Standard 1(Revised), *The Presentation of Financial Statements*, that the application of International Financial Reporting Standards, with additional disclosure when necessary, is presumed to result in financial statements that present fairly the financial position, financial performance and cash flows of an organisation. There may be rare circumstances, however, where compliance with a particular accounting requirement leads to misleading information. In this case, the organisation can depart from that requirement in order to achieve a fair presentation. In doing so, it must give reasons for departing from that particular requirement and the effect of doing so.

1.7 Uses and Users

So far in this chapter we have discussed the process of accounting and the concepts and assumptions that accountants use in preparing periodic financial statements. We will finish this chapter by explaining the purpose of preparing financial statements and the possible users of financial statements as set out in the Conceptual Framework with revisions in IAS 1, *Presentation of Financial Statements*, effective from 1 January 2005.

The Conceptual Framework explains that it is concerned only with general purpose financial statements. These statements are prepared and presented at least annually by companies to meet the common information needs of a wide range of users. Two objectives of financial statements are identified:

(1) To provide information about the financial position, performance and changes in financial position that is useful in making economic decisions;
(2) To show the results of the stewardship of management, or the accountability of management for the resources entrusted to it.

Similar language is used in IAS 1 and both documents refer to other types of information that can be useful but is outside the scope of IFRSs.

The two uses are often referred to as the decision model and the stewardship model. To a large extent they are incompatible and it is extremely difficult to prepare general purpose financial statements that achieve both objectives. To explain the arguments we will summarise them into two extreme viewpoints, although there are various ranges of opinion.

It is argued that the decision model must provide information that is relevant and the most interested users would be the providers of capital, i.e., shareholders and lenders. Advocates of the stewardship model contend that what is most important is the reliability of the information and that there is a moral, if not a legal, obligation for entities to provide information to a wide range of users who may be interested in their activities; current employees are a good example.

The conflict between relevance and reliability impacts on the method of measurement you use, particularly for items on the balance sheet. If you adopt the stewardship model you would prefer the information to be extremely reliable, and traditionally, accountants have used the historic cost concept that we discussed earlier. If you believe in decision usefulness you would want the information to be relevant, which means that the value of assets must be their present value and not the historic cost that may be 50 years out of date.

This debate has been around for many decades and there has been a move away from historic cost accounting to various methods for measuring current values. This has led to heated discussions on the various methods used for current valuations, their reliability or lack of it and the unintended consequences on the financial performance and position of companies in various economic climates.

We will discuss these issues in subsequent chapters but an agreement is difficult to obtain, particularly on an international basis. There are different views on who the users of financial statements are, or should be, and on the information they need. The Conceptual Framework identifies the following as the potential users and the reasons for which they require information.

There are three basic types of decisions taken by shareholders who invest in a company. They wish to know whether to buy more shares, hold on to shares they already own, or sell part or all of the shares they own. In making these decisions, the investor will not only be considering the potential future of an individual company but the prospects for the stock market. In trying to predict the future, the shareholders will have one or both of two objectives. One is to achieve a regular and attractive income through the dividends received from the company. The other is to achieve a capital growth in shares when the company becomes successful and therefore its share price on the stock market increases. The owner of the shares can sell these at a profit.

Employees and their unions wish to assess the security of their jobs, employment opportunities and the security of their pensions. From the unions' position, they will be attempting to negotiate pay increases and other benefits for their members. Knowledge of the financial status of the company will be invaluable in these negotiations as the trade union wishes to evaluate the company's "ability to pay". Individual employees may be interested in their career prospects and security of employment within the company. Obviously, the future looks more attractive to an employee in a successful company.

Lenders wish to assess whether their loans and the interest will be paid. If the lender is short-term, it is likely to be interested in the current cash position of the company and how likely it is to change in the future. Long-term lenders will need information on the future stability of the company and the probability of the interest on the loan being paid and the loan principle being repaid at the end of its term. The long-term lender may also wish to assess the probability of the loan being repaid if the company goes bankrupt.

Suppliers and other trade creditors (Accounts payable) wish to know whether they will be paid and if the entity is likely to be a long-term customer. Some suppliers are particularly dependent on one or two large customers. If those companies go out of business, then the supplier will go out of business. If the customer is expanding, the supplier can feel confident about the future.

Customers want to know about the future of the entity, particularly if they have warranties or may require replacement parts or repairs in the future.

Governments and their agencies need to regulate and tax business entities and use the information in national planning and for statistics.

The public are often affected by the activities of large entities, whether it be through the donations the entities make to charities, the training they offer, the involvement with community activities or the pollution they cause.

In recent years, with the increasing globalisation of accounting standards, there have been some suggestions to revise the Conceptual Framework. The argument being put forward is that the primary users of financial statements are the providers of capital and that the information should be directed towards their needs which are decision making. Other groups are considered to be secondary users and should find benefits from the information made public.

1.8 Different Approaches to Measurement

The Conceptual Framework identifies four different methods for determining how to measure the transactions and events to be recognised and shown in the financial statements. Since the Framework was issued, there have been other proposals and some changes in the terms used. Each method has its advocates and its detractors and we currently use a mixed approach, with historic cost accounting being the most dominant method. The four methods given in the Framework are summarised and explained below.

Historical cost

This is also known as historic cost. Traditionally, this has been the approach favoured by accountants. Using this method, assets are recorded at the amount paid for them at the time of their acquisition. Liabilities are recorded at the amount of proceeds received in exchange for the obligations or the amount of cash to be paid to satisfy the liability in the normal course of business.

The great advantage of historical cost is its reliability. You know exactly how much was paid for the asset and there will in all probability be a paper trail that can be used to verify the cost. You know how much you have to pay to settle any liability you have incurred.

The disadvantage of the historic cost approach is the poor input that the information gives to users for decision making, particularly after the passage of time. Companies may have acquired premises, land and machinery over the years. If they were recorded at historic cost they will remain in the records at that amount. After several years, because of changes in prices, the values the assets are shown at will be out of date. Some companies still have properties in their accounts that were purchased over 50 years ago.

Current cost

This is sometimes referred to as replacement value or current entry value. For assets, it is the amount that would have to be paid if the same or similar asset was acquired currently; in other words, how much it would cost to replace that asset. Liabilities are valued at the amount of cash that would be needed to settle the liability.

Realisable value

This is sometimes known as current exit value. Assets are shown at the amount that could be obtained if the assets were sold in an orderly disposal, i.e., not in a bankruptcy. Liabilities are valued at the amount of cash that would be needed to settle the liability.

Present value

This is sometimes known as value in use. Assets are shown in the balance sheet at the discounted value of the future cash flows that the asset is expected to generate in the normal course of business. Liabilities are carried at the present discounted net value of the future cash flows expected to be required to settle the liabilities in the normal course of business.

We will use an introductory example to demonstrate how these concepts might be applied.

Example
Company A needs a loan but the only asset it has is a machine that is used in production. Company A knows that the bank manager will want to use the machinery for security and will ask its value. The company has managed to obtain the following information:

Historical cost
The machine cost $250,000 five years ago and is expected to continue to produce for a further five years. The machine will have no scrap value at the end of that time.

Current cost
As prices have increased over the last five years, it would cost $300,000 to replace the machine. This would be basically the same model.

Realisable value
As industry is booming and the machine has been well-maintained, the company is confident that it could sell the machine for $175,000.

Present value
The company believes that, after deducting all costs of running the machine, it will receive $100,000 in cash each year for the next five years from the output it will sell.

The problem is to decide what the value of the machine is. If we use historic cost we have the reliable purchase cost of $250,000, but the machine is half-way through its useful life. As we explain in Chapter 4, the company will depreciate the machine so the amount shown in the company's accounts is likely to be $125,000. They will have written off half of the cost of the machine over the last five years and will write off the remaining half over the next five years. But the amount of $125,000 is not intended to show the "Value" of the machine, but is an indication of the proportion of the original cost that has been already written off in the financial statements.

The current cost is the value of a new machine, but the machine the company owns is five years old. We could arrive at a calculated, but arbitrary, value by taking just half of the value of the new machine to represent the age of the old machine. This gives a value of $150,000.

The realisable value of $175,000 seems to be a useful guide to the value. Of course, there are often many circumstances where the company is unable to sell the machine. Also, how confident are we that there are likely purchasers willing to complete the transaction? This also poses the question as to why does the company not sell the machine as it would receive $25,000 more than the amount it has in its books? The answer to that is in the final method of measurement.

By keeping the machine and continuing to sell the output, the company will receive a cash surplus of $100,000 for the next five years. It is obviously better for the company to keep the machine rather than to sell it. There is one refinement that we need to make to this amount and that is the calculation of the present value of the future cash flows known as "discounting".

In Chapter 6 we discuss present values but at this stage we will explain the context. In making its predictions, the company is deciding that it will receive $100,000 each year for the next five years. The problem is that $100,000 in five years' time is not worth as much as $100,000 now. If you had $100,000 now you could invest it and by year 5 you would have significantly more than $100,000.

We need, therefore, to take all of the future cash flows of $100,000 and turn them into present values. For example, at 10% interest you would only need to invest $90,900 now to receive $100,000 in one year's time. That future $100,000 is therefore discounted to its present value of $90,900.

In future chapters we will be looking again at the various methods of measurement, but you can appreciate the difficulty in determining the "value" of an asset. You can produce values that are more up-to-date and more relevant to users' needs, but you are going to sacrifice the reliability of historic cost.

1.9 Capital Maintenance and Profit

In Chapter 3 we will look at the Statement of Income and the calculation of profit or loss. We will see that this raises some problems, and the Conceptual Framework mentions this issue but does not explore it. The difficulty is related to the use of historical accounting and a simple example will help.

Imagine that you purchased a machine for $5,000 which will last for 5 years. The cost of the machine is your capital — the amount that you have invested. Each year you sell the output from the machine. You pay for your running costs and make a profit of $1,200. At the end of five years you will have accrued a total profit of $6,000, but your machine needs replacing. The cost of a new machine is now $6,000, so did you really make a profit?

This is a very simple example but highlights the issue that in operating business, you need to ensure that you maintain your Capital. The Conceptual Framework identifies the following two types of capital maintenance:

Financial capital maintenance

This assumes that profit is earned only if the financial (or money) amount of the net assets at the end of the period exceeds the financial (or money) amount of net assets at the beginning of the period. In other words, you are as well off at the end of the financial period as you were at the beginning. Historical cost accounting uses financial capital maintenance in money terms.

Physical capital maintenance

This assumes that profit is earned only if the physical productive capacity (or operating capability) of the business at the end of the period exceeds the physical productive capacity at the beginning of the period. Historical cost accounting is not useful in this respect and we need to look at another form of measurement.

1.10 Chapter Summary

☞ Accounting involves recognising, measuring, recording and disclosing the economic transactions and events of a business entity.

☞ Financial statements summarise the financial performance of an entity over a period of time and its financial position as on a particular date.

☞ Accountants use various assumptions and concepts, many of which are formalised in a regulatory framework referred to as GAAP.

☞ Increasingly, countries are adopting the accounting standards issued by the IASC, now known as the IASB, to form the main part of their regulatory framework.

☞ There are two objectives of general purpose financial statements: to assist users in making decisions and to assess the stewardship of management.

☞ The underlying assumptions of financial statements are accruals and going concern.

☞ There are ten desirable characteristics of information. The greatest tension is between the characteristics of relevance and reliability.

☞ Several potential users of financial statements have been identified, but there is now a school of thought that the primary users are the providers of capital and financial statements should meet their needs.

☞ Although historic cost remains the main approach to measurement, various alternatives have been proposed to make measurement more current and more relevant.

This book is about "International Accounting", but often the same or very similar business and accounting activities are described using different English words. This is particularly true if you compare US and UK usage. To help you overcome this, we provide a guide to the most common terms in Table 1 and the relevant International Accounting Standard where appropriate.

As well as different uses of English terms, the International Accounting Standards Board decided in 2007 to change the titles of the main financial statements. This change is not mandatory so companies may still use the previous titles if they wish, although new or revised accounting standards will adopt the revised titles. The changes are shown in Table 2.

Table 1.   Meaning of various terms

Terms	Simple Explanation	International Accounting Standard
1. Revenue 2. Turnover 3. Sales	This is the economic inflow, usually payments or promise of payment, that an entity receives in a financial period	IAS 18 Revenue
1. Non-current assets 2. Long-lived assets 3. Fixed assets	A resource controlled by an entity that is expected to provide future economic benefits and that will be kept in the business for a long period, e.g., land, buildings, machinery	IAS 16 Property, Plant and Equipment
1. Accounts receivable 2. Debtors	People or other groups that owe money to the entity	
1. Accounts payable 2. Creditors	People or other groups that are owed money by the entity	
1. Shares 2. Stock	Money invested in the business in the form of risk capital	IAS 33 Earnings per Share
1. Finance leases 2. Capital leases	A financial agreement entered into by an entity for the use of an asset which appears on the balance sheet as an asset and a liability	IAS 17 Leases
1. Profit and loss account 2. Income statement 3. Statement of financial performance 4. Statement of Comprehensive Income	A financial statement giving the financial performance of an entity over a period of time	IAS 1 Revised

Table 2.   Revision of IASB terminology

Old Terminology	New Terminology
Income statement	Statement of Comprehensive Income
Statement of recognised Income and Expense	Items in one specific section of the Statement of Comprehensive Income
Balance sheet	Statement of Financial Position
Cash flow statement	Statement of Cash Flows

In subsequent chapters we will explain the purpose, structure and content of these statements. We will use both the old and the revised terminology so that you become familiar with all the terms.

Progress Test

1. Which one of the following statements is correct?

   a) Substance over form means that the commercial reality of the transaction must always be shown in the financial statements
   b) Materiality means that only items that are at least 10% of the total revenue of the company need be shown in the financial statements
   c) The relevance of information must always take priority over its reliability

2. Which of the following statements best describes the term "going concern"?

   a) The ability of a business to continue into the foreseeable future
   b) When current assets less current liabilities give a negative figure
   c) When income less the expenses of the business gives a negative figure
   d) The business is likely to be taken over in the next 12 months

3. Which one of the following terms best describes financial statements whose basis of accounting recognises transactions and other economic events as they occur?

   a) Cash basis of accounting
   b) Invoice basis of accounting
   c) Accruals basis of accounting
   d) The going concern basis of accounting

4. If a business decides to change its method of depreciating non-current assets, it would be contrary to the:

   a) matching concept
   b) prudence concept

    c) going concern concept

    d) consistency concept

    e) none of these

5. Which of these characteristics of financial information contribute to reliability, according to the IASB's Framework for the Preparation and Presentation of Financial Statements?

    a) Neutrality

    b) Prudence

    c) Completeness

    d) Timeliness

6. Which ONE of the following is the best description of "reliability" in relation to information in financial statements?

    a) Comprehensibility to users

    b) Freedom from material error

    c) Including a degree of caution

    d) Influence on the economic decisions of users

7. Which ONE of the following best describes information that influences the economic decisions of users?

    a) Relevant

    b) Reliable

    c) Understandable

    d) Prospective

8. Which of the following are the four principal qualitative characteristics of financial information as set out in the IASB's Framework for the Preparation and Presentation of Financial Statements?

    a) Fair presentation, relevance, reliability and comparability

    b) Relevance, comparability, materiality and understandability

    c) Relevance, reliability, comparability and understandability

    d) Materiality, comparability, reliability and fair presentation

9. According to the IASB's Framework for the Preparation and Presentation of Financial Statements, which of the following characteristics should make financial information relevant to users?

    a) Predictive value and confirmatory value

    b) Completeness

c) Faithful representation
d) Comparability

10. The accounting concept that tends to understate asset values and overstate profits in times of rising prices is:

a) going concern concept
b) prudence concept
c) realisation concept
d) historical cost concept

2

The Growth of Standard Setting and the International Accounting Standards Board

Learning Objectives

At the end of this chapter you should be able to:

☞ Discuss the development of national standard setting
☞ Explain the reasons for international accounting convergence
☞ Describe the structure and operation of the IASB
☞ Describe the procedure for issuing an international accounting standard
☞ Describe the structure and organisation of international accounting standards
☞ Explain the procedures for companies adopting international accounting standards for the first time
☞ Explain the role of auditing in standard setting.

2.1 Introduction

It was not until the 1970s that, in various countries, standard setting bodies and committees were established and the term *accounting standards* came into widespread use. The Accounting Standards Steering Committee (ASSC) in the United Kingdom was established in 1970. The U.S. FASB succeeded the Accounting Principles Board (APB) on 1 July 1973, two days after the IASC was formed. The process is still continuing. The Malaysian Accounting Standards Board (MASB) came into being in 1997.

Before 1970, it was normally the professional accounting bodies that issued guidelines, briefing notes and other documents to their members to help them. This system, however, was not sufficiently robust to ensure that published financial statements provided information that gave a faithful representation of the activities of the entity. The move to a more formal process with standard setters normally being independent of the professional accounting bodies and, in most countries, having some form of legal authority did much to improve the quality of financial statements.

In this chapter we will discuss the development of national standard setting bodies and some of the reasons for the differences in the accounting standards they have issued. The difficulties arising from these differences in standards will be examined and we will then trace the growth of international accounting standards. In the latter part of the chapter we will examine the operation of the IASB and the impact it has had on accounting throughout the world. We will also consider the procedures that companies should follow on abandoning their own national accounting standards and adopting international accounting standards.

Whilst reading this chapter it is important for you to remember that international accounting standards are dynamic and changes are continuously taking place, both in the number of standards being issued and in the companies adopting them. Canada, India, and Korea will adopt IFRSs in 2011 and several other countries have stated their intentions to converge with IFRSs in the future. There are also new standards being introduced and revisions being made to existing standards. In the last section of this chapter we give details of all the standards that have been issued as at 30 June 2009.

2.2 The Development of National Standard Setting

The demands and pressures of national political and economic environments largely formed the way that countries established their own standard setting body in the first instance. The structure, operation and authority of the national standard setters are shaped within existing national practices and conventions.

Standard setters work within a coalition of interests including reporting organisations, shareholders, the media, political groups, and others. The powers of these interested parties differ, and the need and desire of the accounting standard setters to gain the support of particular factions also vary. For example, the United States is notable because of the considerable statutory authority of the Securities and Exchange Commission (SEC) to participate in the standard setting process and the extent to which lobbying takes place. In the United Kingdom, support is more indirect, with the legislation requiring organisations to comply with accounting standards but with little direct government influence in the development of standards.

Of course, when countries use different accounting standards to regulate the financial statements produced by organisations operating within their borders, there is difficulty in comparing the financial statements of a company in one country with a company in another country. Much has been written on the reasons for countries having different financial accounting and reporting regulations and the main reasons put forward are:

(1) the source of external financing for companies
(2) the legal system in the country
(3) types of business organisations and ownership
(4) culture.

The source of external finance

> **Definition — equity**
>
> Equity is the residual interest that remains after deducting both long-term and current liabilities from total assets. The term is used to refer to the common shares of the company.

Businesses, when they first start, usually obtain financing from the founders or owners. This initial financing is referred to as capital or share capital for a small business, but you will find that the term "equity" is used as companies grow larger. Share capital is the amount invested in the business by the shareholders.

As companies become larger they cannot rely on the existing owners of the company to invest more. Companies have to seek external finance to fund that growth. The external finance can come from either individuals or organisations wishing to invest in the company or financial institutions willing to lend money to the company.

In some countries, such as the United States, the United Kingdom and Australia, the funding has frequently come from individuals or groups. These shareholders make an investment in the company and, if the company is profitable, they receive a dividend and their "share" of the company grows in value. In such countries there is usually a powerful stock exchange that regulates some aspects of companies' activities.

In other countries, such as Germany, France and Italy, the funding has often come in the form of loans from banks, family or other organisations. In these circumstances the lenders demand regular interest and will want the loan repaid at some date. They also normally have access to the financial records of the company.

Definition — stock exchange

A market for the sale and purchase of securities such as company shares in which the prices are influenced by supply and demand. The first stock exchange was established in Amsterdam in 1602. The basic function of stock exchanges is to allow public companies, governments and other incorporated bodies to raise capital by selling securities to investors. The secondary function, where the greatest activity takes place, is to provide a market in which investors can buy and sell securities already in issue.

Legal system

Countries have usually developed or adopted one of two legal systems. One is the common law system which is developed case-by-case and there are no general rules set out that could be applied in several cases. Countries such as England, Singapore and New Zealand have a common law system. Where a country has common law, accounting rules are not part of the law and are developed by the professional accounting bodies and/or standard setters.

By contrast, countries such as France, Portugal and Japan have a code law system. Where there is a code law system there is a wide set of rules to give guidance in all situations. Accounting regulations are often part of the law and are controlled by the government either directly or indirectly.

Types of business organisations and ownership

This is related to the different sources of finance and the size and complexity of the business. In some countries, small family- or privately-owned businesses are a significant part of the economy. When funding comes from the banks or a similar institution, the lender will be able to demand access to certain information as part of the agreement to lend money. Similarly, when the state has a significant interest in the company, such as in China, then financial information will be provided to the state.

In other countries there are large companies with their shares listed on the stock exchange. The shareholders are many and are not able to demand certain financial information. They must, therefore, rely on accounting regulations and stock exchange requirements to ensure they receive financial statements that meet their needs.

Culture

Culture is regarded as highly influential on the financial accounting and reporting system in a country, but it is difficult to define the direction and power of its influence. Research has classified countries according to cultural differences and there have been attempts to relate "accounting values" to the cultural classification. This research has helped us to understand why differences in accounting regulations in a country may arise, but has not been of much help in resolving technical accounting differences.

Although the above factors have been important in the past in explaining the different national regulations, they are overshadowed by the needs of an increasingly globalised world. For companies, particularly multinational ones, it is expensive and complex to draw up different sets of accounts for the various countries in which they operate. For investors, it is almost impossible to compare a company in one country with a similar company in another country.

Companies that conduct transactions with foreign suppliers and customers would find that a shared accounting language enhances ease of business and understanding. Investors, both large and small, need to be able to compare the financial statements of companies in different countries. For international capital markets to operate efficiently and effectively, international accounting standards are essential. Given all these reasons for introducing international accounting standards, the question that can be asked is why it did not happen sooner.

Definition — capital markets

A market in which long-term capital is raised by industry, commerce, the government, and other institutions. The money comes from private investors, insurance companies, pension funds, and banks. Stock exchanges are part of the capital market.

2.3 The Impetus for International Accounting Standards

In the latter half of the twentieth century, there were some highly publicised examples of very profitable companies in Europe that wanted to list shares on the New York Stock Exchange (NYSE). In order to do so, the profitable companies had to redraft their financial statements in accordance to U.S. GAAP. In some instances, the previously declared profit for a financial year turned into a loss. Thus, a conceptual inconsistency exists as the activities of a particular company in a specific financial period can show either a profit or a loss depending on which national accounting regime applies.

Possibly the most famous case is that of Daimler Benz AG, a German company that wished to list its shares on the US Stock Exchange in the early 1990s. To do so it had to reconcile the profit it had shown for 1993 using German GAAP with what the profit would have been if it had used U.S. GAAP. The net income, or profit, the company had reported in its German financial statements was DM615 million. After the company had made all the adjustments to comply with U.S. GAAP, the reported net income turned to a net loss of DM1,839 million. Such a huge difference demonstrated that the accounting at the international level did not make sense. To say that Daimler Benz either made a good profit or massive loss depending on which country's regulations you used is not acceptable.

Although Daimler Benz highlighted the problem, the issue of significant differences in national accounting standards had been recognised at an early stage. In 1973, national accountancy bodies from Australia, Canada, France, Germany, Mexico, the Netherlands, the United Kingdom and Ireland, and the United States established the International Accounting Standards Committee (IASC). The objectives of the IASC were:

- to formulate and publish, in the public interest, accounting standards to be observed in the presentation of financial statements and to promote their worldwide acceptance and observance;
- to work generally for the improvement and harmonisation of regulations, accounting standards, and procedures relating to the presentation of financial statements.

The above objectives were extremely ambitious for an organisation that was resourced very modestly and had no enforcement powers. The IASC intended to achieve these objectives by:

- ensuring that published financial statements comply with international accounting standards (IASs) in all material respects;
- persuading governments and standard setting bodies that published financial statements to comply with IASs;
- persuading authorities controlling securities markets and the industrial and business community that published financial statements to comply with IASs.

It is important to emphasise that the IASC was not established primarily to promote the growth of international capital markets. The reverse was the case and it was the increasing globalisation of markets and business that led to increasing pressure for international accounting standards. However, that pressure took many years to develop to the stage which we have now reached.

2.4 The International Accounting Standards Committee (IASC)

It is uncertain whether the IASC had, as its long-term aim, the achievement of standardisation with all accounting regimes being the same, or harmonisation where some differences are acceptable. In its early years, with scarce resources and little power, the IASC concentrated mainly on the harmonisation of financial reporting on a worldwide basis.

One major factor in promoting the role of the IASC was the reaction of the emerging economies. Many were attempting to establish themselves in international trade or to move away from command economies. The IASC offered a quick and viable way for establishing an appropriate and acceptable accounting regime. The standards offered significant flexibility, thus easing the process of adoption. The other benefit was that they carried none of the possible political implications from adopting the standards of one particular country.

A second factor assisting the IASC was the increased encouragement from several organisations and countries to pursue the goal of international harmonisation more rapidly and effectively. For example, the European Union (EU) had for many years been seeking accounting harmonisation throughout the EU by issuing Directives that were binding on all member states. In 1978, the Fourth Company Law Directive dealing with the annual accounts of companies was passed. The Seventh Directive passed in 1983 extended this to the preparation of consolidated accounts. However, progress was slow and the process cumbersome. Towards the end of the 1980s, the European Commission gave increasing support to the efforts of the IASC.

Definition — consolidation

The process of adjusting and combining financial information from the individual financial statements of a parent company and its individual subsidiary companies to prepare consolidated financial statements.

These developments encouraged the IASC to take a more proactive approach. It refined its earlier objectives and defined its role as:

- developing robust standards to satisfy the needs of international capital markets and the international business community;
- producing and helping to implement accounting standards that satisfy financial reporting needs of developing and newly industrialised nations;
- achieving greater compatibility between national accounting requirements and international accounting standards.

In 1995, the IASC embarked on an ambitious program in the next stage of its development — an agreement with the International Organisation for Securities Commissions (IOSCO) to issue a core set of standards. The "core standards" project resulted in fifteen new or revised standards and was completed in 1999 with the issue of *IAS 39, Financial Instruments: Recognition and Measurement.* These core standards reduced the number of alternative methods available to companies and established benchmark treatments and permitted alternatives.

IOSCO spent a year reviewing the results of the project, releasing a report in 2000. The report recommended that IOSCO members allow multinational issuers to apply IASC standards for cross-border listings. However, it also allowed its members to require reconciliation, disclosure, and interpretation, where necessary, to address outstanding substantive issues at a national or regional level.

Although the IASC was successful in the core standards project, in retrospect, it is easy to see that the work it was attempting to undertake was impossible due to the way that the organisation was structured and resourced. The IASC recognised the problems confronting it.

Firstly, too many of its standards allowed alternative choices in accounting treatment and were open to different interpretations. Thus, companies could claim to be following international accounting standards but still draw up financial statements that were not comparable.

Secondly, a major weakness in the operation of the IASC was that it did not have enforcement powers or mechanisms to obtain compliance. Thus, consensus could only be achieved by issuing standards containing sufficient flexibility to obtain widespread acceptance.

Thirdly, there were also structural and resource problems beyond the power of IASC to remedy. The members of the IASC were from various national professional accounting bodies. Many of them had no responsibility for standard setting in their own countries, thus reducing IASC's ability to influence and persuade national standard setters.

Finally, there was the question of how much independence the IASC needed from the professional accounting bodies to conduct its activities. The technical contribution of the professional accounting bodies was essential but was regarded by some as placing the IASC under the direct influence of one particular interest group. There were other interest groups represented, for example, analysts and academics, but professional accounting bodies were perceived as dominant. To some extent, this perceived dominance also weakened the possibility of achieving a mechanism for enforcement. Few would wish to allow professional accounting bodies, however well-intentioned, to make the regulations for worldwide accounting as well as having the power to enforce them.

Although there was a desire to make progress, the question whether the IASC could achieve the goals remained. Either a complete overhaul of all aspects of the IASC was required or a new body formed. The latter was the course of action chosen.

2.5 Formation of the International Accounting Standards Board (IASB)

The IASB was established formally in April 2001, but it took many years to arrive at that point. Although there was substantial support for the IASC, a number of organisations were looking for a more rapid and robust approach to internationalisation of accounting. Discussions on how the operation of the IASC could be improved gradually moved to proposals that included the structure and funding of the IASC. One mover in these discussions was a group known as G4+1.

In 1992, the three standard setting bodies of Canada, the United Kingdom and the United States met to discuss some of the accounting issues confronting them. A major problem was the proper treatment for provisions and the three countries agreed to work jointly in seeking a solution. Australia later joined the working group, as did New Zealand. This was the start of the G4+1 and an invitation was given to the IASC (the +1) to join them. The reason for this inclusion was mainly political, as the original English-speaking countries did not wish to be criticised for attempting to set an international accounting agenda unilaterally.

G4+1 addressed a number of major accounting issues from a strong conceptual basis and also became involved with discussions on the structure and effectiveness of the IASC. In the proposals that the group made on the future of the IASC, it appeared to many critics that the G4+1 would have increasing power over international accounting standards. The group denied that this was their intent, but there is no doubt of their influence in the way that international accounting standard setting has been established. In January 2001, it was agreed that the G4+1 group would disband as the IASB was ready to take over from the IASC. The G4+1 group cancelled its proposed future activities and submitted its current work to the IASB as potential future projects.

The activities of G4+1 encouraged the IASC to reflect and review its position. In 1998, a Strategy Working Party set up by the IASC issued a discussion paper. After extensive consultation, the IASC approved a resolution supporting a new structure. An independent organisation, the IASC Foundation (IASCF), would be set up and it would be responsible for four distinct bodies: the Trustees, the IASB, the Standing Interpretations Committee (SIC) and the Standards Advisory Council (SAC). Although the IASCF is the parent entity of the IASB, it is the latter body that is responsible for issuing accounting standards.

The objectives of the IASB are:

- to develop, in the public interest, a single set of high-quality, understandable and enforceable global accounting standards;
- to help participants in the world's capital markets and other users make economic decisions by having access to high-quality, transparent and comparable information;
- to promote the use and vigorous application of those Standards;
- to bring about convergence of national accounting standards and International Accounting Standards to high-quality solutions.

The IASC Foundation is not merely a figurehead. It has 19 individuals who are appointed as Trustees and act under the constitution of the Foundation. They must show a firm commitment to the IASC Foundation and the IASB as a high-quality global standard setter, be financially knowledgeable, and be able to meet the time commitment.

It is the responsibility of the Trustees to appoint the members of the IASB, the SIC, and the SAC. The Trustees' other duties include reviewing external events affecting accounting standards and the strategy of the IASB and its effectiveness in operation. The Foundation also approves the annual budget of the IASB and determines the basis for funding.

The resourcing of the IASB is different compared to the IASC. It is the responsibility of the Trustees to secure sufficient funding for the IASB to operate effectively and the IASB has a budget of approximately US$18 million per year. This funding greatly exceeds the modest funding of its predecessor.

The IASB and IOSCO continue to work together to resolve outstanding accounting and reporting issues and to identify areas where new standards are needed. IOSCO representatives sit as observers on the SIC.

2.6 Structure of the IASB

The IASC Foundation is an independent organisation with the Trustees and the IASB, as well as the SAC and the SIC. Of the 22 Trustees, there are six from North America, six from Europe, six from Asia-Oceania, and four others from any area, as long as geographic balance is maintained. The International Federation of Accountants (IFAC) suggests candidates to fill five of the 19 Trustee seats. International organisations of preparers, users, and academics suggest one candidate from each group. The remaining 11 Trustees are "at-large" in that they are not selected through the constituency nomination process.

The IASB has 16 members and has sole responsibility for setting accounting standards. The foremost qualification for Board membership is technical expertise. The Trustees exercise their best judgment to ensure that any particular constituency or regional interest does not dominate the Board. At least five Board members have backgrounds as practising auditors, at least three have backgrounds in the preparation of financial statements, at least three have backgrounds as users of financial statements, and at least one has an academic background.

The SAC provides a forum for further groups and individuals having diverse geographic and functional backgrounds to give advice to the Board and, at times, to advise the Trustees.

The SIC, later to become the International Financial Reporting Interpretations Committee (IFRIC), reviews accounting issues that are likely to receive divergent or unacceptable treatment in the absence of authoritative guidance, with a view to reaching consensus as to the appropriate accounting treatment. In developing interpretations, the Committee works closely with similar national committees. Members are appointed by the Trustees. In making appointments, the Trustees aim for a reasonably broad geographical representation. Many of the members are practising accountants with technical expertise. Membership also includes representation of accountants in industry and users of financial statements.

On 1 February 2009 an IASCF Monitoring Board was established to serve as a link between the IASCF and the capital markets. This move was a response to the tremendous economic turmoil that had been experienced throughout the world and was aimed to assist those capital market authorities that allow or require the use of IFRS in their jurisdictions. The members are the relevant leaders of the European Commission, the Japanese Financial Services Agency, the US Securities and Exchange Commission, the Emerging Markets Committee of IOSCO, and the Technical Committee of IOSCO.

The responsibilities of the Monitoring Board will be:

- to participate in the process for appointing Trustees and to approve the appointment of Trustees according to the guidelines set out in the IASC Foundation's Constitution;
- to review and provide advice to the Trustees on their fulfilment of the responsibilities set out in IASC Foundation's Constitution. The Trustees will make an annual written report to the Monitoring Board.

The Monitoring Board will have oversight responsibilities in relation to the Trustees and their oversight of the IASB's activities, in particular the agenda-setting process and the "IASB's efforts to improve the accuracy and effectiveness of financial reporting and to protect investors". The oversight responsibilities of the Monitoring Board will neither change the interactions between the Trustees and the IASB nor alter the Trustees' responsibilities as described in the IASCF Constitution.

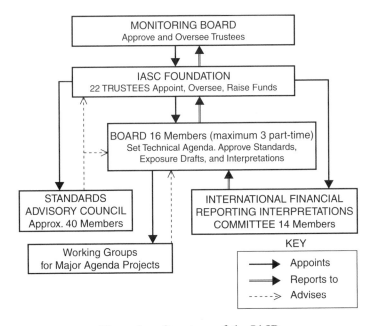

Figure 1.   **Structure of the IASB**

2.7 Funding and Operation of the IASB

One crucial element in establishing the IASB was that it would have sufficient resources to carry out the responsibilities placed upon it. The task of securing those funds rests with the Trustees. In the first year, a budget was set of approximately £12 million and in 2001 a total of 188 corporations, associations and other institutions provided the financial support. Some of these supporters are known as underwriters and they gave five-year pledges of between US$100,000 and US$200,000 annually.

The basis of funding has not changed much over the years. Although there has been an increase in expenditure, the IASCF had managed to build up a reserve fund of £11 million by the date of the 2003 Annual Report and Accounts. It lost US$1 million through the demise of Arthur Anderson, but the Trustees continue to find additional supporters.

There have been concerns expressed on the possible threat to the IASB if it is dependent on certain organisations for part of its resources. This has not, at this stage, presented a major issue and the Trustees are seeking ways of funding operations that would not lead to perceptions of possible influence from fund providers and that the source of funds are regular and reliable.

A preferred model would be to require those parties who benefit from the work of the IASB to fund it. Unfortunately, this would be very difficult to apply at the international level. In addition, the national standard setters have different models for their resourcing so there is not an immediate apparent way for building on those models. For example, the FASB raises two-thirds of its operating costs from the sale of publications, whereas the IASB is closer to a mere 10%.

In 2004, as part of its update on the Constitution Review, the Trustees started to explore ways of ensuring a more stable resourcing platform. At the same time, they are aware that the increasing number of countries using IFRSs places even more demands on the resources. A large part of the work that the IASB does is already being supported by many organisations that contribute time and effort. Without this support, the Board would not be able to continue its operations at the current level.

In many respects, the process of standard setting by the IASB is little different from many national bodies. Board members, members of the SAC, national standard setters, securities regulators, other organisations and individuals and the IASB staff are encouraged to submit suggestions for new topics which might be the subject of a standard.

Having established an accounting issue, there is a lengthy procedure to ensure wide consultation and full consideration of problems and alternative solutions. The IASB may decide to establish an Advisory Committee to give advice on the issues arising in the project. Consultation with the Advisory Committee and the SAC occurs throughout the project. It is also usual for the IASB to issue Discussion Documents that are circulated widely for public response. Field tests, both in developed countries and in emerging markets, may be made as the project progresses to ensure that proposals are practical and workable around the world. The IASB does not have monitoring and enforcement powers and these reside at the national level.

After comments have been received and examined and field tests conducted, the IASB publishes an Exposure Draft for public comment. The Exposure Draft takes the same form and content of what is expected to be the final standard, although there remains an opportunity for changes to be made. After considering comments on the Exposure Draft, the IASB issues a final International Financial Reporting Standard (IFRS).

It is essential that the IASB follows a due process in setting standards. Failure to do so would lead to criticisms and the possible non-acceptance by some countries of standards issued. The formal due process for projects normally, but not necessarily, involves the following steps. The steps that are required by the IASC Foundation Constitution are indicated by an asterisk*:

- ask the staff to identify and review the issues associated with the topic and to consider the application of the Framework to the issues;
- study national accounting requirements and practice and exchange views about the issues with national standard setters;
- consult the Standards Advisory Council about the advisability of adding the topic to the IASB's agenda*;
- form an advisory group (generally called a "working group") to advise the IASB and its staff on the project;
- publish for public comment a discussion document;
- publish for public comment an exposure draft approved by votes of at least nine IASB members, including any dissenting opinions held by IASB members (in exposure drafts, dissenting opinions are referred to as "alternative views")*;
- publish within an exposure draft a basis for conclusions;
- consider all comments received within the comment period on discussion documents and exposure drafts*;
- consider the desirability of holding a public hearing and the desirability of conducting field tests and, if considered desirable, holding such hearings and conducting such tests;
- approve a standard by votes of at least nine IASB members and include in the published standard any dissenting opinions*; and
- publish within a standard a basis for conclusions, explaining, among other things, the steps in the IASB's due process and how the IASB dealt with public comments on the exposure draft.

In April 2001, the IASB announced that future accounting standards would be called "International Financial Reporting Standards" (IFRSs). Standards issued by the IASC that are still in circulation are referred to as "International Accounting Standards" (IASs).

The International Financial Reporting Interpretations Committee (IFRIC) is the successor to the SIC. It is responsible for interpreting requirements of standards that may be capable of being applied in a way other than that intended by the IASB or issues that have not yet been addressed by a standard. It is not the role of IFRIC to provide advice to individuals or groups.

The IFRIC (until 2002 known as the Standing Interpretations Committee) has 14 members appointed by the Trustees for terms of three years. IFRIC members are not salaried but their expenses are reimbursed. IFRIC meets approximately every other month at meetings that are open to public observation. Approval of Drafts or final Interpretations requires that not more than three voting members vote against the Draft or final Interpretation. IFRIC is chaired by a non-voting chair who can be one of the members of the IASB, the Director of Technical Activities, or a member of the IASB's senior technical staff.

The Committee develops Draft Interpretations (numbered D1, D2, etc.) and releases these for public comment. When approved by IFRIC, they are sent to the IASB for review, approval and release as Final Interpretations. Organisations cannot claim that their financial statements comply with IFRSs unless they comply with both the requirements of the standard and any interpretation that has been issued.

Meetings of the IASB, the SAC and the IFRIC are open to public observation. However, certain discussions (primarily selection, appointment and other personnel issues) are held in private. The IASB is investigating the greater use of technology to make it easier for interested parties, who are prevented by geographical distances, to be more involved in its procedures. The IASB liaises directly with eight national standard setting bodies. These are: Australia, Canada, France, Germany, Japan, New Zealand, United Kingdom, and the United States.

For standards to be effective, some form of monitoring and enforcement is required. The IASB does not have direct powers or procedures to ensure this but some mechanisms are already available or are being created. The IASB, however, has to rely on the mechanisms in place in individual countries to ensure enforcement.

The first stage of monitoring for compliance is at the internal level where control systems, including internal audit, can ensure that standards are applied. This is reinforced by external auditors who are independent and have necessary expertise. The commitment of management is also required to ensure that financial statements fairly represent the financial performance and position of the organisation.

Definition — internal audit

An examination of the procedures and records of an organisation carried out on its own behalf to ensure that its own internal controls are operating satisfactorily. The internal audit may also be used to conduct investigations to detect any possible theft or fraud.

A second stage in ensuring compliance with international accounting standards is an audit conducted by an auditor who is independent of the company. An audit will involve an examination of the procedures, processes and records of the company and the financial statements that are drawn from those records. The auditor will express an opinion on those financial statements. There are different national rules on the status of organisations that require an external audit. At a minimum, an external audit is usually required by those companies whose shares are listed on a stock exchange and the auditors are reporting their opinion to the shareholders. Below we provide excerpts from the Auditor's Report of Sinopec which complies with China Accounting Standards and not international accounting standards.

Sinopec

Opinion

In our opinion, the financial statements comply with the requirements of China Accounting Standards for Business Enterprises (2006) issued by the Ministry of Finance of the People's Republic of China and present fairly, in all material respects, the consolidated financial position and financial position of the Company as at 31 December 2008, and the consolidated results of operations and results of operations and the consolidated cash flows and cash flows of the Company for the year then ended.

The final and critical stage is a monitoring and enforcement mechanism held by a regulator. There are models currently employed at the national level. There are security commissions, such as the SEC in the United States, stock exchanges that can de-list companies for regulatory transgressions, and other bodies that have some legal support such as the Financial Reporting Review Panel (FRRP) in the United Kingdom.

These examples are at the national level and there is concern that differences in approach can lead to differing applications and interpretations of international standards. There are indications that effective enforcement mechanisms are beginning to appear that stretch across national boundaries. In 2003, the Committee of European Security Regulators (CESR) issued two enforcement standards that European Union national security regulators are implementing.

2.8 The Principles Approach to Standard Setting

The International Accounting Standards Board has always been adamant that it uses a "principles-based approach" to develop its standards. This can be contrasted with some other countries, particularly the USA, that use a "rules-based approach". This is not just a small matter of terminology but goes to the philosophy underpinning the establishment of standards. The difference explains the problems that some countries have in adopting International Financial Reporting Standards completely. It is not just a case of exchanging one set of regulations for another, but being able to accept the basis on which those regulations have been drawn up.

Underlying this comment is the recognition that we are not comparing two technical systems but two different mindsets. This raises difficulties in explaining the detailed advantages of one approach over another. If it could be clearly shown that one approach is far superior to the other, there would be no problems in encouraging countries to adopt IFRSs. These advantages are not easily identified and even the differences between the two approaches can be challenged.

A simple distinction between the two approaches is that a principles-based approach applies fundamental concepts to ensure financial statements are not misleading. The burden is placed on the preparers and auditors of the financial statements to use their judgment and experience to ensure the financial statements are not misleading. A rules-based approach states that if you follow the rules strictly when preparing financial statements, they will not be misleading.

A principles-based system is heavily dependent on the use of concepts and these are often culturally and contextually derived and can be fuzzy around the edges. This can be illustrated with the term "furniture". In common speech we would consider that this refers to such articles as chairs and tables. It does not mean articles such as pencils and ladders, although these may be made of the same wood as furniture. But are television sets furniture or equipment? If a television set is used in a school for educational purposes we would most likely consider it as equipment. We might also define desks used in a school as equipment. Does this mean that a desk used in a home is equipment or furniture? These are the issues where judgment is required.

A rules-based system is expressed in a certain setting and does not require further explanation or interpretation. You can instruct your broker to sell your shareholdings in a certain company when the market price is above $5.00 per share. This is a rule. To instruct your broker to "buy low and sell high" would place the judgment on the broker to determine what is high and what is low. These are relative terms and can be interpreted differently in different situations.

There have been studies that have suggested that strict adherence to the rules may not always lead to the best approach in the preparation of financial statements. The danger is that detailed rules drive out professional judgment resulting in decisions that are consistent with the rules but inconsistent with the principle of providing the most useful financial information.

There is also the danger that the preparers of financial statements may comply with the rules, and are beyond criticism, but may stretch the limits of what is permissible under the law, even though it may not be ethically or morally acceptable or even good accounting. One example of where the rules have been manipulated is accounting for leases which we discuss in Chapter 8.

If principles-based standards are better, what are the reasons for the endurance of rules-based standards? First, if you appoint regulators, they feel that they have to regulate and will continue to do so in the way that they have done in the past: a form of regulatory inertia. Perhaps more importantly, principles may be regarded as too threatening both to the preparers of accounts and to the auditors. It is easier to claim that you have complied with the rules and save yourself the problem of applying principles to complex and controversial situations.

This could turn into a philosophical discussion but it is a practical problem which confronts those countries adopting International Financial Reporting Standards for the first time. There is a substantial amount written on the principles- versus rules-based approach, but it would seem now that most countries are willing to accept standards that use the principles-based approach.

2.9 The Structure and Organisation of International Standards

Copies of all standards, both IASs and IFRSs, can be found on the IASB website. Many universities, colleges and professional organisations subscribe to this website, so access is available for most students and professional accountants. In addition to the website, the IASB publishes all standards, interpretations and a glossary of terms in a large book of over 2,500 pages. This is sometimes referred to as the "bound volume" and is published annually.

In the Preface to the bound volume, the IASB states that IFRSs (and also IASs) apply to general purpose financial statements of profit-orientated entities. These include those organisations in commercial, industrial, financial and similar activities. All standards refer to "entities" and this includes organisations in corporate or other forms. In other words, it is a very inclusive term and we will use the term in this book when we are discussing the requirements of specific standards. We will also use the terms "business", "company", and "organisation" for examples and case studies to reflect the variety of terms in general business use.

Although IFRSs are not intended specifically for not-for-profit organisations, they may find them appropriate. If we look at the list of companies adopting international standards, several forms of profit and not-for-profit organisations are included.

Standards have paragraphs in **bold** font and in plain font. They have equal authority. The paragraphs in bold font indicate the main principles but they do not have greater authority than other paragraphs.

Individual standards have a similar structure and we will describe how a standard is organised. We will use as our example IAS 2 *Inventories* as that is the first standard you will encounter in the next chapter. The main sections of IAS 2 are:

Objectives

A standard cannot be understood properly without an appreciation of what it is trying to do. In the case of IAS 2 it is to set out the accounting treatment for inventories. It identifies what the problem is and explains how the standard addresses it.

Scope

This explains what transactions and events are covered by the standard and which are excluded. IAS 2, for example, applies to all inventories except work-in-progress in construction contracts, financial instruments and biological assets. Exclusions usually arise because they are dealt with in another standard.

Definitions

The key terms used in the standard are defined. This is extremely important as some standards are very technical and the definitions assist in the correct application of the standards.

Measurement of inventories

In many standards this is the longest section. IAS 2 states that the cost of inventories comprises all costs of purchase, costs of conversion and other costs incurred in bringing the inventories to their present location and condition. There follows several sub-sections explaining what is meant by these terms and how the measurement takes place.

Recognition as an expense

As we will see in the next chapter it is essential that you know when to deal with inventories as an expense, as this will determine the profit for the financial period.

Disclosures

The standard very carefully lists all the information that must be disclosed by an entity in its financial statements. With inventories, the list is fairly short, starting with the disclosure of "accounting policies used in measuring inventories" and ending with "the carrying amount of inventories pledged as securities".

Some standards are primarily concerned with the appropriate disclosure of information and will contain a lengthy list of requirements.

Effective date

It is essential for entities to know when they must start complying with the standard. Usually the IASB permits at least 12 months to allow companies to adopt its accounting records and procedures so that the information can be captured. It is also usual for the standard to encourage entities to adopt the standard early if they so wish.

Appendices

In the appendices there is a basis for conclusions explaining the reasons for the IASB's requirements. With some standards there may be several examples of how the standard should be applied in different circumstances.

2.10 The Current Position with Standards

We can consider the present position with international standards both from the view of the standards themselves and also from the view of the countries using them. As we explained above, the IASB is a standard setting body and it is the responsibility of countries to decide whether they will adopt international accounting standards and which organisations will use them.

As you can imagine, on a global basis there is considerable variation, even with those countries that have adopted international accounting standards completely. A good reference of the countries using international standards can be found on www.iasplus.com. The European Union adopted International Accounting Standards in 2005 for the consolidated accounts of listed companies. A survey published by the European Union Commission in April 2005 analysed the different approaches amongst member states. This report shows considerable variation in how the individual countries had decided to adopt international standards. The following is an extract of a table in the report showing the practices of the first five countries listed in alphabetical order:

Use of options in the IAS regulation by member states

	Companies	Publicly traded companies		Non-publicly traded companies	
		Consolidated	Legal entity	Consolidated	Legal entity
Austria	All	Required	Not permitted	Permitted	Not permitted
Belgium	Credit institutions	Required	Not permitted	Required	Not permitted
	Other	Required	Not permitted	Permitted	Not permitted
Cyprus	All	Required	Required	Required	Required
Czech Republic	All	Required	Required	Permitted	Not permitted
Denmark	All	Required	Permitted	Permitted	Permitted

The table shows the position for publicly traded companies, i.e., those listed on a stock exchange, and non-publicly traded companies. These are further divided into consolidated companies (where a group of companies are issuing their financial statements as if they were one organisation) and a legal entity which is a separate company. These five countries all followed EU policy and publicly traded companies issuing consolidated accounts are required to follow international standards. With the remaining categories of companies, the countries have adopted different policies. There is nothing wrong with them doing this, but you need to be aware that there are these different applications.

You will also need to be cautious of countries that claim their standards are similar to or the equivalent of international accounting standards. On deeper investigation you may find that there are significant differences. If you are unsure of the status of a company's financial statement, the best solution is to refer to its Annual Report and Accounts. Look at both the Report by the Auditors and also the Notes to the Accounts, particularly the statement on Accounting Policies. If a company's financial statements comply completely with international standards, you will find this is stated. We show extracts below from Marks and Spencer's Annual Report 2008. They are one of the largest general retailers in the UK.

Extracted from the Notes to the Accounts

1 *Accounting policies*

Basis of preparation

The financial statements have been prepared in accordance with International Financial Reporting Standards (IFRS) as adopted by the European Union and with those parts of the Companies Act 1985 applicable to companies reporting under IFRS.

Marks and Spencer

Extracted from the Auditor's Report

Opinion

In our opinion:

- the financial statements give a true and fair view, in accordance with IFRSs as adopted by the European Union, of the state of the Group's and the Parent Company's affairs as at 29 March 2008 and of the Group's and the Parent Company's profit and cash flows for the year then ended.

Marks and Spencer

For a comparison, we show the extract from the Annual Report 2008 for Aluminium Corporation of China. You can see that they are following Hong Kong Financial Reporting Standards. These are very similar to International Financial Reporting Standards, but you would have to be cautious when analysing the financial statements.

Extracted from the Auditor's Report

The directors of the Company are responsible for the preparation and the true and fair presentation of these consolidated financial statements in accordance with Hong Kong Financial Reporting Standards issued by the Hong Kong Institute of Certified Public Accountants and the disclosure requirements of the Hong Kong Companies Ordinance.

Aluminium Corporation of China

Extracted from the Notes to the Accounts

These financial statements have been prepared in accordance with Hong Kong Financial Reporting Standards ("HKFRS"). These financial statements have been prepared under the historical cost convention, as modified by the revaluation of available-for-sale financial assets and financial assets and liabilities at fair value through profit and loss (including derivative instruments).

Aluminium Corporation of China 2008

As far as standards themselves are concerned, there is some confusion for new students because of the change of names and the apparent duplication of some individual standards. The present position is that the IASC issued 41 standards between 1975–2000. The standards were numbered consecutively starting with 1 and each standard also had a descriptive title, for example IAS 7 Cash Flow Statements. Most of the IASC standards are still in force.

When the IASB took over from the IASC, it "adopted" the IASs still in force and started to issue its own standards called International Financial Reporting Standards (IFRSs). Once again these standards are numbered consecutively starting with 1 and have a descriptive title, for example, IFRS 7 Cash Flow Statements.

When referring to all the standards that have been issued, the term International Accounting Standards or International Financial Reporting Standards may be used. It is essential, however, to use correctly the term IAS or IFRS when referring to a specific standard, e.g., IAS 2 Inventories or IFRS 2 Share-Based Payment.

Table 1 lists the numbers and titles of all the standards currently in force and the chapter number in this book which mainly explains that standard.

2.11 IFRS 1 First-Time Adoption of International Financial Reporting Standards

This chapter has been mainly about the global movement away from national standards to the adoption of international accounting standards. Although a country may decide to adopt international standards, it is the individual companies that have to

Table 1.   Standards in force in 2009

Number	Title	Chapter
IAS 1	Presentation of Financial Statements	1/12
IAS 2	Inventories	3
IAS 7	Statement of Cash Flows	5
IAS 8	Accounting Policies, Changes in Accounting Estimates and Errors	7
IAS 10	Events After the Reporting Period	7
IAS 11	Construction Contracts	11
IAS 12	Income Taxes	8
IAS 16	Property, Plant and Equipment	4
IAS 17	Leases	8
IAS 18	Revenue	3
IAS 19	Employee Benefits	8
IAS 20	Accounting for Government Grants and Disclosure of Government Assistance	–
IAS 21	The Effects of Changes in Foreign Exchange Rates	13
IAS 23	Borrowing Costs	4
IAS 24	Related Party Disclosures	10
IAS 26	Accounting and Reporting by Retirement Benefit Plans	–
IAS 27	Consolidated and Separate Financial Statements	10
IAS 28	Investments in Associates	10
IAS 29	Financial Reporting in Hyperinflationary Economies	13
IAS 31	Interests in Joint Ventures	10
IAS 32	Financial Instruments: Presentation	9
IAS 33	Earnings per Share	12
IAS 34	Interim Financial Reporting	12
IAS 36	Impairment of Assets	6
IAS 37	Provisions, Contingent Liabilities and Contingent Assets	7
IAS 38	Intangible Assets	6
IAS 39	Financial Instruments: Recognition and Measurement	9
IAS 40	Investment Property	11
IAS 41	Agriculture	11
IFRS 1	First-Time Adoption of IFRS	2
IFRS 2	Share-Based Payment	9
IFRS 3	Business Combinations	10
IFRS 4	Insurance Contracts	–
IFRS 5	Non-Current Assets Held for Sale and Discontinued Operations	11
IFRS 6	Exploration for and Evaluation of Mineral Resources	11
IFRS 7	Financial Instruments: Disclosures	9
IFRS 8	Operating Segments	13

deal with the change in their financial reporting practices and policies. Guidance to this transition is found in IFRS 1.

Before we look at this standard, we need to discuss the process of a country adopting international standards. It is a lengthy and complex process involving different institutions and the regulatory requirements in the country itself. At the very least, agreement must be received from the stock exchange authorities. We will use the example of Canada as an overview of the timing.

On 4 January 2006, the Canadian Accounting Standards Board (AcSB) adopted a strategic plan to introduce International Financial Reporting Standards into Canada. The date for publicly accountable enterprises (PAEs) to commence publishing their financial statements is for financial years beginning on or after 1 January 2011. To achieve convergence with IFRSs, the Board's schedule for the period from 2006 to 2011 is to:

2006–2008   Obtain training and thorough knowledge of IFRS. This involves the accounting profession, users of accounts and educational institutions that offer accounting courses.

By early 2008   Progress review by AcSB to ascertain what problems companies and the various other interested parties are finding.

By 31 December 2008   Enterprises to assess accounting policies with reference to IFRSs and develop a plan for convergence and to disclose that plan.

By 31 December 2009   The same disclosure as required in 2008, but with greater degree of quantification of the effects of the change to IFRSs.

1 January 2010   First year for collection by companies of comparative information for inclusion with 2011 financial statements under new IFRS-based requirements.

31 December 2010   Last year of reporting under current Canadian GAAP.

1 January 2011   Changeover. First year reporting under new IFRS-based standards.

31 March 2011   Enterprises issuing interim financial statements prepare their first IFRS-based statements for the three months ended 31 March 2011.

31 December 2011   End of first annual reporting period in accordance with new IFRS-based requirements.

Most countries planning for convergence will have a similar time frame and the above schedule emphasises the extra workload on companies and the short period in which they have to make the change. IFRS 1 sets out the procedures that an entity must follow when it adopts IFRSs for the first time as the basis for preparing its general purpose financial statements. The standard specifies very carefully the terms it uses to pinpoint the key dates:

First IFRS financial statements — First annual statements explicitly and unreservedly stating that they are IFRS-compliant.

Transition date — Beginning of the earliest period comparative figures, that are IFRS-compliant and presented in the first IFRS financial statements.

Opening balance sheet — The entity's balance sheet at the date of transition to IFRS.

Reporting date — End of the latest period covered by the financial statements.

If you examine these definitions carefully you will see that a company has to prepare well in advance before it can issue IFRS-compliant financial statements. For example: If a company prepares its first IFRS financial statements for the year ending 31 December 2014, with one year of comparative financial statements, the date of **transition** to IFRS will be 1 January 2013, and the opening IFRS balance sheet will be prepared at that date.

The general principle of the standard is that all IFRSs effective at the reporting date are to be applied retrospectively to the opening IFRS balance sheet, the comparative period and the reporting period.

In its opening IFRS balance sheet, a company should:

- Include all assets and liabilities that IFRS requires
- Exclude any assets and liabilities that IFRS does not permit
- Classify all assets, liabilities and equity in accordance with IFRS
- Measure all items in accordance with IFRS.

There are, however, both mandatory exemptions and optional exemptions permitted. The four mandatory exemptions which prevent a company from applying IFRSs retrospectively are:

- Estimates made previously cannot be changed unless they were made in error (IAS 8)
- Derecognition of financial assets and liabilities
- Hedge accounting
- Assets classified as held for sale and discontinued operations.

There are several exemptions where a company can choose whether it wishes to apply IFRSs retrospectively. These optional exemptions are:

- Business combinations
- Use of fair value or revaluation as deemed cost for specific items
- Employee benefits (defined pension plans)
- Compound financial instruments
- Assets and liabilities of subsidiaries, associates and joint ventures
- Cumulative translation difference
- Stock-based payment transactions.

IFRS 1 was first issued in June 2003 and helped European companies in their transition to IFRS-compliant financial statements in 2005. The standard has been amended many times and this made it more complicated to apply. In 2008 the IASB issued a more readable version and subsequent amendments were made in July 2009.

2.12 Chapter Summary

☞ For many years, individual countries developed their own accounting standards. For several reasons, the standards differed substantially, which meant that the financial statements of a company in one country could not be compared with those of another company in a different country.

☞ The difficulties in comparing financial statements on a global basis were first addressed in 1973 with the establishment of the IASC. This organisation issued several International Accounting Standards but suffered from a lack of resources and permitting too much flexibility in its standards.

☞ In 2001 the IASC was succeeded by the International Accounting Standards Board. The IASB adopted all the International Accounting Standards in issue but decided that any standards that it issued would be called International Financial Reporting Standards.

☞ The IASB has been successful in its role of promoting international standards globally and many countries are using them, mainly for companies that are quoted on the stock exchange.

☞ The process for a country adopting international accounting standards is lengthy and involves considerable discussions with various bodies inside the country.

☞ IFRS 1 sets down the requirements for a company transitioning to IFRSs.

Progress Test

1. Which TWO of the following are parts of the "due process" of the IASB in issuing a new IFRS?

   a) Issuing an interpretation as authoritative interim guidance
   b) Establishing an advisory committee to give advice
   c) Reviewing compliance and enforcement procedures
   d) Developing and publishing a discussion document for public comment

2. Which one of the following is responsible for reviewing accounting issues that are likely to receive divergent or unacceptable treatment in the absence of authoritative guidance with a view to reaching consensus as to the appropriate accounting treatment?

   a) SAC
   b) AIASB
   c) IASCF
   d) IFRIC

3. IFRIC issues interpretations as authoritative guidance. For which TWO of the following should IFRIC consider an interpretation?

   a) Issues where unsatisfactory or conflicting interpretations have developed or seem likely to develop
   b) Newly identified financial reporting issues not specifically addressed in IFRSs
   c) Narrow industry-specific issues
   d) Areas where members of the IASB cannot reach unanimous agreement

4. Which TWO of the following are the roles of the IASCF?

   a) Reviewing broad strategic issues affecting accounting standards
   b) Providing interpretations of standards
   c) Approving annually the budget of the IASB and determining funding
   d) Issuing IFRSs

5. Which of the following statements best describes the term "going concern"?

   a) The ability of an entity to continue in operation for the foreseeable future
   b) When current assets less current liabilities become negative
   c) The potential to contribute to the flow of cash and cash equivalents to the entity
   d) When the income and expenses of an entity are negative

6. Which of the following terms best describes assets recorded at a value that represents the immediate purchase cost of an equivalent asset?

   a) Historical cost
   b) Realisable value
   c) Present value
   d) Replacement value

7. IFRSs approved by the IASB include paragraphs in **bold** font and plain font. In relation to the bold font paragraphs, which of the following statements is correct?

   a) Bold font paragraphs should be given greater authority than the paragraphs in plain font
   b) Bold font paragraphs indicate the main principles of the standard
   c) Plain font paragraphs can be ignored
   d) Plain font paragraphs are interpretations of the standard

8. Which of the following are the objectives of the IASB?

   a) To develop, in the public interest, a single set of high-quality, understand-able and enforceable global accounting standards
   b) To help participants in the world's capital markets and other users make economic decisions by having access to high-quality, transparent and com-parable information
   c) To promote the use and vigorous application of those Standards
   d) To bring about convergence of national accounting standards and International Accounting Standards to high-quality solutions

9. Which of the following statements about the IASB Conceptual Framework are correct?

   a) The Framework discusses the qualitative characteristics of financial statements
   b) The Framework normally prevails over IFRS where there is a conflict between the two
   c) The Framework discusses the objectives of financial statements

10. Which one of the following statements is true for a company adopting IFRSs for the first time?

    a) Only the standards that a company wishes to use need be adopted
    b) A company must apply all IFRSs retrospectively
    c) There are mandatory exemptions to retrospective application of IFRSs but no optional exemptions
    d) There are both mandatory and optional exemptions to retrospective appli-cation of IFRSs

3

The Basics of the Statement of Income

Learning Objectives

When you have studied this chapter you should be able to:

☞ Illustrate the difference between profit and cash
☞ Define the purpose of the Statement of Comprehensive Income
☞ Construct a simple Function of Expense Income Statement
☞ Explain the importance of IAS 2 *Inventories* in arriving at gross profit
☞ Apply recognition of revenue according to IAS 18 *Revenue*.

3.1 Introduction

Both users external to a business and managers working within in it are interested in profit. They want to know what the financial performance of the business has been over a period of time and whether it has been profitable or made a loss. This information is contained in the Statement of Comprehensive Income. This is a new title recently introduced by the IASB and also an expansion of the previous statement that was known as the Income Statement, Profit and Loss Account or Earnings Statement. The Statement of Comprehensive Income has two parts to it and in this chapter we will concentrate on the first part: the Income Statement. In a later chapter we will examine both parts of the Statement of Comprehensive Income.

In this chapter we will start first by explaining the difference between profit and cash and how the accounting concepts of matching and accruals, explained in Chapter 1, are applied. We will then explain the construction of a simple Income Statement and the importance of calculating correctly the Gross Profit. This will incorporate consideration of the requirements of IAS 2 *Inventories*.

The main requirements for the presentation of a published Statement of Comprehensive Income are included in IAS 1 *Presentation of Financial Statements*. We will consider the contents and structure of an Income Statement when we discuss the purpose of the statement.

In calculating the financial performance for a period, we will examine the problems of defining revenue correctly. This is an area where significant fraud and errors in reporting are made. Although the basics of defining revenue are fairly straightforward, there are problems in certain industries and different types of transactions that have to be considered. The guidance for correctly identifying revenue is given in IAS 18 *Revenue*.

In this chapter, and the other chapters concerned with financial statements, we will concentrate on the information required to be disclosed by International Accounting Standards. Companies will have various working documents and internal financial statements that are much more complete than the one they are required to publish by the International Accounting Standards Board. In examining the statements required to be published, our explanations will examine, at the simpler level, some of the internal calculations conducted by companies.

As we are using simple examples to explain the construction and concepts of the Income Statement, the amounts we use are small. This means that the impact of some of the calculations do not appear that significant. You must remember that large companies are dealing in millions of pounds, dollars, renminbi, rupees or whatever is their national currency. We reproduce below the Income Statement for AstraZeneca, one of the leading pharmaceutical companies. You will appreciate that with amounts of such magnitude, even a minor error or a shift in the economy can have a substantial impact on the "bottom line" or profit.

Condensed Consolidated Income Statement
For the year ended 31 December

	2008 $m	2007 $m
Revenue	31,601	29,559
Cost of sales	(6,598)	(6,419)
Gross profit	25,003	23,140
Distribution costs	(291)	(248)
Research and development	(5,179)	(5,162)
Selling, general and administrative costs	(10,913)	(10,364)
Other operating income and expense	524	728

Operating profit	9,144	8,094
Finance income	854	959
Finance expense	(1,317)	(1,070)
Profit before tax	8,681	7,983
Taxation	(2,551)	(2,356)
Profit for the period	6,130	5,627

3.2 Comparing Profit and Cash

The first hurdle in understanding the Statement of Financial Performance is to realise that profit and cash are very different things in accounting. This is explained by a simple example.

Example 1

1. In the month of January an antiques trader buys an old oil painting for $2,000 in an auction. He pays for it immediately in cash. When he returns to his home he discovers the painting is quite valuable and he is able to sell it immediately for $5,000 cash. Assuming that the antiques trader has no other business transactions in January, how much cash surplus will he have from this one transaction?
2. You can easily work this out in your head as he pays $2,000 cash and receives $5,000, so he must have a cash surplus of $3,000. Now imagine that he does not receive the cash for the painting in January but is promised that he will be paid in March. What would be his cash deficit at the end of January?
3. Once again, this is a simple transaction where you can easily calculate that he will have a cash deficit (i.e., cash goes out but no cash comes in) of $2,000 — the amount of cash that he has paid out.
4. Looking at the circumstances in No. 2, how much profit or loss will he make in the month of January? We have purposely kept this example simple so you can calculate the amount in your head without worrying about drawing up a financial statement of any kind. Before you do your calculation, we will remind you of the definition of the accruals assumption which states:

Definition — accruals assumption

Financial statements must be prepared on the accruals basis. Transactions and other events are recognised as they occur and not when cash or any other consideration such as cheques is given or received. These transactions and events must be recorded in the accounting records when they occur and not when payment is made or received.

If you apply the accruals assumption you will see that the profit amount is $3,000, although there is a cash deficit of $2,000. We have taken the amount that the trader has agreed to receive for the painting of $5,000 and deducted from this the amount he paid of $2,000. The trader may be concerned that he has a cash deficit, but as far as the Income Statement is concerned he has made a profit.

Example 2

We will now look at a slightly more complex example. If you have not done accounting before, the use of the accruals concept may be slightly confusing but it is essential for understanding the different financial statements as issued by a business. To help you with the following example, we have drawn up the structure of the financial statements and you will have to insert the correct figures.

Ella Chan is a student and has a small business of buying used textbooks and selling them to her friends. In the period 1 September to 31 December she buys 150 textbooks at $25 each, and she has paid for 120 of them at the end of December. She will pay for the remainder in January.

During the same financial period she manages to sell all the textbooks for $40 each. At the end of the period she is still owed for 10 books and she expects to receive the cash in February. To advertise her business she uses a local newspaper. This costs her $15 per month and at the end of the period she still owes for the month of December.

Complete the following financial statements:

Ella Chan
Statement of cash flow 1 September to 31 December

	$
Cash received	
140 textbooks at $40 each	
Cash paid	
120 books at $25 each	$3,000
Advertising for three months	$<u>45</u>
Cash surplus	

Ella Chan
Income Statement 1 September to 31 December

	$
Sales	
150 textbooks at $40 each	
Expenses	
150 books at $25 each	
Advertising for four months	
Profit for period	

Obviously, in practice, financial statements do not show the details of the number of items sold and purchased, but it helps you at this early stage. As long as you have followed the accruals principle, then your financial statements would look as follows. We have omitted the detailed workings.

Ella Chan
Statement of cash flow 1 September to 31 December

		$
Cash received		
		5,600
Cash paid		
Books	$3,000	
Advertising for three months	$45	3,045
Cash surplus		2,555

Ella Chan
Income Statement 1 September to 31 December

		$
Sales		
		6,000
Expenses		
Purchase of books	$3,750	
Advertising for four months	$60	3,810
Profit for period		2,190

The difference between cash and profit can be explained by the cash that Ella owes for textbooks and the cash she is owed from her customers. We can draw a simple table to show this.

Ella Chan
Reconciliation of cash and profit

		$
Cash surplus for the period		2,555
Add cash due from customers (10 books at $40 each)		400
		2,955
Deduct cash owed for textbooks (30 books at $25 each)	$750	
Advertising for one month	$15	765
Profit for period		2,190

As we move through this chapter and continue to other chapters, the examples will become more complex. The essential lesson at this stage is that the accruals assumption is applied to the Income Statement and that will give us the figure of profit. The amount of cash surplus or deficit for the period, however, is likely to be significantly different from the profit figure.

The fact that the company is owed cash and owes its suppliers is very important. We will address these issues when we examine the Statement of Financial Position and the Cash Flow Statement in later chapters.

3.3 The Purpose of the Income Statement

The objective of financial statements is to provide information about the financial position, financial performance and cash flows of a business that is useful to a wide range of users in making economic decisions. Financial statements also show the results of the management's stewardship of the resources entrusted to it. To meet this objective, the Income Statement provides information about a business's income, expenses and profit for a specific financial period.

IAS 1 Presentation of Financial Statements permits two forms of presentation of the full Statement of Comprehensive Income. Either a single Statement of Comprehensive Income can be used or two statements. If two statements are presented, the first statement will give the different components of profit or loss and we will refer to this as the Income Statement. The second statement starts with the profit or loss figure for the period shown in the Income Statement, and then gives the other components of comprehensive income.

We will assume that a company has decided to present two statements and we will look at the structure and contents of the first statement that gives the components of profit and loss. In other words, the statement will give the total revenue for the financial period and the expenses that have been incurred in generating that revenue. The accruals assumption will be used, not movements of cash in and out of the business.

In presenting the Income Statement under IAS 1, a company can choose to use either the function of expense method or the nature of expense method. There are advantages and disadvantages for both methods, and it is the responsibility of management to select the method which provides the most relevant and reliable financial information.

With the nature of expense method, the expenses incurred by the company are shown according to their nature, for example, purchase of materials, transport costs, employee benefits and advertising costs. The following shows the items that may appear on such a statement. There will be some terms you are unfamiliar with, but we will discuss these at a later stage.

Revenue	X
Other income	X

Changes in inventories of finished goods and work-in-progress	X
Raw materials and consumables used	X
Employee benefits expense	X
Depreciation and amortisation expense	X
Other expenses	<u>X</u>
Total expenses	(<u>X</u>)
Profit before tax	X

With the function of expense method, sometimes known as the cost of sales method, expenses are classified according to their function, for example, distribution and administration. As a minimum, the company must disclose the cost of the goods that it has actually sold. In doing this, the company will also show its gross profit and this can be relevant information to the users. The following example shows the items that may appear in such a statement:

Revenue	X
Cost of sales	(<u>X</u>)
Gross profit	X
Other income	X
Distribution costs	(X)
Administrative expenses	(X)
Other expenses	(<u>X</u>)
Profit before tax	X

The standard allows either presentation, but most users would possibly find the function of expense method the most informative. Unfortunately, it appears that most companies use the nature of expense method.

3.4 Constructing a Function of Expense Income Statement

We are choosing to explain this method as it introduces the calculation for "cost of sales", sometimes referred to as "cost of goods sold". In our earlier example of Ella Chan we assumed that she sold every book she had bought in the one financial period. This is unrealistic. At the end of a financial period, a company will have goods that it has made or bought to resell still unsold. These are known as the closing inventory or closing stock.

Obviously, if you have not sold some goods in the financial period, then you cannot make a profit on them. You can only make a profit on the goods that you sell in that financial period. To express this more formally, when inventories are sold, the carrying amount of those inventories must be recognised as an expense in the period in which the related revenue is recognised.

To carry out this matching exercise of goods bought and sold, accountants use a specific calculation that has the advantage of both giving them the costs of the goods actually sold but also acts as a check on the accounting record. It also provides the gross profit for the period. We will demonstrate this calculation by taking the purchase of goods and their resale by the Imperial Bicycle Company over a three-month period. In this example, the accruals assumption will be used and any movements of cash are ignored.

The Imperial Bicycle Company

The Imperial Bicycle Company has a business in the Middle East. It imports bicycles from China at $80 each and sells them at $120 each. For the first three months of 2010, the number of bicycles it purchases and sells is:

Month	Number purchased	Number sold
January	100	90
February	150	130
March	140	150

We will do the calculations for each month separately, showing how we have arrived at the figures. Instead of the term "Sales", we will use the term "Revenue" as that is the one used in the standard. You may find both used in practice.

Imperial Bicycle Company
Calculation of gross profit for January

	$	$
Revenue (90 bicycles @ $120)		10,800
Cost of goods sold		
Purchases (100 bicycles @ $80)	8,000	
Deduct closing inventory (10 bicycles @ $80)	800	7,200
Gross profit		3,600

With this simple model it is easy to calculate that Imperial makes a gross profit of $120 − $80 = $40 for each bicycle. If it sells 90 bicycles, the gross profit must be $40 × 90 = $3,600. The great advantage, however, is that the Cost of Goods Sold calculation allows all the figures to be checked as follows:

1. There should be an invoice that Imperial has received for the 100 bicycles it has purchased.

2. There should be a record that 100 bicycles were physically received by Imperial in good condition.
3. There should be records that 90 bicycles were purchased by customers. These records should also show whether payment was made at the time of purchase or whether the amount is still owed to Imperial.
4. Finally, and very importantly, on the last day of January, Imperial can physically count the number of bicycles it has remaining — its closing inventory. If there are not 10 bicycles but only 9, we can assume that one has been stolen, lost or so badly damaged it had to be scrapped.

If Imperial finds that it only has 9 bicycles remaining, its Cost of Gross Profit calculation would be as follows:

Imperial Bicycle Company
Calculation of gross profit for January (one bicycle missing)

	$	$
Revenue (90 bicycles @ $120)		10,800
Cost of goods sold		
Purchases (100 bicycles @ $80)	8,000	
Deduct closing inventory (9 bicycles @ $80)	720	7,280
Gross profit		3,520

You can see that the gross profit has decreased by the $80 attributable to the missing bicycle. The calculation of this amount of closing inventory is so critical that there is a standard, IAS 2 Inventories, which explains the correct procedures. Before we look at that standard, we will show the calculation for February and March.

Imperial Bicycle Company
Calculation of gross profit for February

	$	$
Revenue (130 bicycles @ $120)		15,600
Cost of goods sold		
Opening inventory (10 bicycles @ $80)	800	
Purchases (150 bicycles @ $80)	12,000	
	12,800	
Deduct closing inventory (30 bicycles @ $80)	2,400	10,400
Gross profit		5,200

A few notes on the above before looking at March:

1. At the beginning of February, Imperial has the 10 bicycles to sell that remain unsold from January.
2. An additional 150 bicycles were purchased, so it has 160 bicycles it could sell. As the information is not given, we have calculated that as 130 bicycles were sold, there should be 30 bicycles in closing inventory. In practice, this is a figure that needs to be checked.

Finally, the calculation for March:

Imperial Bicycle Company
Calculation of gross profit for March

	$	$
Revenue (150 bicycles @ $120)		18,000
Cost of goods sold		
Opening inventory (30 bicycles @ $80)	2,400	
Purchases (140 bicycles @ $80)	11,200	
	13,600	
Deduct closing inventory (20 bicycles @ $80)	1,600	12,000
Gross profit		6,000

You should have had no difficulty with March. Once again, in the absence of information we have calculated the closing inventory figure. You will notice that the closing inventory amount for one month is the opening inventory amount for the following month.

In the simple example above, it is possible to calculate that the total gross profit should be the gross profit of each bicycle ($40) multiplied by the 150 bicycles sold. The gross profit is very important for users as it is a good measure of how well a company performs at buying and selling goods. We can express this performance in percentage terms by calculating the gross profit margin, also known as the gross margin ratio.

Definition — gross profit margin

This is calculated by expressing the gross profit as a percentage of revenue and is a good measure of the performance of a company in buying and selling goods.

$$\text{Gross profit margin} = \frac{\text{Gross profit}}{\text{Revenue}} \times 100$$

If we take the above formula and apply it to one bicycle, the gross profit margin is:

$$\frac{\$40}{\$120} = 33.3\%.$$

If you calculate this gross profit margin for each of the three months it will always be 33.3%, as the company has been able to maintain its selling price, purchase costs and inventory control. If any of these factors had changed, we would have a different gross profit margin and this would be a warning signal. If you calculate the gross profit margin for January as if the bicycle had been stolen, the answer is:

$$\frac{\$3,520}{\$10,800} = 32.6\%.$$

This may not appear to be a significant decline, but it would be worrying for investors as it suggests that there are some problems in the company.

Because of the importance of the gross profit figure, there is a temptation for companies to manipulate the figures to increase their gross profit. They can either inflate the revenue figure or increase the closing inventory amount. Additionally, because of the complexity of business, they may have some difficulties in determining what the correct amount should be. To prevent these uncertainties, there are two standards, IAS 2 *Inventories* and IAS 18 *Revenue*, which set out the procedures to follow for measuring revenue and inventories. We will look at IAS 2 first.

3.5 IAS 2 Inventories

Definition — inventories

These are goods held for sale in the normal course of business, or items in the course of production, or raw materials or supplies that will be used in production or in providing services.

Looking at the above definition, we can apply it to a manufacturing company at the end of a financial period. There will be goods it has manufactured in the warehouse ready to go to customers. Remember that production does not stop at the end of the financial period. The production process will be in operation and there will be goods that are partly completed. These items in the course of production present some accounting difficulties that we need not concern ourselves with at this level. Finally, the company will have raw materials in its stores waiting to go through the production process.

The amount of funds a large company can have tied up in inventories can be significant, as can be seen from the following excerpt from the Notes to the Accounts of GlaxoSmithKline, a leading pharmaceutical company:

	2008 £m	2007 £m
Raw materials and consumables	1,127	1,105
Work-in-progress	1,295	771
Finished goods	1,634	1,186
	4,056	3,062

The profit of a company can be inflated or reduced if an error is made in the calculations or if the management wishes to commit fraud. The management can increase the closing inventory figure by inflating either the number of items or the value of each item, or both. If you look at January, the closing inventory amount was 10 bicycles @ $80 each = $800. An unscrupulous company may decide to pretend that there were 12 bicycles or ignore the fact that one bicycle was stolen. This type of fraud is usually easy to detect by the auditors.

There may be an intention to mislead the users of the financial statements, or it may be because of uncertainty or ignorance that inventory amounts are incorrect. IAS 2 *Inventories* sets out the procedure for calculating the value of inventory to ensure that there is consistency in the approach that management uses. The standard is not designed to specifically prevent fraud.

The objective of IAS 2 is to prescribe the accounting treatment for inventories. It provides guidance for determining the cost of inventories. The standard states that inventories include assets held for sale in the ordinary course of business (finished goods), assets in the production process for sale in the ordinary course of business (work-in-progress), and materials and supplies that are consumed in production (raw materials).

A key principle in the standard is that inventories are required to be stated at the lower of cost and net realisable value (NRV). We will discuss NRV later, but first we will look at what is included in the cost. It includes all of these items:

- costs of purchase (including taxes, transport, and handling) net of trade discounts received
- costs of conversion (including fixed and variable manufacturing overheads)
- other costs incurred in bringing the inventories to their present location and condition.

The phrase "to their present location and condition" is very important and lays down the boundary beyond which further costs cannot be added. You cannot include:

- abnormal waste
- storage costs
- administrative overheads unrelated to production
- selling costs
- foreign exchange differences arising directly on the recent acquisition of inventories invoiced in a foreign currency
- interest cost when inventories are purchased with deferred settlement terms.

In some industries there may be some problems in identifying the cost, or the internal accounting system may not capture the cost. The standard makes particular provisions for these. In particular, it refers to the retail industry where it is the practice to reduce the sales value of inventory by the percentage gross margin to arrive at an approximation of cost. This method is acceptable.

Although the standard sets out specifically what is meant by cost, in practice there can be difficulties in determining the value of inventory when prices are fluctuating. This can be illustrated by a simple example.

Tyre example

A tyre company purchases in the month of January the following tyres that are all exactly of the same model and size, but it is a time of rising prices:

> Day 1 — 200 tyres @ $80 each
> Day 18 — 250 tyres @ $90 each
> Day 24 — 100 tyres @ $100 each

On the last day of the month it sells 400 tyres. What is the value of the closing inventory?

Assuming that no tyres have been stolen, the closing inventory will be 150 tyres. The problem is whether we use $80, $90 or $100 each tyre or some combination. The standard sets out two main methods as follows.

First-in, first-out (FIFO)

Definition — first-in, first-out

This method assumes that items purchased or manufactured first are sold first. The result of this is that the value of inventory at period end is the most recently purchased or produced.

This assumes that the first tyres purchased are the first tyres sold. The 400 tyres sold would therefore be 200 tyres costing $80 and 200 tyres costing $90. Our closing inventory would be valued as follows:

Remaining 50 tyres costing $90 each	= $4,500
100 tyres costing $100 each	= $10,000
Value of closing inventory	= $14,500

An example of the FIFO method is taken from the 2008 Annual Report of Smith & Nephew:

Inventories

Finished goods and work-in-progress are valued at factory cost, including appropriate overheads, on a first-in first-out basis. Raw materials and bought-in finished goods are valued at purchase price. All inventories are reduced to net realisable value where lower than cost.

Weighted average

Definition — weighted average

This method calculates the average cost of items at the beginning of the period and the cost of similar items purchased or produced during the period.

Taking the above example but using the second method, we need to calculate the weighted average of purchases on a continuing basis and, using this figure, the closing inventory. It is best shown in the form of a table:

Number of tyres	Cost of each tyre	Total value	Cumulative value	Weighted average cost of each tyre
200	$80	$16,000	$16,000	$80
250	$90	$22,500	$38,500	$85.56
100	$100	$10,000	$48,500	$88.18

As the sale takes place at the end of the month, the 400 tyres will have a value of $88.18 × 400 = $35,272. The closing inventory will have a value of $88.18 × 150 = $13,227.

An example of the use of weighted average is the following extract from the Notes to the 2009 Annual Report of Tesco:

Inventories

Inventories comprise goods held for resale and properties held for, or in the course of, development and are valued at the lower of cost and fair value less costs to sell using the weighted average cost basis.

It is easy to realise that a company of any size will need to maintain computerised records. Not only will sales normally take place throughout the month, requiring frequent calculations, but costs may go down instead of up. This presents a problem when the company is considering the value of its closing inventory.

Definition — net realisable value

Net realisable value (NRV) is the estimated sales value of the goods minus the additional costs likely to be incurred in completing production, if necessary, and any other costs necessary to make the sale.

The standard requires that a company should state its closing inventory at the lower of cost or net realisable value. The net realisable value can be lower than the original cost because:

- The inventories have been damaged whilst in store
- The inventories have become obsolete
- The selling prices have declined below the original cost
- The costs of completing production or making the sale have increased.

Although a company may purchase or manufacture goods with the intention of selling them at a profit, this may not happen. Occasionally in some industries, or with certain goods, or in certain economic climates, the amount a company could achieve by selling its inventory is lower than what it cost originally. One example is where the goods are fashionable, such as certain clothes items. If the demand for these clothes falls, shops will have to lower their prices considerably to sell their goods. The selling price could be even lower than the original cost to them. In this instance, any closing inventory must be valued at the net realisable value. The impact of restating inventories can be seen from Unilever's Annual Report 2008:

Extract from Note 13

Inventories with a value of €134 million (2007: €101 million) are carried at net realisable value, this being lower than cost. During 2008, €246 million (2007: €177 million) was charged to the income statement for damaged, obsolete and lost inventories. In 2008, €23 million (2007: €25 million) was utilised or released to the income statement from inventory provisions taken in earlier years.

Returning to our example of tyres. Imagine that a new process has been invented so that the tyres that we have can be sold to the public at only $75 each. How much is our closing inventory worth now? It does not matter whether you use the First-in First-out method or the weighted average, the net realisable value is lower than the cost of the old tyres.

The standard stipulates that the difference between the cost and the net realisable value should be recognised as an expense in the period in which it occurs; in other words, it must go to the Statement of Comprehensive Income. Of course, it is possible that in a later period, the selling price that can be obtained for the goods will increase above the original cost. In these circumstances, the original writedown can be reversed in the Income Statement in the period in which it occurs.

Comparing FIFO and weighted average methods

We will now look at a slightly more complex example and compare the two methods. The information we have about a company is as follows:

> Day 1 — purchases 200 items at $10 each
> Day 2 — purchases 200 items at $12 each
> Day 3 — sells 250 items at $20 each
> Day 4 — purchases 100 items at $13 each

Once again we will use tables to illustrate the calculations:

FIFO example

Day	Activity	Calculation	Inventory value $
1	Purchases	200 items @ $10 each	2,000
2	Purchases	200 items @ $12 each	2,400
	Balance		**4,400**
3	Sales	200 items @ $10 each	(2,000)
		50 items @ $12 each	(600)
	Balance		**1,800**
4	Purchases	100 items @ $13 each	1,300
	Balance		**3,100**

FIFO Income Statement (days 1–4)

	$	$
Sales		5,000
Cost of goods sold		
Purchases	5,700	
Less closing inventory	3,100	2,600
Gross profit		**2,400**

FIFO proof

Sold 250 items @ $20 each	= $5,000
Cost of 250 items	
200 @ $10 + 50 @ $12	= $2,600
Gross profit	**$2,400**

Weighted average example

Day	Activity	Calculation	Average cost of each item	Inventory value $
1	Purchases	200 items @ $10 each		2,000
2	Purchases	200 items @ $12 each		2,400
	Balance	**$4,400/400**	**$11**	4,400
3	Sales	250 items @ $11 each		(2,750)
	Balance	**$1,650/150**	**$11**	1,650
4	Purchases	100 items @ $13 each		1,300
	Balance	**$2,950/250**	**$11.80**	2,950

Note that with the Weighted Average method, the balance (carrying amount) of our inventory is calculated by taking the total amount and dividing by the number of items. It is this carrying amount per item that is used to calculate the succeeding closing balance. Thus, at the end of Day 3 we have total inventory valued at $1,650 ($11 for 150 items). To this we add our purchases that cost $1,300, so the total balance for our inventory is $2,950. This represents 250 items, so the average cost per item is $11.80.

Weighted average Income Statement (days 1–4)

	$	$
Sales		5,000
Cost of goods sold		
Purchases	5,700	
Less closing inventory	2,950	2,750
Gross profit		**2,250**

Weighted average proof

Sold 250 items @ $20 each	= $5,000
Cost of 250 items	
250 @ $11 each	= $2,750
Gross profit	**$2,250**

If we do a summary comparing the two methods, the figures are as follows:

FIFO/Weighted average summary

Method	Purchase costs $	Closing inventory $	Cost of goods sold $	Gross profit $
FIFO	5,700	3,100	2,600	2,400
Weighted average	5,700	2,950	2,750	2,250

The main points to note are:

1. Under both methods, the revenue amounts are exactly the same.
2. Under both methods, the costs of purchases are the same.
3. It is the closing inventory, cost of sales and gross profits that are different.

Given that we have different amounts, the question arises as to which is the correct method. The answer is that they are both correct as they are both permitted under the standard. However, once a company has determined the policy which it will use, it must continue to use it. This complies with the consistency assumption that we used in Chapter 1. In the long-term, the differences in reported profit will even out, but it is essential that the users appreciate which method is being applied.

Net realisable value

Our final example in this section on IAS 2 is concerned with the calculation of net realisable value. For our example, we will use the case of Aziz who imports shawls.

Aziz imports shawls and at the year end has calculated the closing inventory value using the FIFO method:

100 luxury shawls that cost $100 each	= $10,000
200 everyday shawls that cost $80 each	= $16,000
50 domestic shawls that cost $40 each	= $2,000
Total value	**= $28,000**

When he conducts a physical examination of the inventory, he finds that the luxury shawls are defective. The normal selling price of these shawls is $160 and Aziz decides that he will have to repair the shawls at a cost of $30 each. The domestic shawls have a normal selling price of $60. They also have a defect and Aziz calculates that it will cost $25 for each of the domestic shawls to be repaired. The everyday shawls, imported from a different manufacturer, are in good condition. However, Aziz believes that the market has declined and he will have to reduce the selling price to $100 instead of the normal price of $120 each.

What is the value of Aziz's closing inventory if IAS 2 is applied?

The standard states that the NRV is the estimated sales value of the goods minus the additional costs likely to be incurred in completing production. The easiest way to tackle these types of questions is to take each item of inventory and carry out a calculation separately. Fortunately, Aziz has used the FIFO method which is permitted under the standard, so we must concentrate on determining whether the cost is higher than the net realisable value. The calculations are shown in the following table for each shawl:

Type of shawl	Normal selling price	Cost of repairs	NRV	FIFO value
Luxury	$160	$30	$130	$100
Everyday	$100	—	$100	$80
Domestic	$60	$25	$35	$40

The above table shows that the net realisable value for luxury and everyday shawls is higher than the cost. With domestic shawls, the net realisable value is lower than cost, so the inventory must be valued using the NRV. The calculation for closing inventory will therefore be 50 domestic shawls at $35 each, and not 50 shawls at $40 each.

It is important to note that it is only the additional cost required to sell the inventory that is deducted from the selling price, and not the costs that are normally incurred in the business.

3.6 IAS 18 Revenue

Definition — revenue

Revenue arises from the sale of goods, the provision of services, and the use of assets yielding interest, royalties and dividends. It is the gross inflow of economic benefits, for example, cash, receivables, and other assets arising from the ordinary operating activities of an enterprise.

In some countries, revenue is referred to as sales or turnover, but the IASB uses the term "revenue". The main issue in accounting for revenue is ascertaining the financial period when revenue is to be recognised. This is a far more complex task than it would first appear. It is surprising how many businesses still find that they have misstated revenue in their financial statements and subsequently have to make adjustments. One assumes that these are honest errors and not attempts to mislead.

The appropriate allocation of revenue is essential for calculating the correct profit figure for a financial period. IAS 18 defines revenue and identifies the two criteria for the recognition of revenue:

1.   it is highly likely that future economic benefits will flow to the business, and
2.   that these benefits can be measured reliably.

The standard defines the circumstances when these two criteria are satisfied and provides guidance on the practical application of the criteria. Taking the first criterion, which is one of recognition, the standard separates revenue from the sale of goods and revenue from the provision of services.

Revenue from the sale of goods should only be recognised when:

*   the seller has transferred to the buyer the significant risks and rewards of ownership;
*   the seller retains neither continuing managerial involvement to the degree usually associated with ownership nor effective control over the goods sold;
*   the amount of revenue can be measured reliably;
*   it is probable that the economic benefits associated with the transaction will flow to the seller;
*   the costs incurred or to be incurred in respect of the transaction can be measured reliably.

An example that meets these criteria is taken from the 2008 Annual Report of Smith & Nephew:

> ### Revenue
>
> Revenue comprises sales of products and services to third parties at amounts invoiced net of trade discounts and rebates, excluding taxes on revenue. Revenue from the sale of products is recognised upon transfer to the customer of the significant risks and rewards of ownership. This is generally when goods are delivered to customers.

Revenue from the provision of services should be recognised when:

- the amount of revenue can be measured reliably;
- it is probable that the economic benefits will flow to the seller;
- the stage of completion at the balance sheet date can be measured reliably;
- the costs incurred or to be incurred in respect of the transaction can be measured reliably.

If these criteria cannot be met, a cost-recovery basis should be used with revenue being recognised only to the extent that the recoverable expenses are recognised. Revenue from interest, royalties and dividends, assuming that these are probable economic benefits that will flow to the business and the amount of revenue can be measured reliably, are recognised as follows:

- Revenue interest: on a time proportion basis that takes into account the effective yield;
- Royalties: on an accruals basis in accordance with the substance of the relevant agreement;
- Dividends: when the shareholders' rights to receive payment are established.

Revenue should be measured at the fair value of the consideration that is received or receivable. There are examples, however, where companies, to promote trade, will allow customers to defer their payment for one or two years and the company does not charge interest. In these cases, the fair value of the consideration that is receivable for the goods is really less than the amount of cash to be received in two years' time. The company should, therefore, separately report the interest element from the cash received for the sale of goods.

Although in practice the recognition and measurement of revenue can cause problems, at this stage of your studies you should have few difficulties if you remember two important points:

1. You are using the accruals assumption. In other words, you ignore cash.
2. You are calculating the revenue generated in a specific financial period. This means that sometimes you will have to allocate the revenue over the periods that will benefit from it.

The following two examples should help you to understand these points.

Tuition revenue

Acme College is a private college with a financial year end on 31 December. It commences business on 1 September 2009 with 10 students undertaking a six-month course in Business Studies. The tuition fee for each student is $6,000 for the six-month course and they are expected to pay the full amount on 1 September. Eight students have paid in full. Of the two remaining students, one has paid half the fee and one has paid one-third of the fee. What is the amount of revenue that will appear in the Statement of Comprehensive Income?

The first point is to ignore the cash paid or not paid. Cash is very important but does not directly affect our calculation of revenue for the Income Statement. On the accruals basis, we have 10 students. The fee is $6,000 for six months, but by 31 December 2009 they will have only completed 4 months of the course. The amount of revenue is $6,000/6 months × 4 months × 10 students = $40,000. The remaining $20,000 will be shown as revenue in the financial statement for the year ended 31 December 2010.

Maintenance contract

Digital Services Inc. sells and maintains IT equipment for large companies. In the year ended 31 December 2009 it sells equipment to a company for $500,000. It also enters into an agreement with them for the maintenance of the equipment for a 5-year period starting in 2009. Digital Services charges a fee of $250,000 for the 5-year contract. What is the revenue for 2009?

Once again, this is a question of timing. The equipment was sold in 2009, so Digital Services can recognise the sale of $500,000 in that year. The maintenance contract, however, is for a 5-year period, so only one-fifth, i.e., $50,000 of the total amount, can be recognised in 2009. The remaining $200,000 will be recognised at $50,000 each year for the life of the contract.

Although the recognition and measurement of revenue seems to be a simple task, in practice there are several difficulties because of the complexity of the transactions in certain industries. In Chapter 2 we discussed the work of the International Financial Reporting Interpretations Committee. It does not issue many interpretations, but the problems revolving around revenue have resulted in the following:

- IFRIC 18 Transfers of Assets from Customers
- IFRIC 15 Agreements for the Construction of Real Estate
- IFRIC 13 Customer Loyalty Programmes
- IFRIC 12 Service Concession Arrangements
- SIC 27 Evaluating the Substance of Transactions in the Legal Form of a Lease
- SIC 31 Revenue — Barter Transactions Involving Advertising Services

3.7 Case Study

So far in this chapter we have concentrated on the accruals concept and the Statement of Income. We have ignored cash. However, cash is vitally important for a business and must be managed carefully. All businesses, even very small ones, need to keep a record of the cash coming into and going out of the business.

There is an accounting standard, IAS 7 Statement of Cash Flows, that sets out the financial information that a company must disclose. We will look at that statement in a later chapter. At this stage we will use an example of a simple working document that most companies keep.

In the following case study we will be introducing you to some new terms and we will explain them as they are used. Most of these will be further examined in later chapters.

"High as a Kite"

Andy Stewart starts a business with $6,000 buying and selling kites that are intended to be flown by adults. He names the business "High as a Kite". He purchases the kites for $25 each and sells them for $50 each. He does not pay the suppliers of the kites immediately but pays in the month after he has received the kites. His customers take two months' credit, i.e., if they purchase a kite in January they do not pay until March.

He rents a small shop in Glasgow, Scotland for $500 every three months, to be paid on the first day of the quarter.

He spends $200 per month on advertising and this is paid in the month following the month in which the expenses were incurred.

In the first six months of trading, the number of kites he purchases and sells is:

Month	Number of kites purchased	Number of kites sold
January	20	20
February	25	20
March	30	25
April	50	40
May	50	30
June	40	30
Total	**215**	**165**

Comment

In this example, we are going to concentrate on the cash and show you how it flows in and out of the business. To do this we will use a Cash Flow Statement. This will show the **amount** of cash flowing in and out of the business and the **timing** of these cash flows. Before we look at the full Cash Flow Statement, we want you to calculate the cash flows for sales and purchases on a monthly basis in the following table:

Cash Flows — Sales and Purchases

	Jan	Feb	Mar	April	May	June	Total
Sales							
Purchases							

Your calculations should look like this — as long as you have remembered the timing of the movements of cash. Andy Stewart does not pay his suppliers until the month following and his customers take two months' credit.

Cash Flows — Sales and Purchases

	Jan	Feb	Mar	April	May	June	Total
Sales	—	—	1,000	1,000	1,250	2,000	5,250
Purchases	—	500	625	750	1,250	1,250	4,375

Having inserted the cash flows for sales and purchases, you can now complete the full Cash Flow Statement by inserting the cash flows for Rent and Advertising.

We want you to also insert the subtotal for Cash In and Cash Out and the difference between subtotals A and B.

High as a Kite
Cash Flow Statement — January to June

	Jan	Feb	Mar	April	May	June	Total
CASH IN							
Sales	—	—	1,000	1,000	1,250	2,000	5,250
Subtotal A			**1,000**	**1,000**	**1,250**	**2,000**	**5,250**
CASH OUT							
Purchases	—	500	625	750	1,250	1,250	4,375
Rent							
Advertising							
Subtotal B							
Difference A – B							

If you have entered the amounts correctly, your final cash flow should look like the following. We have added a final row which gives the cumulative amount of cash. In other words, the amount of the cash difference, either a surplus or a deficit, for the month is added to the previous month. The deficit of $700 for the month of February is added to the deficit of $500 for January to give a cumulative deficit of $1,200. In March we have a cash surplus of $175 and that reduces our deficit to $1,025. Our cumulative figure at the end of June agrees with the difference between Cash In and Cash Out shown in the Total column.

High as a Kite
Cash Flow Statement — January to June

	Jan	Feb	Mar	April	May	June	Total
CASH IN							
Sales	—	—	1,000	1,000	1,250	2,000	5,250
Subtotal			**1,000**	**1,000**	**1,250**	**2,000**	**5,250**
CASH OUT							
Purchases	—	500	625	750	1,250	1,250	4,375
Rent	500	—	—	500	—	—	1,000
Advertising	—	200	200	200	200	200	1,000
Subtotal	**500**	**700**	**825**	**1,450**	**1,450**	**1,450**	**6,375**
Difference	(500)	(700)	175	(450)	(200)	550	(1,125)
Cumulative		(1,200)	(1,025)	(1,475)	(1,675)	(1,125)	

The above Cash Flow Statement dramatically illustrates the importance of cash. In real life, Andy would go bankrupt very quickly. In January there is just cash going out and the same in February. Although there is a small cash surplus of $175 for the month of March, Andy ends the six months with a cumulative cash deficit of $1,125.

Because of the critical importance of cash, most businesses will draw up a cash flow forecast. This is not a financial statement that shows past cash movements but a prediction of **future** cash flows. This enables businesses to take corrective action before the problem arises. In Andy's case, he has several alternatives to improve his cash position such as:

1. to ask his customers to pay cash when they purchase the kite;
2. to try to agree with his suppliers on a longer period of credit, and/or to pay his rent and advertising costs even later;
3. to get a loan from the bank.

Whatever Andy decides to do, he will need a cash flow forecast. Note that in the above we have used the terms "cash deficit" and "cash surplus". The Cash Flow Statement tells us nothing about profit or loss. For that we need to draw up an Income Statement.

High as a Kite
INCOME STATEMENT — January to June

	$	$
Revenue (165 @ $50)		8,250
Less cost of goods sold		
Purchases (215 @ $25)	5,375	
Less closing inventory (50 @ $25)	1,250	4,125
Gross profit		**4,125**
Less operating expenses		
Rent	1,000	
Advertising	1,200	2,200
Earnings		**1,925**

To help you compare the cash and income statement differences, we have inserted the number of kites bought and sold, although in practice these numbers would not be shown on a financial statement. We have also used the term Earnings rather than Profit.

3.8 Bad and Doubtful Debts

One issue we have not yet discussed is those customers who do not pay. We have explained that the sale of the item or provision of the service, on an accruals basis, will be shown as revenue on the Income Statement. If the sale is on credit and the customer will pay at a later date, there can be some delay for the amount owed to show on our Cash Flow Statement. The amount owed to the company is known as Accounts Receivable.

When it comes to the end of a financial period, a company will analyse its Accounts Receivable and judge whether it will be able to collect the money. If the customer has died, gone missing, or become bankrupt, it is highly unlikely that the company will be able to collect the money. In these circumstances, the company will make a charge to the Income Statement of the amount of the bad debt as an expense.

The writing off of these bad debts will have two effects. First, the amount of profit for the period will be reduced by the amount of the bad debt. Secondly, the amount owing to the company by customers, the Accounts Receivable, will be reduced by the amount of the bad debt. In the next chapter we will demonstrate the impact of this on the balance sheet.

Although the company may be able to identify those amounts of money it will not be able to collect, there may be other amounts owing by customers where the company is uncertain whether it will be able to collect the money. Remember that the company has put the full amount of revenue in the Income Statement, so it is calculating its profit for the period as if it will be able to collect the money.

This is where the caution of the accountant comes into effect. Looking at the total amount of the Accounts Receivable, the accountant may estimate that 3% will not be collected. This figure of 3% will be based on past records or the experiences within the industry. Having identified this amount, a charge will be made to the Income Statement for the doubtful debts, thus reducing the profit. Frequently companies refer to this amount as a provision for doubtful debts, but be careful. In a later chapter we will see that the term "provision" has a special meaning in the accounting standards.

In Chapter 5 we will demonstrate the impact of both bad debts and doubtful debts on the Income Statement and balance sheet.

3.9 Chapter Summary

☞ The IASB has changed the title of the Income Statement to the Statement of Comprehensive Income and extended the information to be provided. In this chapter we concentrate on the Income Statement.

☞ The Income Statement uses the accruals basis. It presents the results of transactions regardless of whether cash movements have occurred.

☞ Cash is critical to an organisation and it will produce a Cash Flow Statement. The Statement required by IAS 7 will be examined in a later chapter.

☞ Most companies have a working document that shows the timing and amount of cash coming into and going out of the business. They frequently prepare these to show predictions of cash movements. These working documents give control of cash movements to companies.

☞ Companies can choose either of two presentations for the Income Statement — the nature of expense method or the function of expense method. The latter method provides the figure of gross profit.

☞ It is essential that companies correctly show the cost of goods sold in generating revenue for the period. To do this, amounts for opening and closing inventory must be correct.

☞ IAS 2 Inventories sets out the methods for valuing inventories and the most commonly used methods are First-In, First-Out and Weighted Average. Companies are not permitted to use Last-In, First-Out.

☞ Revenue can be very difficult to measure in some industries and the guidelines are given in IAS 18.

Progress Test

1. On 1 January a company has an opening inventory of $30,000. During the course of the year it purchases a further $40,000 of goods. The sales for the year are $60,000 and this includes a gross profit percentage of 25%. At the end of the year the factory is damaged by fire. Only $20,000 of inventory in a good condition is rescued. What is the value of the inventory damaged in the flood?

   a) $70,000
   b) Nil
   c) $5,000
   d) $15,000

2. Which of the following statements about the valuation of inventory are correct, according to IAS 2 Inventories?

   a) Inventory items are normally to be valued at the higher of cost and net realisable value
   b) The cost of goods manufactured by an entity will include materials and labour only. Overhead costs cannot be included
   c) LIFO (last-in, first-out) cannot be used to value inventory
   d) Selling price less estimated profit margin may be used to arrive at cost if this gives a reasonable approximation to actual cost

3. Which two of the following conditions apply to the recognition of revenue for transactions involving the rendering of services?

   a) The costs incurred for the transaction and the costs to complete the transaction can be measured reliably
   b) The enterprise retains neither continuing managerial involvement nor effective control over the transaction
   c) The significant risks and rewards of ownership have been transferred to the buyer
   d) The amount of revenue can be measured reliably

4. A company has an opening inventory of $1,000 and during the period purchases $4,000 of goods. At the end of the period, it calculates its cost of sales amount at $4,500. What is its closing inventory?

   a) $5,000
   b) $1,500
   c) $500
   d) $3,000

5. A company purchases $400 of goods during the financial period. Its opening inventory is $100 and its closing inventory is $50. What is the cost of sales figure?

   a) $600
   b) $550
   c) $450
   d) $150

6. During the financial period, a company had the following information:

   Opening inventory $50
   Purchases $680
   Cost of sales $520

   What was the closing inventory at the period end?

   a) $800
   b) $210
   c) $270
   d) $570

7. A company has an opening inventory of $1,020 and a closing inventory of $1,550. Its cost of sales was $9,680. What was the purchases figure?

   a) $10,210
   b) $10,700

    c) $2,570
    d) $11,230

8. A company has a cost of sales of $450 and a gross profit of $150. What is its sales figure?

    a) $300
    b) $150
    c) $600
    d) None of these

9. A company has the following information for the financial period:

Sales	$17,000
Gross profit	$3,500
Net profit	$250

What is the total expenses figure?

    a) $20,500
    b) $13,500
    c) $3,750
    d) $3,250

10. A company had a fire in its offices and most of its records have been damaged. It has been able to supply the following information:

Opening inventory	$14,960
Closing inventory	$18,815
Cost of sales	$159,715

What is the amount of purchases?

    a) $14,960
    b) $163,570
    c) $178,530
    d) None of these

4

The Basics of the Statement of Financial Position

Learning Objectives

At the completion of this chapter you should be able to:

☞ Explain the accounting equation
☞ Identify the structure and contents of a simple Statement of Financial Position
☞ Differentiate between current and non-current assets
☞ Calculate annual and cumulative depreciation
☞ Explain the main requirements of IAS 16 Property, Plant and Equipment
☞ Apply IAS 23 Borrowing Costs in given circumstances.

4.1 Introduction

In the previous chapter we examined the Statement of Income and how this helps users understand the financial performance of a company over a period of time. However, this is not the only aspect of the "financial health" of the business that is of interest. When users are investigating a business they will want to know what is its "financial strength". Sometimes people will refer to what the business *owns* and what it *owes*, although this is not really an accurate description.

Information on the financial strength of the business is contained in the Statement of Financial Position, frequently known as the Balance Sheet. It provides financial information of the business at a specific point of time, that is, the end of the financial period. The Balance Sheet can be imagined as a snapshot or photograph of the business as it captures the financial position of the business on the last day of the financial period.

Of course there are connections between the Income Statement, Statement of Cash Flow and the Statement of Financial Position. We will look at these more closely in subsequent chapters. In this chapter we will examine the basis and main contents of the Statement of Financial Position. We will also look at IAS 1 Presentation of Financial Statements so that we understand how the information is communicated.

4.2 The Accounting Equation

The basis of the Statement of Financial Position is the accounting equation. To understand this equation, you must remember that the business is a separate entity from its owners. When a business is first established, it has nothing. The owners of the business will have to invest money in it, known as capital, so that the business can, in turn, acquire those items it requires to operate such as machinery, premises, and materials. These are known as assets. It may be that the owners do not have sufficient funds to make the business fully operational, so it will have to borrow funds from other sources such as banks to acquire assets.

At any one point in time, therefore, the assets that the business has will have been acquired by using the capital invested by the owners and the funds borrowed from other sources. The relationship between the assets, capital and other liabilities in the business forms what is known as the *accounting equation* which is stated thus:

$$\textbf{Assets = Capital + Liabilities.}$$

The application of the equation can be illustrated in the very simple example below.

Lazio and two friends decide to open a Pizza Shop. They have found premises that cost $100,000 and the cost of the equipment is $40,000. The bank has loaned the business $50,000 and Lazio and his friends have invested $90,000 in the business. Applying the accounting equation, we have:

Assets	=	Capital	+	Liabilities
($100,000 + $40,000)		($90,000)		($50,000)

This information would be presented formally as a Statement of Financial Position or Balance Sheet as follows:

Statement of Financial Position on Day 1

	$		$
Assets		Capital	90,000
Premises	100,000	Liabilities	50,000
Equipment	40,000		
	140,000		140,000

The presentation we have used is known as the "horizontal" format. This has the advantage of clearly illustrating the accounting equation with the assets being on one side and totalling the same amount as the capital and liabilities. However, most companies usually present the financial statement in a "vertical" format and we will examine this later in the chapter. At this stage we need to consider the balance sheet not just on the first day of operations but how it changes as the business grows. To do that, we will take the case of Will Games.

Case study — Will Games

Before we look at this case study, we will refresh your memory on Chapter 3. In that chapter we discussed the Income Statement and emphasised that it was constructed using the accruals assumption and did not recognise the movements of actual cash. This means that a business can have revenue of $25,000 on its Income Statement but, if some of the customers did not pay, the business is owed money. The amount that the business is owed is referred to as either Accounts Receivable or Debtors and is an asset. It is an asset because the cash belongs to the business and it is waiting to be paid.

Similarly, a business may purchase goods from a supplier on credit. In the Income Statement we will show the full value of the goods even though the business still owes the money. The amount owed by the business is known as Accounts Payable or Creditors and will be shown as an amount owing on the Statement of Financial Position.

We will now work through the following transactions for Will Games, constructing a horizontal format balance sheet as at the end of each day.

Will Games starts a business with $10,000.
On the first day, fixtures are purchased for $5,500 and goods for resale for $3,500.
On Day 2, the business buys a further $1,000 of goods but on credit.
On Day 3, the business sells for $3,000 cash, goods it had purchased for $2,500.

Will Games
Statement of Financial Position on Day 1

	$		$
Fixtures	5,500	Capital	10,000
Goods	3,500		
Cash	1,000		
	10,000		10,000

Comments

1. Will invested $10,000 into the business and that is the Capital.
2. The business uses $9,000 of the capital invested to purchase fixtures and goods.
3. The remaining cash unspent is an asset that the business has and appears on the balance sheet.

Will Games
Statement of Financial Position on Day 2

	$		$
Fixtures	5,500	Capital	10,000
Goods	4,500	Accounts payable	1,000
Cash	1,000		
	11,000		11,000

Comments

1. The only change on Day 2 is the business purchases a further $1,000 of goods but does not pay for them.
2. The amount for goods is now increased to $4,500 to give a total of assets of $11,000.
3. The business now owes $1,000 to its suppliers and this will appear on the right-hand side of the balance sheet as a liability.
4. If we were carrying out an audit of Will's business on Day 2 we would want to ensure that the business had inventories to the value of $4,500 and had cash of $1,000. We would also make certain that the business had a liability of $1,000.

Will Games
Statement of Financial Position on Day 3

	$		$
Fixtures	5,500	Capital	10,000
Goods	2,000	Profit	500
Cash	4,000	Accounts payable	1,000
	11,500		11,500

Comments

1. These transactions introduce some new concepts but as long as you apply the accounting equation, they should cause few difficulties.
2. The business has sold goods that cost $2,500 so the amount shown for goods on our balance sheet must be decreased to $2,000 — the value of the goods that the business now owns.
3. Customers paid cash of $3,000, so the amount of cash the business has is now $4,000.
4. The difference of $500 between the cost of the goods and what they were sold for is profit, and profit belongs to the owners of the business. The business owes the $500 to Will Games and this is shown on the balance sheet which now balances.
5. If the business paid the profit to Will, it would no longer appear on the balance sheet as something it owed and the cash balance would decline by $500 — the balance sheet still balances.

One major point to observe as we will meet this again in Chapter 10 is that the original capital figure remains the same. It can only change if the owners invest more capital into the business or, in some circumstances, if capital is withdrawn. If Will Games retains any profit in the business to make it grow, then that profit is shown on a separate line.

When we examine the balance sheet of companies, they will have a Capital or Equity amount. This will be the amount initially invested by the owners of the business and is calculated by multiplying the number of shares issued by the price per share. This is known as the "face" value or "par" value of the share. A company that has in issue 2,000 shares at a par value of $1 per share will show its total equity at $2,000.

With companies that are listed on the stock exchange, their share prices can change daily and this is public information. These changes are not reflected in the Equity amount on the balance sheet which remains at par value. Of course, a company after several years may decide to issue 1,000 more shares when the market price is high, let us say $1.50. The company will issue these new shares at the higher price. The par value of the shares is still $1 and the amount added to equity in the balance sheet will be $1,000. The difference of 50 cents between the par value and the market price will be shown separately in a share premium account.

4.3 The "Vertical" Statement of Financial Position

In the above section we concentrated on a simple version of the "horizontal" format for the balance sheet. In this section we will illustrate the "vertical" format. It is drawn up using the same principles and applying the accounting equation as using the horizontal format, but the structure of the presentation of the information differs.

The vertical format is most frequently used by companies, and assets and liabilities are classified into different groupings to make the information more useful to the reader of the financial statement. We will start this section by looking at the definitions and classifications of assets and liabilities.

Definition — asset

An asset is "a resource controlled by the enterprise as a result of past events and from which future economic benefits are expected to flow to the enterprise".

This definition is more complex than the simple statement that an asset is "what a business owns". The definition recognises that a business may not own an asset but may have entered into an agreement with another party that it can use or has control of an asset. This control will arise from an event in the past, such as entering into a formal agreement. The final, and very important, part of the definition is that future economic benefits are expected to flow to the enterprise.

A business will acquire control of premises, equipment, fixtures and other assets in the expectation that they will lead to benefits either in the form of cash or other assets, or in the form of cost savings. For example, a company may purchase some expensive computer-controlled equipment that will substantially reduce its production costs.

IAS 1 *Presentation of Financial Statements* classifies assets into current and non-current assets and these must be shown separately on the Statement of Financial Position. We have already seen examples of non-current assets such as premises, machinery, and equipment. These are items that will last a long time and are used for business operations. It is not intended that they will be immediately resold in the short-term.

The standard does not define non-current assets but states that if an asset does not fall under the definition of a current asset, it must be non-current. We need to look at the definition of a current asset. The standard states that a current asset is an asset that meets **any** of the following criteria:

- It is expected to be sold or used in the entity's normal operating cycle. For example, raw materials will be used in production; goods will be bought and resold at a profit.
- It is held primarily for the purposes of trading.
- It is expected to be realised within 12 months after the balance sheet date. For example, money owing to the company will be paid.
- It is cash.

For our purposes, there should be few problems in separating current and non-current assets, but in some complex industries there can be problems.

Definition — liability

A liability is a present obligation of an entity resulting from past events, the settlement of which is expected to be an outflow from the entity of resources embodying economic benefits.

Once again, for our purposes the above definition presents few difficulties, although in practice there may be problems. As with assets, the standard defines what it means by current liabilities, and all other liabilities are non-current. A liability is current when it satisfies **any** of the following criteria:

- It is expected to be settled in the entity's normal operating cycle.
- It is held primarily for the purposes of trading.
- It is due to be settled within 12 months of the balance sheet date.
- The entity does not have an unconditional right to defer settlement of the liability for at least 12 months after the balance sheet date.

We can now take the balance sheet for Will Games on Day 3 and convert it to the vertical format using the classifications for assets and liabilities:

Will Games
Statement of Financial Position on Day 3

	$	$
Non-current assets		
Fixtures		5,500
Current assets		
Inventories	2,000	
Cash	4,000	6,000
		11,500
Current liabilities		
Trades payable		1,000
Capital and reserves		
Capital	10,000	
Retained profits	500	10,500
		11,500

The standard does not lay down any order or format in which the items must be presented, so you will see variations in practice. Although the above is a simplified example, it does give a basic structure used by most companies. In a later chapter we will examine the format laid out in the standard.

Sometimes a company will use the vertical format for the balance sheet but reorder the separate elements to emphasise the amount of working capital. In Chapter 14 we will discuss the importance of working capital management. At this stage we will explain the presentation:

> **Definition — working capital**
>
> The amount of funding required for the organisation's day-to-day operations. It is the sum of current assets minus the sum of current liabilities.

If you consider the accounting equation expanded to show the main elements of a balance sheet, it looks like this:

Non-current assets + current assets
= Capital and reserves + long-term liabilities + current liabilities.

We can reorder this and instead of adding current liabilities to the right-hand side of the equation, we can deduct it from the left-hand side. The accounting equation still balances. Taking Will Games' vertical balance sheet, we can reorder the elements to show the working capital as a separate amount:

Will Games
Statement of Financial Position on Day 3

	$	$
Non-current assets		
Fixtures		5,500
Current assets		
Inventories	2,000	
Cash	4,000	
	6,000	
Less **Current liabilities**		
Trades payable	1,000	5,000
		10,500
Capital and reserves		
Capital		10,000
Retained profits		500
		10,500

From the above we can see that Will has invested $5,500 in non-current assets and $5,000 in working capital. The funding for that investment comes from the Capital put into the business by Will and from the profits that have been earned and kept in the business.

"High as a Kite" revisited

In Chapter 3 we had the example of "High as a Kite" and constructed a Cash Flow Statement and a Statement of Income. We can take the information from those two statements to construct the Balance Sheet or Statement of Financial Position. We can also use some of the terminology you are most likely to find on the financial statements published by large companies.

Below is the layout of the Statement of Financial Position and we have left the amounts blank. Refer to the financial statements in Chapter 3 and use the following notes to help you to complete the Statement of Financial Position. The answer to this example is at the end of this chapter.

Notes

1. The business started by purchasing fixtures and fittings that cost $3,000 and this is a non-current asset.
2. Under current assets we have inventories and this amount is taken from the Income Statement, where the closing inventory (i.e., those at the end of June) is $1,250.
3. On the Income Statement we have revenue of $8,250. The Cash Flow Statement shows that the business has only received $5,250 by the end of June. This means that the business is owed $3,000 by its customers and this will be shown as Accounts Receivable.
4. The amount of cash to be entered on the Statement of Financial Position confuses some students, but if you look at the Cash Flow Statement, the amount of cash remaining at the end of June is $1,875.
5. Andy Stewart invests $6,000 into the business. This is the capital, but we have used the term "Equity" as this signifies the investment by the shareholders of the company.
6. On the Income Statement we show a profit of $1,925. We have placed this under Equity and named it Retained Earnings.
7. Looking again at the Income Statement, purchase of goods came to $5,375 but suppliers were only paid $4,375 as shown on the Cash Flow Statement. Similarly, Advertising was $1,200 on the Income Statement but only $1,000 had been paid. The amounts still owing by the business are shown on the Balance Sheet under Current Liabilities.

High as a Kite
Statement of Financial Position
As at 30 June

	$	$
ASSETS		
Non-current assets		
Fixtures		
Current assets		
Inventory		
Accounts receivable		
Cash		
Total assets		
EQUITY AND LIABILITIES		
Equity		
Retained earnings		
Current liabilities		
Accounts payable		
Advertising		
Total equity and liabilities		

This example shows how the Cash Flow Statement, Income Statement and Balance Sheet are related and show different aspects of the company's financial performance, financial position and cash flow.

4.4 Depreciation

So far we have looked at the structure and main contents of the balance sheet, but we need to go further. One part of the balance sheet that causes some problems is non-current assets. For many companies, the total amount of non-current assets is highly significant so it is important that they are entered into the balance sheet correctly. There is also an additional aspect that we have not yet discussed: the depreciation of non-current assets.

In the examples we have discussed so far, the business has purchased a non-current asset and we have shown the cash paid in the Cash Flow Statement and the same figure in the Balance Sheet. This means that the business has the use of the asset to generate profit, but nothing is shown in respect of that use in the Income Statement. It also means that the cost of the asset will stay in the balance sheet forever, although it is wearing out, unless we do something about it.

Definition — depreciation

Depreciation is the allocation of the original cost of a non-current asset to the Income Statement over its useful economic life.

Before we look at the requirements of IAS 16 Property, Plant and Equipment, we will give a simple example of depreciation.

Depreciation example

A business purchases some equipment for $5,800 on 1 January. It believes the equipment will last for 10 years, at the end of which time it can be sold for the scrap value of $800.

To calculate the annual amount of depreciation that will be charged to the Income Statement, we will use the formula:

$$\text{Annual depreciation charge} = \frac{\text{Original cost} - \text{scrap value}}{\text{Life of asset}} = \frac{\$5,800 - \$800}{10 \text{ years}}$$

$$= \$500 \text{ each year.}$$

The annual depreciation charge will have an impact on the Income Statement and on the Balance Sheet as follows:

	Charge to Income Statement	Balance Sheet Carrying Amount
Original cost		$5,800
End of year 1	$500	$5,300
End of year 2	$500	$4,800
End of year 3	$500	$4,300
Years 4–9	$3,000 ($500 × 6 years)	$1,300
Year 10	$500	$800

At the end of year 10 the non-current asset will be shown at $800 and can be sold for scrap and will no longer appear on the Balance Sheet. The Income Statement will also have been charged each year with the $500 use it has made of the asset.

It is important to remember that the depreciation charge for the period appears only in the Income Statement — it is not a flow of cash. The amount of cash paid for the asset appears in the Cash Flow Statement when the payment is made.

Undoubtedly, the use of the depreciation method does involve predictions on the life of the asset and what the scrap value will be in 10 years' time. At best, depreciation is an estimate that allows us to make a charge to the Income Statement annually and also show on the Balance Sheet how much of the original cost of the asset still has to be depreciated.

Sometimes you will see that the carrying amount is referred to as the carrying value or written down value. Both of these terms are misleading as we are not trying to show what the current value or market price of the asset is. The figure on the Balance Sheet represents that remaining original cost of the asset that has not yet been charged to the Income Statement. You may wish to refer back to Chapter 1 and the discussion on the deficiencies of historic cost.

To make certain that you understand the treatment of depreciation and to refresh your memory on the three financial statements and their interrelationship, we will work through another example of a small business. We are using examples of small businesses to keep the figures simple, but exactly the same methods and principles are used by large businesses.

Case study — IMB

Dawn Welsh has been a collector of music boxes for a number of years. A Japanese company has introduced a new range of music boxes and Dawn believes that there is a market for these in Canada. She establishes contact with the Japanese supplier and agrees a purchase price of $20 per box. Payments must be made in cash, as she has no credit standing with the supplier. After comparing with prices in a number of stores, she calculates that the selling price of each box is $30.

Dawn has savings of $3,000 and decides to invest all of this in the business, which she will call "International Music Boxes". Dawn rents a space at a local shopping mall at $100 per month and purchases a stall from a friend for a bargain price of $1,000. She spends some time renovating the stall until it looks like new. She believes that the stall will last for 10 years but will have no value at the end of that time. She decides to charge depreciation on a straight-line basis as in IAS 16. Dawn's only other costs are advertising in the local press at $50 per month and some miscellaneous costs of $20 per month. She has a deep distrust of banks and deals only in cash, keeping any surplus money in an antique slop pot under her bed.

IMB commences trading in January 2009. For the first three months, the numbers of music boxes she purchases and sells are:

	Purchases	Sales
January	20	20
February	30	25
March	30	32

Prepare:

A Cash Flow Statement and an Income Statement for the first three months of trading, and a Balance Sheet as on the last day.

Comments

1. Complete the Cash Flow Statement first. Remember that the purchase of the stall is a cash outflow.
2. Calculate the amount of depreciation to be charged to the Income Statement for one quarter. Remember that the Income Statement is on an accruals basis.
3. The final statement to prepare is the Balance Sheet. Remember to deduct the depreciation for one quarter from the original cost of the stall.
4. Use the differences between the Cash Flow Statement and the Income Statement to calculate the amounts the business is owing or is owed at the year end.
5. Do not forget that the cash figure on the Balance Sheet under Current Assets is taken from the final cash amount on your cash flow forecast.

4.5 IAS 16 Property, Plant and Equipment

For most entities, expenditure on property, plant and equipment is substantial and raises issues on the timing of the recognition, the determination of their carrying amounts and the depreciation charge. The proper and consistent treatment of these issues is critical to ensure that the financial statements are not misleading. The standard sets out guidance on these issues for property, plant and equipment.

If you refer to our earlier definition of an asset, you will find that the standard is consistent. Property, plant and equipment must be recognised as assets when the future economic benefits associated with the asset flow to the enterprise and the cost of the asset can be measured reliably. One particular feature of the standard is that recognition should be originally at cost but subsequently may be carried at either cost or a revalued amount. In both cases, accumulated depreciation and any accumulated impairment losses should be deducted. In practice, the great majority of companies use cost, but it is important to remember that revaluation of the non-current assets is an option.

Costs include:

- costs incurred initially to acquire or construct an item of property, plant and equipment to bring it to working condition for its intended use;
- costs incurred subsequently due to additions to the original property, plant and equipment or to replace part of it or to service it. Routine servicing should be charged to the Income Statement as an operating expense, but if the asset is improved so that additional economic benefits will flow, the additional costs can be recognised as part of the asset.

As a general rule, costs that add to the value of the finished asset may be added to the original cost and shown on the balance sheet. In addition, costs that are unavoidably incurred in purchasing, installing or preparing an asset may be included as cost.

Examples of costs that are normally recognised for each class of asset are as follows:

- Land — purchase price, legal fees and preparation of land for intended use.
- Buildings — purchase price and costs incurred in putting the buildings in a condition for use.
- Plant and machinery — purchase price, transport and installation costs.

Abnormal costs such as rectifying installation errors, design errors, wastage, and idle capacity should not be considered as a part of the original cost of the asset but should be treated as an expense in the Income Statement.

Depreciation should be applied on a component basis. This means that each part of an item of property, plant and equipment with a cost that is significant in relation to the total cost of the item is depreciated separately. For example, if you have a building, you may depreciate the structure of the building over 50 years, the roof over 30 years and the windows over 10 years. It is the responsibility of the company to determine the useful economic life of an asset.

Companies need to be careful to the extent that they apply component depreciation as it could involve considerable work with no benefit. The standard refers to the components being significant in relation to the total cost of the asset. You should also remember that depreciation is based on estimates. If you have an asset that you believe may last for 25 years and it has a significant component that may last for 24 years, it is more sensible to depreciate everything over 25 years. The following are practical guidelines to depreciation practice:

- Only separately identify significant components.
- Insignificant components can be grouped together.
- Do NOT provide for future major repairs — this could be an indication that it is a component and should be depreciated separately.
- Assess whether component depreciation is significant to the user.

Depreciation applies to both the cost and revalued bases and must be applied in a systematic manner over the asset's useful life. The depreciation charge commences when the asset is available for use and continues until the asset is derecognised regardless of periods of idleness.

There are two main methods for calculating a provision for depreciation. The method we have already used in this chapter is known as the *straight-line method* of depreciation because it spreads the cost (or revalue amount) evenly over the life of the asset. It is calculated using the following formula:

$$\frac{\text{Cost} - \text{Residual value}}{\text{Useful economic life}}.$$

The residual value is an estimate of expected net proceeds from the sale of the asset (disposal value less any costs of sale) at the end of its estimated useful economic life. In the example we used earlier the figures were as follows:

A business purchases some equipment for $5,800 on 1 January. It believes the equipment will last for 10 years, at the end of which time it can be sold for the scrap value of $800.

$$\text{Annual depreciation charge} = \frac{\text{Original cost} - \text{scrap value}}{\text{Life of asset}} = \frac{\$5,800 - \$800}{10\ \text{years}}$$

$$= \$500\ \text{each year}.$$

The straight-line method is simple and easy to use, and apportions the cost of the asset evenly over the period in which it is used. Most companies find that this method satisfies their needs.

An alternative method which is allowed under IAS 16 is the *reducing balance method* which reduces the annual charge for depreciation over the life of the asset. This is also based on the cost of the asset, an estimate of any residual value and the length of its useful economic life. However, with this method, a depreciation rate (a percentage) is used. In the first year, any residual value is deducted from the original cost of the asset and then the depreciation rate is applied. In subsequent years, the depreciation rate is applied to the carrying amount of the asset in the preceding year.

We can show the impact of these two different methods with the following example.

Depreciation methods example

Sue Stirling owns a fashion shop selling high-class clothes for the older woman. She started the business on 1 January 2003. She does not know which depreciation method to use and calculates the effect of both methods.

The fixtures and fittings, which cost $40,000, on a straight-line basis over the expected life of 10 years with no residual value. Equipment, which cost $18,000, on a straight-line basis over 5 years with no residual value.

Using the reducing balance method, she has decided to depreciate at 20% for both the fixtures and fittings, and the equipment.

Depreciation calculation — Fixtures and fittings

Depreciation method	Straight line 10%	Reducing balance 20%	Add (or reduce) depreciation charge
Original cost	40,000	40,000	
Depreciation to 31 December 2003	4,000	8,000	4,000
Written down value	36,000	32,000	
Depreciation to 31 December 2004	4,000	6,400	2,400
Written down value	32,000	25,600	
Depreciation to 31 December 2005	4,000	5,120	1,120
Written down value	28,000	20,480	
Cumulative depreciation			
31 December 2003	4,000	8,000	
31 December 2004	8,000	14,400	
31 December 2005	12,000	19,520	

Depreciation calculation — Equipment

Depreciation method	Straight line 20%	Reducing balance 20%	Increase (or reduce) depreciation charge
Original cost	18,000	18,000	
Depreciation to 31 December 2003	3,600	3,600	—
Written down value	14,400	14,400	
Depreciation to 31 December 2004	3,600	2,880	(720)
Written down value	10,800	11,520	
Depreciation to 31 December 2005	3,600	2,304	(1,296)
Written down value	7,200	9,216	
Cumulative depreciation			
31 December 2003	3,600	3,600	
31 December 2004	7,200	6,480	
31 December 2005	10,800	8,784	

To comply with the consistency concept, once chosen, the same method of depreciation should be used every year, unless there is good reason to change it. If the straight-line method is chosen, the annual depreciation charge to the Income Statement will be the same each year. This is not the case with the reducing balance method, where the annual depreciation charge is higher in the early years and lower in later years.

For some assets, such as vehicles and machinery, the lower depreciation charges in later years offset the higher maintenance costs that are likely as the asset ages. Thus, the reducing balance method allows the overall cost of such assets to be spread fairly evenly. However, many companies choose the straight-line method because of its ease of application.

So far, we have concentrated on the straight-line and reducing balance methods of depreciation, but the standard also refers to the units of production method. This calculates the annual depreciation charge on the basis of the expected use or output of the asset. The following example illustrates this method.

Production method of depreciation example

A company acquires a machine at a cost of $10,000. It estimates the residual value of the machine as nil. The machine is an important part of the production process and it is estimated that the machine will be able to produce 100,000 units before it can no longer produce.

The expected life of the machine is therefore not based on the passage of time but on the amount of units it produces. The depreciation cost per unit is calculated as:

$$\frac{\text{Cost of machine}}{\text{Total production units}} = \frac{\$10,000}{100,000} = 10 \text{ cents per unit.}$$

Year	Number of units produced	Annual depreciation charge $	Carrying amount of assets $
Start			10,000
1	5,000	500	9,500
2	8,000	800	8,700
3	10,000	1,000	7,700

If the company's estimates are correct, at the end of its useful economic life the machine will have produced 100,000 units and the original cost will have been completely charged to the Income Statement by the amount of the annual depreciation. In this example we have used units, but we could have used miles travelled for a vehicle or hours of running time for an engine. One disadvantage of the production method is that the company does have to make careful estimates and maintain accurate records.

Companies should review each year the expected useful life of the asset and the residual value. There may sometimes be a change in the life of the asset and the company must make the necessary adjustments. This change in the life of an asset is not a change in the accounting method but a change in estimate. The following example shows how the adjustment is made.

Illustrative example: Change in useful life

A non-current asset with a useful life of 10 years and no residual value is acquired for $150,000. The annual depreciation charge is $15,000 and at the end of year 4, the carrying value is $90,000. The remaining useful life is revised to 3 years.

Original cost of asset	$150,000
Cumulative depreciation charge at end of year 4 ($15,000 × 4)	$60,000
Carrying amount at end of year 4	$90,000

$$\text{New depreciation charge} = \frac{\$90,000}{3 \text{ years}} = \$30,000 \text{ each year.}$$

This change in the estimate of the life of the asset can have a significant impact on a company's annual profit. In the above example, the depreciation charge in the Income Statement is being increased from $15,000 to $30,000 each year.

Under IAS 16, after the initial recognition and measurement on the acquisition of an asset, a company may decide to revalue it. We have explained previously that accountants tend to use historic cost to measure assets. This means that some non-current assets, such as land and buildings, are shown on the balance sheet at a much lower value than their present value in a time of rising prices.

A very few companies have decided to use the option in IAS 16 to revalue some of their assets. If they choose to do so, they must follow the following regulations:

- revaluations should be carried out regularly, so that the carrying amount of an asset does not differ materially from its fair value at the balance sheet date;
- the entire class of assets to which that asset belongs to should be revalued;
- depreciation is charged in the same way as under the cost basis;
- increases in revaluation value should be credited to equity under the heading "revaluation surplus" unless it represents the reversal of a revaluation decrease of the same asset previously recognised as an expense, in which case it should be recognised as income;

- decreases as a result of a revaluation should be recognised as an expense to the extent that it exceeds any amount previously credited to the revaluation surplus relating to the same asset;
- disposal of revalued assets can lead to a revaluation surplus that may be either transferred directly to retained earnings or it may be left in equity under the heading "revaluation surplus".

The following example is from the Annual Report of Enterprise Inns in the UK which owns many public houses selling alcoholic and other drinks and also food:

17. Property, plant and equipment			
	Licensed land and buildings	Landlords' fixtures and fittings	Other assets	Total
	£m	£m	£m	£m
Cost or valuation				
At 1 October 2005	5,051	103	24	5,178
Additions	102	33	8	143
Revaluation	323			323

The requirement to review revaluations regularly can be interpreted as meaning annually or at least when there are indications that there have been changes in the prices in the market. Each class of assets must be revalued to prevent what is known as "cherry picking", i.e., the revaluation of only those particular assets in a class that have increased in value and excluding those in a class that have not increased in value.

Those entities that decide to move to a revalued basis will find that it has an adverse effect on some key financial ratios. The annual depreciation charge will increase, thus lowering earnings, and the higher value of assets will depress the Return on Assets ratio. The higher asset value will have a beneficial effect on leverage ratios.

Definition — derecognition

The removal from the Balance Sheet of assets and liabilities that had previously been recognised in the financial statements of an organisation.

The time will come when either the asset has come to the end of its useful life or the company disposes of it for some other reason. The standard states that the carrying amount of an item of property, plant and equipment shall be derecognised on disposal or when no future economic benefits are expected from its use or disposal. The gain or loss arising from the derecognition goes to profit or loss when the item is derecognised. Gains shall not be classified as revenue.

4.6 IAS 23 Borrowing Costs

When a company borrows money to operate a business, it will have to pay interest. This is usually entered into the Income Statement as an expense of the business. There is an argument that if a company borrows money to acquire or construct a building or some machinery that will last for many years, instead of charging the interest to the Income Statement as an expense, it should add the interest to the cost of the asset. The interest should be treated as other costs in acquiring or constructing a non-current asset.

The effect of these different treatments on the financial statements can be highly significant. Interest that is charged to the Income Statement reduces the profit in that financial year. If the interest is capitalised, that is added to the cost of the asset, the Income Statement is not charged with the interest and the asset increases in value by the amount of the capitalised interest.

For several years there was no guidance on this issue and a company could select a method that would make the financial statements misleading. Under IAS 23, which has recently been revised, borrowing costs that are directly attributing to the acquisition, construction or production of a qualifying asset should be capitalised as part of the cost of that asset.

Borrowings may include:

- interest on bank overdrafts and borrowings;
- amortisation of discounts or premiums on borrowings;
- amortisation of ancillary costs incurred in the arrangement of borrowings;
- finance charges on finance leases;
- exchange differences on foreign currency borrowings where they are regarded as an adjustment to interest costs.

Definition — qualifying asset

A qualifying asset is an asset that necessarily takes a substantial period of time to get ready for its intended use or sale.

Examples of qualifying assets include manufacturing plants; power generation facilities and investment properties; and inventories that require a substantial period of time to bring to a saleable condition, but not inventories that are manufactured on a routine basis or produced in large quantities on a repetitive basis over a short period of time.

Where companies are capitalising borrowing costs, the following regulations apply:

- costs eligible for capitalisation are the actual costs incurred less any income earned on the temporary investment of funds borrowed specifically;
- where funds are part of a general pool, the capitalisation rate is the weighted average of the borrowing costs for the general pool;
- capitalisation commences when expenditures and borrowing costs are being incurred and activities that are necessary to prepare the asset for its intended use or sale are in progress;
- capitalisation ceases when substantially all of the activities are complete;
- capitalisation must be suspended during periods where active development is interrupted;
- where construction is completed in stages, capitalisation should cease when substantially all of the necessary preparatory activities are complete.

It is essential that a company applies the above conditions when it intends to capitalise borrowing costs and the following examples illustrate the points.

Timing

Premium Products Inc. decides to build a new headquarters. It purchases some suitable land on 1 March 2009. On 1 April it takes out a loan to start construction but because of a shortage of building materials, construction does not start until 1 June.

The interest for the period 1 April to 30 May cannot be capitalised because construction on the qualifying asset has not started. The interest will be charged to the Income Statement. From 1 June, interest can be capitalised and will be a part of the full cost of the asset.

Capitalisation and cost of assets

Newgen is building a generator plant at a cost of $5 million. It takes out a loan for the full amount with an interest charge of 10% annually. Work commences on 1 April 2009 and is completed on 31 March 2010. The loan and interest are repaid in full on 30 September 2010. What is the amount of interest to be paid, the amount of interest to be capitalised and the full cost of the asset?

Interest capitalised 1 April 2009–31 March 2010 ($5m @ 10% for 12 months)	$500,000
Construction cost	$5,000,000
Full cost of asset	$5,500,000
Interest to be charged to the Income Statement 1 April 2010–30 September 2010 ($5,000,000 @ 10% for 6 months)	$250,000

A clear example of an accounting policy which complies fully with the standard is the following extract from the Annual Report of Tesco:

> **Borrowing costs**
>
> Borrowing costs directly attributable to the acquisition or construction of qualifying assets are capitalised. Qualifying assets are those that necessarily take a substantial period of time to prepare for their intended use. All other borrowing costs are recognised in the Group Income Statement in finance costs, excluding those arising from financial services, in the period in which they occur.

Reinvestment of loan

A company is erecting a new building at a total cost of $6,000,000. It agrees a loan from the bank of $6,000,000 at a 10% interest rate for one year. The company has to take the full loan immediately but it does not need it for several months. It therefore invests the loan until it is needed and receives interest of $100,000 on this temporary investment.

Interest cost $6m × 10%	=	$600,000
Interest received	=	$100,000
Total borrowings capitalised	=	$500,000
Total cost of construction		
Cost of building before interest	=	$6,000,000
Interest capitalised	=	$500,000
Total cost	=	$6,500,000

Cessation of borrowing costs

A company takes out a loan of $900,000 at 10% interest rate per year for a new building that starts construction immediately on 1 January 2009. The building is completed by 30 June that year but the loan is not repaid until 30 September 2009.

Total interest for 9 months   = \$67,500
Interest capitalised for 6 months = \$45,000
Interest expensed for 3 months   = \$22,500

It can be difficult for a company to determine the rate of interest on the borrowing costs and the guidance is:

- If borrowing can be identified with a specific asset, the amount capitalised is the actual borrowing costs less any income earned on temporary investment.
- If funds are borrowed generally, then use the weighted average costs of capital as the capitalisation rate.
- A company cannot capitalise more than the actual borrowing costs.

4.7 Relationship between the Three Financial Statements

We have now looked at three financial statements:

- The Cash Flow Statement as a working document used for internal purposes and not published for external users. We will look at the public statement in a later chapter;
- The Income Statement which is one part of the Statement of Comprehensive Income;
- The Statement of Financial Position or Balance Sheet.

Although we have been using simple examples, the principles in constructing them are the same as used for the published accounts of large companies. You may have noticed that when we constructed the Balance Sheet, some of the figures from the other two statements were needed. One of the obvious items was the cash position from the Cash Flow Statement. The closing inventory shown in the Income Statement also appeared in the Balance Sheet.

In addition, there were these other relationships:

- The difference between the sales figure shown in the Cash Flow Statement (cash received from cash and credit sales) and the sales figure in the Income Statement (total sales revenue irrespective of when cash is received) is shown as Accounts Receivable in the Balance Sheet.
- The difference between the purchases figure shown in the Cash Flow Statement (cash paid for purchases of inventory) and the purchases figure in the Income Statement (total purchases irrespective of when cash is paid) is shown as Accounts Payable in the Balance Sheet.

We will complete this chapter by looking at the next three months, April to June 2009, for IMB.

IMB Phase 2 — April–June 2009 scenario

The period April to June 2009 was very turbulent for IMB. In April, the supplier increased the cost of the music boxes to $24 per box but allows Dawn 50% payment credit of one month for all purchases, i.e., half of April's purchases will be paid in April and half in May. Dawn believes that she is unable to increase her selling price but thinks that the number of music boxes sold can be increased. In line with this strategy, she increases her advertising spending to $100 per month. In the month of April, 50 music boxes are purchased and, at the end of the month, the closing inventory is 10 boxes.

In May, IMB purchases a further 60 music boxes at $24 each and maintains the selling price at $30 per box. A total of 45 music boxes are sold during the month but, unfortunately, a crate of 5 boxes disappears, assumed stolen, and Dawn has no insurance. All other operating costs are the same in May as for April.

In the month of June, the demand for music boxes declines dramatically. The Japanese supplier offers IMB a special deal of 20 boxes at $15 each, but all outstanding money has to be paid. Dawn accepts this offer.

For the month of June, Dawn reduces her selling price to $18 in the belief that, as she is buying at $15, she is making $3 per box. As demand is down, Dawn decides to reduce her advertising to $50 for the month. Even at this price only 16 boxes are sold and Dawn considers that the remainder can only be sold at $12 each. All other operating costs are the same but Dawn decides that she should be charging depreciation for the stall. For the three months 1 April–30 June, Dawn decides to make a charge of $25 in the Income Statement for depreciation.

You are required to complete the:

- Cash Flow Statement for each of the months April–June
- Income Statement for the period 1 January–30 June
- Statement of Financial Position as at 30 June.

Comments

1. The first statement to complete is the Cash Flow Statement and we provide below a statement showing the figures for the first three months. You will have to complete the statement for the final 3 months of the period.
2. The most complicated part is calculating the inventory at the end of June. It is easiest to do this by working out the monthly figures and we show you the method below.
3. When you account for the depreciation figure, remember that the amount goes in the Income Statement as an expense and will appear on the Balance Sheet as a deduction from the original cost of the asset.

The answers to this question are at the end of this chapter.

Inventory position

	Opening	Purchases	Sales	Closing
Jan–March	—	80	77	3
April	3	50	**43**	10
May	10	60	45	
Stolen			5	**20**
June	20	20	16	**24**
Total		210	186	

Value of inventory at end of June

Opening	20 boxes purchased @ $24 each
Purchased	20 boxes purchased @ $15 each
Total	**40 boxes**
Sold	16 boxes
Closing	*24 boxes @ ?*

In this example we are going to use the FIFO method:

FIFO

20 boxes @ $15	=	$300
4 boxes @ $24	=	$96
Closing inventory	=	$396

IMB

Cash Flow Statement January to March 2009

	January	February	March	April	May	June	Total
CASH IN							
Capital	3,000	0	0				
Sales	600	750	960				
Subtotal	**3,600**	**750**	**960**				
CASH OUT							
Supplier — cash	400	600	600				
Accounts payable	0	0	0				
Rent	100	100	100				
Advertising	50	50	50				

Misc.	20	20	20
Stall	1,000	0	0
Subtotal	**1,570**	**770**	**770**
Difference In/Out	2,030	−20	190
Cash b/f	0	2,030	2,010
Cash c/f	2,030	2,010	2,200

4.8 Chapter Summary

☞ The Balance Sheet reflects the accounting equation by showing what the business owns in the way of assets less what it owes to creditors (assets − liabilities). This is equal to what it owes to the owner (capital + retained profit).

☞ IAS 16 Property, Plant and Equipment sets out the regulations for valuing assets and the treatment of depreciation.

☞ IAS 23 Borrowing Costs specifies the circumstances in which companies can capitalise borrowing costs.

☞ The Cash Flow Statement is based on actual cash flows and shows the cumulative cash position at the end of the accounting period.

☞ The Income Statement is based on the accruals concept and measures the financial performance over the accounting period.

☞ The Statement of Financial Position is based on the accounting equation and measures the financial position at the end of the accounting period.

☞ Depreciation is the allocation of the original cost of a non-current asset over the useful life of the asset. The purchase of the asset is shown on the Cash Flow Statement when payment is made. The annual depreciation charge is shown in the Income Statement, and the Balance Sheet shows the original cost of the asset less the depreciation charged to date.

Answer — "High as a Kite"

Statement of Financial Position
As at 30 June

	$	$
ASSETS		
Non-current assets		
Fixtures	3,000	
Less depreciation	250	2,750
Current assets		
Inventory	1,250	
Accounts receivable	3,000	
Cash	1,875	6,125
Total assets		**8,875**

EQUITY AND LIABILITIES

Equity	6,000	
Retained earnings	1,675	7,675
Current liabilities		
Accounts payable	1,000	
Advertising	200	1,200
Total equity and liabilities		**8,875**

Answer — IMB January to March

IMB
Cash Flow Statement
January to March 2009

	January	February	March
CASH IN			
Capital	3,000	0	0
Sales	600	750	960
Subtotal	**3,600**	**750**	**960**
CASH OUT			
Supplier — cash	400	600	600
Accounts payable	0	0	0
Rent	100	100	100
Advertising	50	50	50
Misc.	20	20	20
Stall	1,000	0	0
Subtotal	**1,570**	**770**	**770**
Difference In/Out	2,030	−20	190
Cash b/f	0	2,030	2,010
Cash c/f	2,030	2,010	2,200

IMB
Income Statement
For January to March 2009

	$	$
Revenue (77 @ $30)		2,310
Cost of goods sold		
Purchases (80 @ $20)	1,600	
Less closing inventory (3 @ $20)	60	1,540

Gross profit		770
Less operating costs	510	
Depreciation	25	535
Profit before interest and tax		**235**

IMB
Balance Sheet
As at 31 March 2009

	$	$
Non-current assets		
Stall	1,000	
Cumulative depreciation	25	975
Current assets		
Inventory	60	
Cash	2,200	2,260
Total assets		**3,235**
Owner's capital		**3,000**
Profit		235
		3,235

Answer — IMB January to June

IMB
Cash Flow Statement
January to June 2009

	January	February	March	April	May	June	Total
CASH IN							
Capital	3,000	0	0	0	0	0	3,000
Sales	600	750	960	1,290	1,350	288	5,238
Subtotal	**3,600**	**750**	**960**	**1,290**	**1,350**	**288**	**8,238**
CASH OUT							
Supplier — cash	400	600	600	600	720	300	3,220
Accounts payable	0	0	0	0	600	720	1,320
Rent	100	100	100	100	100	100	600
Advertising	50	50	50	100	100	50	400
Misc.	20	20	20	20	20	20	120
Stall	1,000	0	0	0	0	0	1,000
Subtotal	**1,570**	**770**	**770**	**820**	**1,540**	**1,190**	**6,660**

Difference In/Out	2,030	−20	190	470	−190	−902
Cash b/f	0	2,030	2,010	2,200	2,670	2,480
Cash c/f	2,030	2,010	2,200	2,670	2,480	1,578

IMB
Income Statement
For January to June 2009

	$	$
Revenue		5,238
Cost of goods sold		
Purchases	4,540	
Less closing stock (24 units)	396	4,144
Gross profit		**1,094**
Less operating costs		
Rent	600	
Advertising	400	
Miscellaneous	120	
Depreciation	50	1,170
Loss		**(76)**

IMB
Balance Sheet
As at 30 June 2009

	$	$
Non-current assets		
Stall	1,000	
Less depreciation	50	950
Current assets		
Inventory	396	
Cash	1,578	1,974
Total assets		**2,924**
Owner's capital		**3,000**
Loss for period		(76)
		2,924

Progress Test

1. Betin Inc. has constructed its Income Statement for the year 2010 and it shows a net profit of $206,000. The accountant notices that some equipment that was

bought for $50,000 on 1 January 2010 had incorrectly been charged to the full to the Income Statement. It is the policy of the company to depreciate machinery over 8 years. What is the net income for 2010 after adjusting for this error?

a) $256,000
b) $156,000
c) $249,750
d) $212,250

2. A company purchased a building for $1,200,000 and depreciated it at 2% per annum. At the end of 10 years the building is revalued at $1,500,000 and is estimated to have a remaining life of 40 years. What is the amount of the revaluation that will be transferred to the revaluation reserve and what is the new depreciation charge?

	Amount of revaluation	New depreciation charge
	$	$
a)	540,000	37,500
b)	540,000	30,000
c)	300,000	37,500
d)	300,000	30,000

3. A business entity purchased a machine for $150,000. It estimated its useful life as 10 years with a residual value of nil. What is the annual depreciation charge and the carrying amount of the machine after three years?

a) Annual depreciation charge ....
b) The carrying amount of the machine after 3 years ....

At the beginning of year 4, it is decided that the remaining life of the machine is only five more years. What would be the annual depreciation charge for the remaining five years?

4. Which of the following best describes the annual depreciation charge to the Income Statement?

a) A method of calculating the current value of an asset
b) The allocation of the original cost of the asset over future financial periods
c) A way of building up a fund of cash to replace the asset
d) A method for decreasing the taxation charged on a company

5. A company purchases a machine for $50,000 on 1 January 2008 which had an expected useful life of four years and an expected residual value of $10,000; the asset was to be depreciated on the straight-line basis. On 1 January 2011, the

machine was sold for $16,000. The amount to be entered in the 2011 Income Statement for profit or loss on disposal is:

a) profit of $6,000
b) loss of $6,000
c) profit of $4,000
d) loss of $4,000

6. Which two of the following can be included in the cost of an item of property, plant and equipment?

a) Initial delivery and handling costs
b) Costs of training staff on the new asset
c) Installation and assembly costs
d) Apportioned general overhead costs

7. If a company purchases a vehicle on credit for making deliveries to customers, it will be classified as a:

a) current liability
b) current asset
c) non-current asset
d) long-term liability

8. A business buys equipment for £20,000 on credit. This transaction will:

a) increase assets and decrease liabilities
b) increase assets and increase liabilities
c) decrease assets and decrease liabilities
d) decrease assets and increase liabilities

9. How is working capital described?

a) Fixed assets plus current assets
b) Fixed assets minus current assets
c) Current assets minus current liabilities
d) Fixed assets plus current assets less current liabilities

10. Which one of the following terms best describes the removal of an asset entirely from an entity's balance sheet?

a) Write off
b) Depreciation
c) Derecognition
d) Impairment

5

The Basics of the Statement
of Cash Flows

Learning Objectives

At the end of this chapter you should be able to:

☞ Explain the importance of the Cash Flow Statement as a working document
☞ Analyse and interpret the working document
☞ Explain specific items on the three financial statements
☞ Describe the main purpose and requirements of IAS 7
☞ Explain the main contents of the published Cash Flow Statement.

5.1 Introduction

In previous chapters we looked at the Cash Flow Statement as a working document. Because of the importance of cash to a business, it is essential that cash inflows and outflows are monitored and controlled. Businesses will normally prepare a Cash Flow Forecast for a period of time — possibly one year. In this document they will predict the flows of cash in and out of a business and will be able to determine when they may have a cash flow deficit. In this chapter we will revisit the use of these working documents.

As well as revisiting cash flow statements, we will also examine the connection between the Cash Flow Statement, Income Statement and Balance Sheet. We have discussed some aspects in previous chapters but this is a good time to consolidate that knowledge before we move on to a deeper explanation of international accounting standards in subsequent chapters.

However, cash is not only important to those managing the business on a day-to-day basis; it is also interesting and useful information for those who are external to the business. They will want to get an overview of where the cash came from, how it is spent, and where any cash surplus is invested.

IAS 7 Cash Flow Statements is the International Financial Reporting Standard that explains the financial statement that companies should produce to keep the users of financial statements well-informed. In places, this standard is quite complex and introduces terms that we have not yet explained. The principles of the standard, however, are similar to the working documents we have been examining.

This chapter is in two main sections. In the first part we return to the Cash Flow Statement as a working document, but examine more closely how it is used by businesses. It is an extremely important tool for monitoring, controlling, planning and deciding on the financing of the business. Without full control over the cash, it is possible that a business will go bankrupt.

IAS 7 requires all companies that are using International Financial Reporting Standards to publish a Cash Flow Statement. Unlike the working document, it does not show the movements of cash in and out of a business over a period of time, but gives a summary at the end of a financial period.

5.2 Cash Flow Statements and Forecasts — The Working Documents

We have already worked through the principles of cash flow statements in Chapter 3 where we distinguished between cash and profit, but it will be useful to recap on that material and provide explanations of the terms used. The first point to remember is that cash flow statements do not reveal anything about the profit or loss of the business — they only tell you about cash. You need to refer to the Income Statement if you wish to know about profit or loss. If you are uncertain on this matter, then refer back to Chapter 3.

As a working document, the Cash Flow Statement shows the amounts of cash coming into and going out of the business over a period of time. For example, we could do a Cash Flow Statement for a period of six months showing the cash movements for each month or even for each week in the six months. These were the types of examples that we looked at earlier.

The cash coming into the business is known as a cash inflow, and the cash going out is known as a cash outflow. The difference between the cash coming in and the cash going out is known as a cash surplus if more cash comes in than goes out. If more cash goes out than comes in, then the difference is known as a cash deficit.

There are no regulations that govern cash flow statements as a working document. It is entirely the wish of a company to decide whether to keep a Cash Flow Statement — and most do. The company will also decide what the format will be. The examples we have been using are very similar to what most companies use. In a small business you may find that there is very little information in the working document and it will just be the main totals of cash coming in and going out. In large companies there will often be a great deal of detail. Needless to say, spreadsheets are used to prepare cash flow statements.

As we have mentioned before, a company will decide on the format of the Cash Flow Statement which best meets its needs. There are several similarities and the following features are usually present. We recommend that you use this format for cash flow statements you are constructing:

- The heading should state the name of the person or organisation and the period to which the cash flow refers.
- The columns should be labelled with the months to which they relate.
- The cash coming in is itemised separately in the first rows and subtotalled.
- The cash going out is itemised separately in the next rows and subtotalled.
- The subtotal of cash out is deducted from the subtotal of cash in, to give the cash surplus or deficit for the month.
- The final rows calculate the cumulative cash position.
- The final column shows the total of all cash movements for that particular item.

As well as a Cash Flow Statement showing past movements of cash, equally important, if not more so, is the Cash Flow Forecast. The format is the same as the cash flow statement, but the forecast shows management's prediction of cash flow movements in the future. The document allows cash flows to be *planned* and gives financial information which can be used in the following ways:

- to establish whether there is enough cash for future activities;
- to ensure that the amount of cash coming in is sufficient to cover the cash going out in the long-term;
- to ensure that there is sufficient cash in the short-term or, if not, that there is enough warning to arrange a bank overdraft or other loan;
- to enable decisions to be made about the investment of any cash surplus.

Example

Kumar Almousa is taking a business programme at his local college. He decides during his winter vacation that he will travel abroad during the following summer. He calculates the cost of his trip and has decided that $5,000 should be sufficient.

He has savings of $1,250 but will need $5,000 by the end of June to be able to afford the summer vacation. He has part-time work and receives $1,000 each month. He predicts that his monthly cash expenditure will be as follows:

- Rent is $200 per month, payable monthly at the start of each month.
- Electricity is $180 every 3 months, payable at the end of each three months.
- Travel is estimated at $50 per month, payable each month.
- Visits to the Health Club are $30 per month, payable at the end of each month.
- General living expenses are expected to total $120 per month, payable monthly.
- Food is estimated at $150 per month, payable monthly.
- The vacation will cost $4,000.

Kumar Almousa: Cash flow forecast January to June ($)

	Jan	Feb	Mar	Apr	May	Jun	Total
Cash inflows:							
Salary	1,000	1,000	1,000	1,000	1,000	1,000	6,000
Total inflows (A)	**1,000**	**1,000**	**1,000**	**1,000**	**1,000**	**1,000**	**6,000**
Cash outflows:							
Rent	200	200	200	200	200	200	1,200
Electricity	—	—	180	—	—	180	360
Travel	50	50	50	50	50	50	300
Health club	30	30	30	30	30	30	180
General	120	120	120	120	120	120	720
Food	150	150	150	150	150	150	900
Vacation	—	—	—	—	—	4,000	4,000
Total outflows (B)	**550**	**550**	**730**	**550**	**550**	**4,730**	**7,660**
Net cash flow (A–B)	450	450	270	450	450	(3,730)	(1,660)
Balances:							
Start of month	—	450	900	1,170	1,620	2,070	
End of month	450	900	1,170	1,620	2,070	(1,660)	

Note how the cumulative cash flow is calculated. If the difference for the net cash flow is negative, you should show the figure in brackets. In calculating the cumulative figure, follow the usual rules of arithmetic: add a positive net cash flow to a positive net cash flow, deduct a negative cash flow from a positive cash flow or add a negative cash flow to a negative cash flow.

The layout shows the difference between cash coming in and cash going out for each month (the net cash flow). It also shows the cumulative cash position (the total amount of cash that Kumar has at the end of each month). The June and Total columns both show that Kumar cannot afford the vacation based on his monthly income: he has a cash deficit of $1,660. He does have savings already of $1,250, so the amount he still needs to take his vacation is $1,660 – $1,250 = $410.

Kumar now has several options open to him that he can plan. They are:

- He could decide to take a cheaper vacation.
- He could find out whether his parents or the bank would be able to lend him the $410.
- He could try to increase his income.
- He could stop going to the Health Club which would save $30 per month.
- He could try to reduce some of his other expenses.
- He could move into cheaper accommodation.

5.3 Cash Flow Forecasts in Business

The type of decisions that Kumar has to make are also made by businesses which predict that they will have a cash deficit problem. The only strategies open to them are:

- obtain a loan;
- increase cash coming in;
- reduce cash going out.

The Cash Flow Forecast is an essential document that allows companies to manage their cash flows. Companies will also keep a Cash Flow Statement of what actually happens. By comparing the two statements as they progress through the financial period, the company can ascertain whether the strategies it adopts to prevent a cash deficit are working. These are not just cash strategies, but also impact on the Income Statement and the Balance Sheet.

The predictions and control of cash flow have an important impact on operations. Reducing the cash flows going out may mean reducing the wages and salaries paid, relocating the business, spending less on training and advertising. To increase cash flows coming in could entail increasing the price of products or increasing the number of products sold.

The Cash Flow Forecast is not only used in continuing businesses, but is essential if a business wishes to start a new venture or if individuals are contemplating starting a new business. The Cash Flow Forecast will allow them:

- to see if the proposed business will generate sufficient cash;
- to decide on the timing of cash inflows and outflows — as a general rule in a business, you want the cash to come in as quickly as possible, but go out as slowly as possible. A business with a shortage of cash may attempt to achieve this by collecting the money it is owed as soon as it can, but delay any payments it has to make;

- to calculate the amount of capital (cash) they need to start the business;
- to ascertain what additional funds they require — the owners of a new business may be able to provide some cash of their own, but a cash flow forecast will show if they will need to obtain a loan from outside sources such as a bank.

Case study — Jim Sparks

Jim Sparks plans to start a business on 1 January manufacturing and selling tennis racquets. His plans include the following:

- Equipment will cost $40,000 and will be purchased and paid for on 1 January.
- Factory rent will be $1,000 per month, payable monthly at the start of each month.
- Costs to run his small workshop are estimated at $2,000 per month, payable monthly during the month in which they are incurred.
- Sales are estimated at $12,000 per month for the first three months, then increasing to $15,000 per month from April onwards. Customers are allowed two months in which to make their payments. For goods sold in January, cash will not be received until the end of March.
- The cost of the materials will be $4,000 per month for the first three months and then $5,000 per month. Suppliers have agreed to allow one month's credit.
- The bank has agreed to grant Jim a loan of $20,000 from 1 January. Interest will be charged at 10% each year, charged to his bank account at the end of each three months.

Jim has two main questions that he needs to answer. First is whether the business will generate more cash than it spends in the long-term. Secondly, how much cash does he have to invest in the business at the beginning?

Jim Sparks: Cash flow forecast for the six months ending 30 June ($)

	Jan	Feb	Mar	Apr	May	Jun	Total
Cash inflows:							
Capital	[ ]	—	—	—	—	—	[ ]
Loans	20,000						20,000
Sales	—	—	12,000	12,000	12,000	15,000	51,000
Total inflows (A)	20,000	—	12,000	12,000	12,000	15,000	71,000
Cash outflows:							
Equipment	40,000	—	—	—	—	—	40,000
Rent	1,000	1,000	1,000	1,000	1,000	1,000	6,000

Workshop	2,000	2,000	2,000	2,000	2,000	2,000	12,000
Materials	—	4,000	4,000	4,000	5,000	5,000	22,000
Interest on loan	—	—	500	—	—	500	1,000
Total outflows (B)	43,000	7,000	7,500	7,000	8,000	8,500	81,000
	(23,000)	(7,000)	4,500	5,000	4,000	6,500	(10,000)
Cumulative cash flow	(23,000)	(30,000)	(25,500)	(20,500)	(16,500)	(10,000)	

The above shows that Jim has the largest cash deficit on a cumulative basis at the end of February. He needs therefore to invest a capital amount of $30,000. The indications are that if his predictions are correct, the business will be making a cash flow surplus on a monthly basis from March onwards. Jim will be able to pay back the loan as quickly as possible, thus reducing the interest charge to the business.

5.4 The Three Financial Statements

We have now discussed the three financial statements: Income Statement, Balance Sheet and Cash Flow Statement. Remember that the Notes to the Accounts which will be in every published Annual Report are regarded as part of the financial statements. We still have one financial statement to examine, but we will leave that until a later chapter when we are looking at international accounting standards in detail.

At this stage you should be aware of the relationship between the three financial statements, but we wish to emphasise the issue of bad and doubtful debts. We will be looking at the requirements of the standards in Chapter 7, so we need to establish the framework now. To illustrate these points, we will use a short case study. We are using the horizontal format for the balance sheet to make the explanation easier.

A company has drawn up the first working documents for its 2009 Income Statement and Balance Sheet as follows:

Income Statement for 2009

	$
Revenue	10,000
Less Cost of goods sold	5,000
Gross profit	5,000
Less Expenses	3,000
Profit	2,000

Balance Sheet as at 31 December 2009

	$		$
Non-current assets	3,000	Capital	4,000
Inventory	500	Profit	2,000
Accounts receivable	1,000		
Cash	1,500		
	6,000		6,000

At the year end the company had only received $9,000 of the $10,000 of the total revenue for the year. It therefore has Accounts Receivable of $1,000 as shown in the Balance Sheet at the year end. The company believes that it will not be able to collect all this money and estimates that it will have a bad debt of $200.

In these circumstances the accountant must use the prudence concept and make an adjustment for the estimated doubtful debt. Companies usually call this a "provision" for doubtful debts, although we will see in Chapter 7 that accounting standards use the term "provision" in a very specific way and that doubtful debts are really an estimate.

If the accountant decides to adjust the financial statements to allow for this doubtful debt, the Income Statement and Balance Sheet will look as follows:

Income Statement for 2009

	$
Revenue	10,000
Less Cost of goods sold	5,000
Gross profit	5,000
Less Expenses	3,000
Doubtful debts	200
Profit	1,800

Balance Sheet as at 31 December 2009

	$		$
Non-current assets	3,000	Capital	4,000
Inventory	500	Profit	1,800
Accounts receivable less			
Doubtful debts	800		
Cash	1,500		
	5,800		5,800

Comments

1. The cash figure does not change — as at the end of December, the company had received $9,000.
2. The Income Statement is adjusted by entering the amount of doubtful debt as an expense. This reduces the profit by $200.
3. The Balance Sheet still balances as Accounts Receivable is now only $800.

If the company finds in 2010 that everybody pays the money that is owed, the provision is reversed. In other words, it would be added to the revenue for 2010 and there would be no Accounts Receivable.

The amount for doubtful debts is so small for a company that it is considered immaterial and you are highly unlikely to find any reference to it in the Annual Report of a company. It is, however, an adjustment that many companies have to make.

5.5 IAS 7 Statement of Cash Flows

Knowledge of cash flow information is helpful to users of financial statements. Stakeholders want to know how a company generates and spends cash to answer such questions as:

*   Can the company generate enough cash to pay its bills, including debt payments?
*   Can the company generate cash in order to earn a sufficient return on investment and pay dividends?
*   Can the company generate enough cash to avoid bankruptcy?

The user can assess both the changes in net assets and the financial structure of the business by evaluating cash flow information in the context of the Statement of Comprehensive Income and Statement of Financial Position. This gives control over the amounts and timings of cash flows for adapting to changing circumstances, and opportunities can also be assessed.

There are persuasive arguments why a cash flow is valuable to users:

*   Cash is crucial for survival. Companies can go bankrupt even when they are making a profit.
*   Cash is more understandable than profit which is calculated on the accruals basis, which may not be familiar to the financially unsophisticated user.
*   Cash is less subjective than profit for forecasting because Income Statements contain several non-cash entries such as depreciation and provisions. These are based on the judgment of the company.

- Loan repayments depend on cash availability, so lenders can assess whether the company is likely to repay its loans.
- Cash satisfies the stewardship function as managers are responsible for safeguarding the assets of the company.
- Cash can be objectively verified by independent auditors who can physically count the cash or request a bank to confirm the amounts held in the name of the company. As we have seen in Chapters 1 and 4, the valuation of most non-current assets can be problematical.
- Inter-company comparison is improved because cash is a definite figure, regardless of the accounting regulations and practices that might be used.

There are some arguments against the value of cash flow information or, at least, minimising its importance:

- Profits are a familiar measure to the financially sophisticated user of financial statements. If you do not understand the concepts and regulations regarding the Income Statement, you should not be an investor.
- There is a need to forecast profits. We will explain in Chapter 14 how profit is an important measure for analysing and interpreting the financial performance of a company.
- The maintenance of operating capacity is not shown. You will recall in Chapter 1 that we explained that accounting does little to ensure capital maintenance.
- Management information systems used in a company for planning, control and decision making are usually based on accrual accounting. If it meets internal needs, accrual accounting should also satisfy the needs of external users.

IAS 7 was issued by the IASB to meet the needs of users. A Cash Flow Statement shows historical changes in cash and cash equivalents by classifying the cash flows during the period from operating, financing and investing activities. The information enables users to assess the entity's ability to generate cash and cash equivalents and to use those cash flows. IAS 7 includes an example of a Cash Flow Statement for all entities other than financial institutions. An example of a Cash Flow Statement for a financial institution is also illustrated in the standard.

Definition — cash equivalents

These are short-term, highly liquid investments that are readily convertible to known amounts of cash and which are subject to an insignificant risk of changes in value.

In discussing the working documents, we concentrate on cash, meaning notes and coins as well as cheques and other means of payment that can immediately be converted into cash. Businesses, if they have a cash surplus, will wish to invest it to earn interest. They can do this through a long-term investment where they commit to leave their investment, without making any withdrawals, for an extended period of time. A business may also decide to put part or all of its surplus funds in a short-term investment, possibly something that will mature in under three months.

For example, if you had deposited money in an account with a bank which had to stay there for six months, this would not be a cash equivalent. Deposits tied up for a specific period are known as time deposits or fixed deposits. As a general rule, three months from the date of making the investment is regarded as short-term.

You must be careful, however, if you have made an investment in the shares of another company (known as an equity investment). Shares are liable to change their value, even in a few days, and therefore the amount is not capable of being converted into known amounts of cash with an insignificant risk of changes in value.

Under the standard, short-term investments are regarded as the equivalent of cash. The standard states that cash and cash equivalents are:

- cash on hand and deposits that can be withdrawn immediately in cash without suffering any penalties;
- short-term, highly liquid investments that are readily convertible to a known amount of cash and that are subject to an insignificant risk of changes in value;
- bank overdrafts that are repayable on demand and are an integral part of cash;
- equity investments if they are in substance a cash equivalent (e.g., preferred shares acquired within three months of their specified redemption date).

The cash flow is structured on three types of activities identified by the IASB:

- *Operating activities* — Cash flows related to the production and delivery of goods and services;
- *Investing activities* — Cash flows related to the buying and selling of long-term assets;
- *Financing activities* — Cash flows related to acquiring capital, repaying debt, and paying investors through dividends.

5.6　The Direct and Indirect Methods

The standard requires the statement to classify the cash flows under several main headings. The first main heading is *Cash flows from operating activities*, and this is the first heading. It is also the only main classification where the standard allows two different methods for presenting the information.

Examples of cash flows from operating activities are:

- cash receipts from sale of goods and services;
- cash receipts from royalties, commissions;

- cash payments to employees;
- cash payments to suppliers of goods and services.

Under IAS 7, *Cash flows from operating activities* can be drawn up using either the direct method or the indirect method. The direct method is the one most preferred by the IASB and this shows each major class of gross cash receipts and gross cash payments. The indirect method, which is permitted by the IASB and which most companies use, adjusts the net profit or loss for the effects of non-cash transactions. Let us look at the information provided in the direct method.

Both methods will give a figure for the cash flow from operating activities. The direct method, however, provides the details of the cash flows that make up the total of cash flows from operating activities. The indirect method makes adjustments to the net profit or loss for the period (e.g., adding back depreciation) to arrive at the total cash flow figure.

If a company chooses to use the direct method, it will normally have the following main headings in its Cash Flow Statement. We have inserted amounts so that you can see what are the deductions and additions:

Cash flows from operating activities — Direct method

	$000
Cash collected from customers	800
Interest and dividends received	50
Cash paid for operating expenses, such as employee salaries and wages	(250)
Cash paid to suppliers	(150)
Cash for other operating expenses	(100)
Interest paid	(50)
Taxes paid	(50)
Net cash flow from operating activities	250

You may not find all of these separate headings on a published cash flow statement or you may find more detail. It will depend on the cash activities of the company. The important point is that all of the above represents movements of cash that are related to the operating activities of the company. Under the indirect method, we are still using the main heading of *Cash flows from operating activities*, but we will not give cash movements. Instead, we will adjust the net income figure from the Income Statement by non-cash movements.

Below we give a worked example, but it is useful to remind you first of the types of adjustments you have to make and why.

Cash from customers

In the above extract we show the actual cash received from customers, but in the Income Statement, using the accruals concept, we show the total amount of revenue regardless of whether cash has been received. This total amount shows not only the cash received but the amount still owing to the company because the customers have not yet paid. If our Income Statement shows a total revenue of $1,000,000 but we know that we are still owed $200,000, how much cash have we received? The amount of cash we have received for the period is $800,000.

Cash paid to suppliers

Once again, our Income Statement will show the total amount due to suppliers on an accruals basis. Let us imagine it is $200,000 for the financial period. However, if we know that we still owe suppliers $50,000 for the period, the total amount of cash actually paid will be:

Amount according to the Income Statement	$200,000
Deduct cash not yet paid for period	$50,000
Amount of cash paid to suppliers in the period	$150,000

Depreciation

We explained in Chapter 4 that when a business purchases a non-current asset, in our Income Statement we would charge depreciation which is an allocation of part of the original cost of the asset. Depreciation is not a cash movement — the cash movement is when the company pays for the asset. As depreciation is deducted from revenue to calculate our net income figure, we must add back depreciation to the net income.

We are now going to demonstrate a simple example, but there is a final complication. Companies have continuing operations and their activities go from year to year with a balance sheet constructed at the end of each year. If we want to know the amount of cash we have not collected from our customers for the year, we must take the amount for Accounts Receivable at the beginning of the year and deduct this from the amount at the end of the year. The difference will show the amount of cash we did not receive during the year.

Similarly with cash paid to suppliers. We must take the amount for Accounts Payable shown on our balance sheet at the end of the year and deduct the amount at the beginning of the year. Let us put all this together into one simple example.

Talal Inc. has the following information:

	$000
Net Income	600
Depreciation charged in Income Statement	100
Accounts receivable at beginning of year	250
Accounts receivable at end of year	350
Accounts payable at beginning of year	200
Accounts payable at end of year	350

Below we show the cash calculations and this is explained afterwards line by line:

Cash flows from operating activities — Indirect method

	$000
Net Income	600
Adjustments for	
Depreciation	100
Increase in accounts receivable	(100)
Increase in accounts payable	150
Net cash flow from operating activities	*750*

Comments

1. The net income of $600,000 has been calculated on an accruals basis. It is not cash.
2. On the Income Statement, depreciation is a deduction from revenue but it is not a cash item. We must therefore add this amount on to the net income for the year.
3. Our revenue on the Income Statement was on an accruals basis. Our Accounts Receivable has increased by $100,000 in the year and this represents the cash we did not receive. Our amount of revenue stated on an accruals basis is therefore higher than the amount of cash we received by $100,000. If our revenue is higher, then our net income is higher. We must therefore reduce our net income by $100,000 to adjust for the cash we did not receive.
4. On the Income Statement we would have shown our purchases of goods and materials on an accruals basis and we would have deducted this amount from the revenue to arrive at our net income. However, our Accounts Payable has increased by $150,000. On our Income Statement we have therefore deducted $150,000 more than what we paid in cash. Our net income must therefore be increased by $150,000 to calculate the cash figure.

Although we have stated that the majority of companies use the indirect method, there are examples of companies using the direct method. Below we show the headings from China Petroleum and Chemical Corporation's Annual Report 2008. Their financial statements were prepared using China Accounting Standards and not International Standards, but they are very similar.

Cash flows from operating activities:
Cash received from sale of goods and rendering of services
Rentals received
Grants received
Other cash received relating to operating activities
Sub-total of cash inflows
Cash paid for goods and services
Cash paid for operating leases
Cash paid to and for employees
Value added tax paid
Income tax paid
Taxes paid other than value added tax and income tax
Other cash paid relating to operating activities
Sub-total of cash outflows

5.7 The Main Headings

We have looked in detail at the heading *Cash flows from operating activities*, but the standard requires the total cash flows to be classified under the following three main headings:

- **Cash flows from operating activities**
  The main revenue-producing activities of the enterprise, for example, cash received from customers and cash paid to suppliers and employees.
- **Cash flows from investing activities**
  The acquisition and disposal of long-term assets and other investments that are not considered to be cash equivalents, for example, acquisition of plant and equipment.
- **Cash flows from financing activities**
  Activities that alter the equity capital and borrowing structure of the enterprise, for example, cash from issuing shares.

We have already looked at the types of information that come under the operating activities heading, so we will give illustrations of the types of disclosures under the other two headings:

Cash flows from investing activities

Purchase of a subsidiary company
Purchase of property, plant and equipment
Capitalised development costs
Cash payments to construct property, plant and equipment
Proceeds from sale of property, plant and equipment
Proceeds from sale of intangible and any other non-current assets
Cash payments to acquire shares or debentures in other entities
Cash receipts from sales of shares or debentures in other entities
Cash flows out as loans made
Cash flows in from repayments of loans made
Interest received
Dividends received
Net cash used in investing activities

You will appreciate from the above that "purchases" represent cash going out, and "receipts" and "proceeds" represent cash coming in.

Cash flows from financing activities

Proceeds from issue of share capital
Proceeds from long-term borrowings
Payment of finance lease liabilities
Dividends paid

Interest and dividends can come under several headings, and the standard states that interest and dividends received and paid may be classified as operating, investing or financing cash flows but must be treated consistently. Tax cash flows can also cause a problem, and the standard states that these flows relating to income are normally classified as operating unless they can be specifically identified under another heading. There are also various regulations concerned with foreign currency cash flows and we will examine these in Chapter 13.

> **Definition — debenture**
>
> A long-term loan usually taken by an organisation and repayable at a fixed date. Some debentures are irredeemable securities. Most debentures pay a fixed rate of interest which must be paid before a dividend is paid to shareholders.

Worked example

The following is the summarised Income Statement and Balance Sheet of Monet Arts Inc.:

Income Statement for the year ended 31 December 2009

	$000	$000
Sales		650
Raw materials	70	
Employee costs	100	
Depreciation	110	280
		370
Interest payable		30
Profit before tax		340

Balance Sheet

	2009 $000	2009 $000	2008 $000	2008 $000
Non-current assets				
Cost	1,650		1,450	
Depreciation	334	1,316	224	1,226
Current assets				
Inventory	20		20	
Accounts receivable	76		60	
Cash	368	464	94	174
		1,780		1,400
Share capital		600		600
Retained earnings		640		300
Long-term loans		400		380
Accounts payable		140		120
		1,780		1,400

Statement of Cash Flows for the year ended 31 December 2009

	$000	$000
Net cash flow from operating activities		
Operating profit	370	
Depreciation	110	
Increase in accounts receivable	(16)	
Increase in accounts payable	20	484

Cash flows from investing activities

Acquisition of non-current assets	(200)

Cash flows from financing activities

Increase in loans	20	
Interest	(30)	(10)
Increase in cash and cash equivalents		274
Cash and cash equivalents at 1 January 2009		94
Cash and cash equivalents at 31 December 2009		368

In preparing a Statement of Cash Flows from the Income Statement and the Statement of Financial Position, remember that we are trying to adjust our profit, which is a non-cash figure, into a cash figure. Possibly the easiest adjustment to understand is the adding back of depreciation because from the earlier examples in this chapter you know that depreciation is charged to the Income Statement but is not cash. Our comments on all the adjustments are given below:

Comments

1. The operating profit of $370,000 is not a cash figure and has to be adjusted.
2. Depreciation of $110,000 is added back. This is shown on the Income Statement and confirmed by the cumulative amounts of depreciation shown on the Balance Sheet.
3. Accounts receivable increased by $16,000 which is cash we did not receive, so it must be deducted from the profit figure.
4. Accounts payable increased by $20,000, so it must be added to the profit figure.
5. From the Balance Sheet we see that the cost of non-current assets increased by $200,000, so that is cash going out.
6. With financing activities we received $20,000 from an increase in loans as shown on the Balance Sheet, and we paid out $30,000 for interest.

Before we speculate on likely future changes to IAS 7, we will summarise the main adjustments to be made to operating profit to calculate the net cash flow from operating activities. Apart from depreciation, the other items are calculated by deducting the figure on last year's balance sheet from the figure on this year's balance sheet to show the increase or decrease.

Additions to profit

Movement	Reason
Depreciation	It is deducted in the Income Statement to calculate profit but it is not cash
Decrease in inventory	Inventory has been sold that was acquired in a previous period, so we have more cash than profit
Decrease in accounts receivable	Customers have paid from sales made in a previous period, so we have more cash
Increase in accounts payable	We have not paid suppliers fully for this financial period, so we have more cash

Deductions from profit

Movement	Reason
Increase in inventory	We have purchased more inventory, so we have less cash
Increase in accounts receivable	Not all customers have paid for the sales shown on the Income Statement
Decrease in accounts payable	We have paid more to suppliers than for the period's receipts of goods, so we have less cash

5.8 Likely Future Changes

As we stated in an earlier chapter, the IASB is constantly trying to improve standards and this brings about amendments and improvements. In addition, for several years the IASB and the Financial Accounting Standards Board in the US have been trying to converge their two sets of standards. The aim is to produce mutually agreed standards. These modifications to existing standards are sometimes of little importance, but there has been discussion between the two bodies about the Cash Flow Statement.

It is too early to say what the results of these discussions will be, but there are two proposals that could have a substantial impact on the appearance and content of the Cash Flow Statement. First is the alternative direct and indirect methods. Secondly, and not so important for our present purposes, is the definition and inclusion of cash equivalents in the Cash Flow Statement.

The IASB has always preferred the direct method for disclosing information. As we have explained above, this shows cash flows based on how much cash is actually paid or received. It is generally agreed that the users of Statements of Cash Flows would prefer the direct method. Unfortunately, the majority of companies use the indirect method which starts with net income and makes adjustments to arrive at the cash flow.

Companies argue that it is much easier to obtain information from their existing records for the indirect method. It is also argued by a few that the direct method may mean that information is disclosed that is commercially sensitive. Whatever the strength of these arguments, current discussions suggest that there will be an attempt by the standard setters to introduce an amendment so that only the direct method can be used.

There is also some confusion regarding the definition of cash equivalents, and this may also be clarified. There are a few other smaller changes that are being considered, but the move to only accepting the direct method would be a major change.

5.9 Chapter Summary

☞ The Cash Flow Forecast and Cash Flow Statement are critical methods used by companies to monitor, control and plan their liquidity.
☞ The Cash Flow Forecast allows a company to determine what actions can be taken if a cash deficit is predicted and the decisions to be made if there is predicted cash surplus.
☞ The working documents used by a company are confidential and not published. Companies are obliged under IAS 7 to report their cash flows.
☞ The main headings on the IAS 7 statement are cash flows from operating activities, investing activities and financing activities.
☞ IAS 7 permits both the direct and indirect method for operating cash flow.

Progress Test

1. Which two of the following items could appear in a Statement of Cash Flows?

   a) Surplus on revaluation of non-current assets
   b) Proceeds of issue of shares
   c) Bad debts written off
   d) Dividends received

2. Part of a company's draft Cash Flow Statement is shown below:

	$000
Operating profit	8,500
Depreciation charges	(2,000)
Increase in inventory	(180)
Increase in accounts payable	230

Which one of the following statements is correct?

a) Depreciation charges should have been added, not deducted
b) Increase in inventory should have been added, not deducted
c) Increase in accounts payable should have been deducted, not added

3. Which ONE of the following items should be presented under "Cash Flows from Investing Activities"?

a) Redemption of debentures
b) Development costs capitalised in the period
c) Employee costs
d) Property revaluation

4. Which TWO of the following can be classified as cash and cash equivalents under IAS 7?

a) Loan notes held due for repayment in 90 days
b) Equity investments
c) A bank overdraft
d) Redeemable preference shares due in 180 days

5. Which two of the following items could appear in a company's Cash Flow Statement?

a) Debenture interest received
b) Conversion of debentures into shares
c) Proceeds of debenture issue
d) Debenture interest owed

6. IAS 7 requires cash flows to be classified into operating, investing and financing activities. Which one of the following is classified as an operating activity?

a) Employee costs
b) Redemption of debentures
c) Sales proceeds of subsidiary
d) Disposal proceeds of a major item of plant

7. IAS 7 requires cash flows to be classified into operating, investing and financing activities. Which ONE of the following is classified as a financing activity?

a) Redemption of debentures
b) Development costs capitalised in the period
c) Sales proceeds of subsidiary
d) Disposal proceeds of a major item of plant

8. Which ONE of the following statements about the calculation of operating cash flows using the indirect method is incorrect?

   a) Loss on sale of operating non-current assets should be deducted from net profit before taxation
   b) Increase in inventory should be deducted from operating profits
   c) Increase in payables should be added to operating profits
   d) Depreciation charges should be added to net profit

9. The following figures are to be included in the calculation of net cash from operating activities:

	$
Depreciation charges	980,000
Increase in inventories	130,000
Decrease in receivables	100,000
Increase in payables	80,000

   What will the net effect of these items be in the Cash Flow Statement?

		$
a)	Addition to operating profit	1,290,000
b)	Subtraction from operating profit	850,000
c)	Addition to operating profit	870,000
d)	Addition to operating profit	1,030,000

10. Which ONE of the following comments about Cash Flow Statements is correct?

    a) A Cash Flow Statement prepared using the direct method produces a different figure for operating cash flow from that produced if the indirect method is used
    b) A surplus on revaluation of a non-current asset will not appear as an item in a Cash Flow Statement
    c) A profit on the sale of a non-current asset will appear as an item under "Cash Flows from Investing Activities" in a Cash Flow Statement

6

Intangible Assets and Impairment of Assets

Learning Objectives

At the end of this chapter you should be able to:

☞ Describe intangible assets and the purpose of IAS 38 Intangible Assets
☞ Distinguish between acquired and internally generated intangible assets
☞ Explain the accounting procedures for intangible assets
☞ Define impairment, value in use and recoverable amount under IAS 36 Impairment of Assets
☞ Calculate the amount of impairment of an asset
☞ Explain the procedures for Cash-Generating Units.

6.1 Introduction

In Chapter 4 we introduced the Balance Sheet or Statement of Financial Position. We used the accounting equation to explain how a Balance Sheet "balanced" and we examined its interrelationship with the Cash Flow Statement and Income Statement. We also discussed the main contents and the treatment of non-current assets under IAS 16 Property, Plant and Equipment.

The non-current assets included in IAS 16 are referred to as tangible assets. This means that they have a physical substance. Buildings, land, machinery, vehicles can be seen and touched. There are other assets that are very important to a business because they generate future economic benefits, but they do not have a physical substance. For example, the name "Coca Cola" is extremely well-known and the brand name encourages people to ask for the product. The name itself, however, is an intangible asset.

There are other examples of intangible assets that are equally important. For example, you may have a legal right to conduct a business or manufacture a certain item that nobody else has. This is possibly because you have a legal right in the form of a patent or you may have copyright to a creative piece of work, such as a book. IAS 38 Intangible Assets explains the proper recognition, measurement and disclosure of such assets.

The accounting treatment of intangible assets is very similar to that of tangible assets. When they are acquired, there will be the payment recorded in the Cash Flow Statement. The intangible asset will appear on the Balance Sheet and, mainly, it will be amortised. Below we give the first five lines from the Consolidated Balance Sheet of Diageo's 2008 Annual Report. You can see that the value of intangible assets is much higher than that of property, plant and equipment.

Non-current assets

		30 June 2008
	Notes	£million
Intangible assets	11	5,530
Property, plant and equipment	12	2,122
Biological assets	13	31
Investments in associates	14	1,809
Other investments	16	168

Note 11 of the Annual Report explains what are the intangible assets that make up the total of £5,530 million, and they are Brands, Goodwill, Other Intangibles and Computer Software.

The increasing importance of intangible assets has led to a variety of practices, with some countries ignoring them completely, and companies not covered by international standards have included some intangible assets on the balance sheet which are questionable. There have also been a variety of approaches to the question of depreciating the intangible asset with some companies using different periods of time and others charging no depreciation. IAS 38 attempts to resolve these issues.

In Chapter 4 our explanation of IAS 16 referred to the revaluation method of measurement. There is no obligation for companies to use this and the great majority of companies use historic accounting to measure their assets. A small number of companies use the revaluation method usually because they own buildings that are increasingly significant in value.

The value of assets may go down as well as up, sometimes because of general decline in market value, but there can also be new legislation restricting the use of certain assets and there may also be damage to the asset. These events may decrease the value of the asset to an amount which is much lower than the amount shown in the balance sheet. We will refer to this amount as the carrying value. Where there is this decrease in value, companies are required by IAS 36 Impairment of Assets to make adjustments to their financial statements.

In this chapter we will examine both IAS 38 and IAS 36. In doing so, we will be building on your previous knowledge of the balance sheet, so you may wish to refer back to Chapter 4 to remind yourself of the main points.

6.2 IAS 38 Intangible Assets

Definition — intangible assets

An intangible asset is an identifiable non-monetary asset without physical substance.

The above definition introduces some specific criteria such as identifiable and non-monetary that require further explanation, but first we will list some intangible assets that appear on the balance sheets of companies. This will give you an appreciation of the types of assets we are examining.

> *Examples of intangible assets*
> Fishing quotas
> Airline landing slots
> Taxi licences
> Patents
> Trademarks
> Customer databases
> Brand names
> Computer software

If you consider the above list, you will appreciate that the holders of these assets or those who have control of them can expect to enjoy, most likely, the future economic benefits. All of these items therefore satisfy the definition of an asset. With some intangible assets such as patents, copyright and taxi licences, it is easy to establish how much they cost the company, and the holder of the right can usually choose to sell it or rent it out if they wish.

There are other items not on the list which are definitely a benefit to the company. A company may have highly trained employees, excellent organisational procedures and a high degree of customer satisfaction. It would be extremely difficult to value these assets, although they may be important in making a company successful. Because of the absence of reliable measurement, these assets do not appear on the balance sheet.

Sometimes it is difficult to judge whether a specific intangible asset should be placed on the balance sheet. To overcome this difficulty, the standard states that intangible assets must be identifiable. This means that they must be capable of being separated from the rest of the company and can be sold, licensed, rented or exchanged either individually or together with a related item; or the intangible asset must be identifiable because it arises from contractual or legal rights, even if those rights are not separable from the business.

Definition — brands

Intangible assets such as a product or company name, sign, symbol or design that, if operated in combination, will lead to greater economic benefits from the manufacture and/or sale of a product or service through brand differentiation.

Earlier in this chapter we used the example from Diageo's 2008 Annual Report to demonstrate how important intangible assets are to some companies. The main business of Diageo is in the drinks industry and for those organisations in food and drink, brand names are extremely important and very valuable. The following extract from the Notes to the Annual Report shows how important brand names are to Diageo:

(a) Brands are stated at fair value on acquisition. The principal acquired brands are as follows:

Product	Currency of Investment	Remaining Amortisation Period	Carrying Amount £ million
Johnnie Walker Whisky	Sterling	Indefinite life	625
Smirnoff Vodka	US dollar	Indefinite life	414
Crown Royal Whisky	US dollar	Indefinite life	736
Captain Morgan Rum	US dollar	Indefinite life	604
Windsor Premier Whisky	Korean won	Indefinite life	416

Capitalised brands are regarded as having indefinite useful economic lives and have not been amortised. These brands are protected in all of the major markets where they are sold by trademarks, which are renewable indefinitely. There are not believed to be any legal, regulatory or contractual provisions that limit the useful lives of these brands.

The nature of the premium drinks industry is that obsolescence is not a common issue, with indefinite brand lives being commonplace, and Diageo has a number of brands that were originally created more than 100 years ago. Accordingly, the directors believe that it is appropriate that the brands are treated as having indefinite lives for accounting purposes.

Some intangible assets may be separable, but the standard does not apply to them because they are covered by another standard or there are special conditions applying to them. Examples are:

- financial assets;
- mineral rights and exploration and development costs incurred by mining and oil and gas companies;
- intangible assets arising from insurance contracts issued by insurance companies.

Having explained what we mean by intangible assets, there is a further consideration. Some intangible assets will have been acquired by the company and some will have been internally generated; in other words, the company has developed the intangible asset itself. For example, a drinks company may have developed a new "energy" drink, or a company may have developed software for controlling its operations. We need to look at these two types of intangible assets separately.

IAS 38 Intangible Assets was issued with the objectives of:

- Establishing the criteria for when an intangible asset may or should be recognised;
- Specifying how intangible assets should be measured;
- Specifying the disclosure requirements for intangible assets.

We will now consider the requirements of the standard in respect of acquired intangible assets and internally generated intangible assets.

6.3 Acquired Intangible Assets

This is the easiest group to consider. Initially, an intangible asset should be recognised at cost if all the following criteria are met:

- it is identifiable and controlled by the entity;
- it is probable that there will be future economic benefits; and
- the cost can be measured reliably.

The simplest situation for determining cost on acquisition is where the company has acquired the asset with a single transaction and paid for it. A second situation is where the company acquires an asset by exchanging another for it. In these circumstances, the asset is measured at fair value. Where this is not possible, the asset acquired is measured at the carrying amount of the asset given up.

The third situation is where the intangible asset is acquired in the course of taking over another business: a business combination. In these circumstances, the intangible asset should be recognised at fair value which is the amount for which an asset could be exchanged between knowledgeable, willing parties in an arm's-length transaction.

After initial recognition, a company has a choice of measurement methods. An intangible asset may be carried in the balance sheet at either:

- cost less any accumulated amortisation and impairment losses; or
- a revalued amount (based on fair value) less any subsequent amortisation and any accumulated impairment losses. This method cannot be used at initial recognition.

We will expand on these two methods. Cost is normally easily found as the asset has been acquired and is the purchase price, including taxes and duties but less discounts and rebates. You can also include the directly attributable costs of preparing the asset for use, e.g., employee benefits, professional fees, and costs of testing.

There are certain items that cannot be included in the original cost and these are:

- administration costs;
- costs of introducing new products or services;
- costs of conducting new business;
- costs incurred whilst waiting to use the asset;
- initial operating losses from operation.

If the revaluation model is used subsequent to the initial recognition, there are several criteria that must be met. The fair value method of measurement can only be used if the fair value of the intangible asset can be determined by reference to an active market at the date of the revaluation. An active market is one where the items traded are homogeneous, willing buyers and sellers can be found at any time, and prices are available to the public. The standard considers that active markets are expected to be uncommon for intangible assets, and valuation models and other techniques cannot be used as a substitute.

The entire class of the intangible assets must be revalued at the same time and revaluations must be made regularly to ensure that the carrying amount does not differ from that which would be determined at the year end.

Having determined the cost of the intangible asset, the question arises as to how it will be treated in the financial statements. One method would be to depreciate the intangible asset over its useful economic life in the same way as we depreciate tangible assets such as machinery and equipment. However, we saw in the example of Diageo that some intangible assets have indefinite lives, so we need to consider the alternatives. There are four main methods that we could use and all of these have been proposed and some used at various times throughout the world:

(1) All companies to depreciate their intangible assets over a set period of years. The difficulty is deciding what that length of time should be. It is an arbitrary decision and we could choose 20 years or 50 years, and neither would necessarily reflect the useful economic life of the intangible asset.

(2) Not allow intangible assets to be recognised and shown on the balance sheet. Instead, the amount that the company pays for the intangible asset could be charged directly to the Income Statement.

(3) Put the intangible asset on the balance sheet and leave it there for all time, or at least until the company disposes of the intangible asset.

(4) Put the intangible asset on the balance sheet but have some mechanism that allows the value of the intangible asset to be changed as economic circumstances change.

The IASB has taken the view that some intangible assets are similar to tangible assets and need to be depreciated, although the term "amortisation" is normally used. The IASB also accepts that some intangible assets are different from tangible assets as they can have an indefinite life with no foreseeable limit to the period in which benefits will be generated.

Where the company believes that the asset has an indefinite life, there is no need to depreciate it. The IASB, however, takes the sensible view that even if we are unable to predict the useful life of certain intangible assets, they will not last forever. The standard requires that in these circumstances, the asset must be tested for impairment annually using IAS 36 Impairment of Assets, and we will be discussing this topic in the later part of this chapter. Note that the standard on impairment refers not only to intangible assets but also to tangible assets such as property, plant and equipment. Our considerations in this chapter are focused on intangible assets and their impairment.

For intangible assets that have a predictable useful life, such as patents and copyrights which have a legal length of life, or where the company can predict the useful economic life, the asset should be depreciated over that period. The procedure for depreciating intangible assets is the same as for tangible assets. In other words, the cost of the asset less any residual value is divided by its useful life. This will give the annual depreciation charge to be entered into the Income Statement, and the carrying amount of the asset will reduce each year by the amount of the annual depreciation.

The following example of the useful economic life of some intangible assets is taken from the 2008 Annual Report of Rentokil. The core activities of this company encompass Pest Control, Tropical Plants, Office Cleaning, Parcels Delivery, Conferencing and Facilities Management.

Intangible assets — Finite useful lives

Intangible assets with finite useful lives are initially measured at either cost or fair value and amortised on a straight-line basis over their useful economic lives, which are reviewed on an annual basis. The estimated useful economic lives of intangible assets are as follows:

Customer lists and relationships: 5–16 years
Brands and patents: 2–15 years
Reacquired franchise rights: 3–5 years
Computer software: 3–5 years
Development costs: 5 years

6.4 Internally Generated Intangible Assets

The standard setters are very reluctant to allow companies to recognise internally generated intangible assets and they set out specific criteria for the recognition of certain internally generated assets. Those assets that should not be recognised as intangible assets include internally generated goodwill, brands, and publishing titles. Although these particular intangibles should not be recognised if internally generated, they may meet the general recognition criteria if purchased from another company.

A similar asset may therefore be recognised on the Balance Sheet if purchased, but must be charged to the Income Statement if internally generated. Although some may regard this differing treatment as illogical, the reason for the provision is the uncertainty of measurement with internally generated intangible assets. The result of this regulation is that some very famous brands and publishing titles will only appear on a balance sheet if they have been acquired externally.

Goodwill presents one of the major accounting problems for standard setters. It is accepted that a very successful company will have various characteristics such as a good reputation, very marketable products, excellent service, etc. These various characteristics are frequently grouped together and known as "goodwill". If a company has developed the goodwill itself, it will not appear on the balance sheet as an intangible asset. One can think of many companies with good reputations, but goodwill does not appear on their balance sheets because it has been internally generated.

A company can acquire goodwill and this will be shown on its balance sheet. We will give a very simple example. Imagine that a very large company purchases a smaller but highly successful smaller company. Because it is so successful, the large company is willing to pay a very good price for it. Let us assume that it is one million dollars. The purchase is successful and the large company calculates the fair value of the tangible assets it has acquired.

It calculates the fair value to be $800,000. As the purchase price was $1 million, the large company paid an extra $200,000 and this must have been for the goodwill that the smaller company had generated internally. However, as the large company has paid for the goodwill, it can show it on its balance sheet.

Internally generated goodwill cannot be placed on a company's balance sheet but purchased goodwill can be. Purchased goodwill normally arises in a business combination: where one company acquires another. Because of the importance of goodwill and the controversy around its accounting treatment, we have delayed our full discussion on this to Chapter 10 where we deal with business combinations.

There is some scope in IAS 38 for companies to put their development costs but not research costs on their balance sheet as an intangible asset. The conditions allowing a company to do this are very restrictive and "research" itself cannot be capitalised. This means that these activities must be divided into a research phase and a development phase. Expenditure on research must be charged to the Income Statement in the financial period in which it occurs and includes such costs as:

- the pursuit of new knowledge;
- the search for, or evaluation, and selection of applications of research;
- the search for such items as alternative materials, products and systems;
- the pursuit of possible alternatives for improved such items as materials, products and systems.

The restrictions on the capitalisation of research are so tight that it is better to look at the criteria that must be met in order to capitalise development costs. To be able to put the development costs on the balance sheet as an intangible asset, a company must separate the research and development phase. The expenditure for the development phase can only be capitalised if the following can be demonstrated:

- The technical feasibility of completing the asset so that it will be ready for sale or use;
- The intention to complete the asset and sell it or use it;
- The ability to use or sell the asset;
- That the asset will generate future economic benefits for the company;

- The availability of sufficient technical, financial and other resources to complete the development of the asset;
- The ability to be able to measure reliably the costs of development.

For some companies, the transition from a research phase to a development phase may be difficult to identify. There is also the issue that in some industries, many research projects are started but then abandoned as the results are not looking promising. A project will often start as research and, if unsuccessful, will be terminated.

If the research is successful, the project will enter into a development phase. Usually a business plan is required to prove that a project has entered into the development phase. The fact that the project is successful does not allow the company to go back and capitalise the research costs. They must be written off as they are incurred.

6.5 IAS 36 Impairment of Assets

There is the risk that an entity may be showing an asset at a carrying value on its balance sheet that is greater than its recoverable amount. The recoverable amount is the greater of the asset's net selling price and its value in use. Without this information, users can be misled on the financial strength of the entity and its financial performance. IAS 36 addresses this issue and it applies to:

- Property, plant and equipment
- Intangible assets and goodwill
- Investment property carried at cost
- Subsidiaries, associates and joint ventures.

IAS 36 describes the procedures to be followed to ensure that an asset is not carried at greater than its recoverable amount. The standard also explains the accounting treatment for impairment loss. Entities may find that the requirement to write off impairment losses in the financial period they occur has a significant negative effect on earnings and associated performance ratios.

> **Definition — impairment**
>
> Impairment is when an asset's recoverable amount falls to an amount less than its carrying amount.

Companies must assess annually whether there has been an indication of impairment of all its assets. The key word is "indication" and that relieves companies from conducting a full impairment test. Companies do have to annually assess recoverable amounts for:

- Intangible assets with indefinite lives
- Intangible assets not ready for use
- Goodwill arising through a business combination.

Looking at the first stage of assessing indications of impairment, companies should carry out a review of its assets at the end of each year. The external indications of a possible impairment are:

- An abnormal fall in the asset's market value;
- A significant change in the technological, market, legal or economic environment of the business in which the assets are used;
- An increase in market interest rates or market rates of return on investments likely to affect the discount rates in calculating the value in use of the assets;
- The carrying value of the net assets being more than its market capitalisation.

The internal indications of impairment are:

- Evidence of obsolescence or physical damage;
- Adverse changes in the use to which the asset is put;
- The asset's economic performance.

If there are no indications of impairment, the company need take no action. If there are indications of impairment, the company must make an estimate of the recoverable amount of the asset. Figure 1 illustrates how impairments are identified.

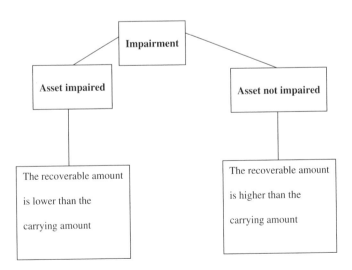

Figure 1.   Identifying impairment

Some of these terms need defining before we can go further and illustrate their application:

Definition — recoverable amount

Recoverable amount is the higher of *fair value* less costs to sell and *value in use.*
Fair value is a sale at arm's length with willing buyer/seller.
Value in use is the discounted future cash flows expected from an individual asset or a cash-generating unit.

In simple terms, recoverable amount is either the amount you would expect to receive if you sold the asset (fair value) or what you would expect to gain if you retained the asset as part of your business (value in use). Value in use is a concept that we have not explained but you may have encountered it during your other studies as it is based on the time value of money. The two major steps that a company would take in arriving at the value in use of an asset are as follows:

- Estimate the future cash flows anticipated over the remaining life of the asset. This is the Cash Flow Forecast that we explained in the previous chapter, but it is related to one asset. The company has to determine the cash inflows and cash out-flows for that asset to find the cash surplus or deficit each year for its remaining years of use.
- The next stage is to calculate the present value of those cash surpluses and deficits. To do this, a company will apply a discount rate to those cash flows and calculate the present value of those future cash amounts.

Having calculated the fair value and the value in use, the company will choose the larger amount. In other words, if it will be better off by keeping the asset it will do so and this will be known as its recoverable amount. Figure 2 illustrates this procedure.

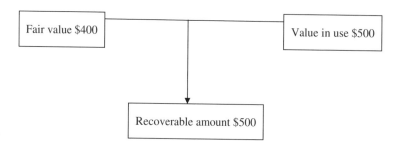

Figure 2.   Calculating impairment

If the company has the asset on its Balance Sheet at a carrying amount of $600, then the asset will be impaired by $100 and this amount must be charged to the Income Statement as an expense. The procedure therefore is:

1. Compare the fair value of the asset with its value in use. The higher amount is the recoverable amount.
2. Compare the recoverable amount with the carrying amount of the asset in the Balance Sheet.
3. If the carrying amount is higher than the recoverable amount, the difference must be charged to the Income Statement.
4. If the carrying amount is lower than the recoverable amount, then no action must be taken.

The application of the impairment test is shown in the following extract from the 2009 Annual Report of Cadbury Schweppes:

> **Cadbury Schweppes Annual Report 2009**
> **Impairment review**
>
> The Group carries out an impairment review of its tangible and definite-life intangible assets when a change in circumstances or situation indicates that those assets may have suffered an impairment loss. Intangible assets with indefinite useful lives are tested for impairment at least annually and whenever there is an indication that the asset may be impaired. Impairment is measured by comparing the carrying amount of an asset or of a cash-generating unit with the "recoverable amount", that is, the higher of its fair value less costs to sell and its "value in use". "Value in use" is calculated by discounting the expected future cash flows, using a discount rate based on an estimate of the rate that the market would expect on an investment of comparable risk.

6.6 Calculation of Impairment

Having gone through the basic procedure, we will take a simple example of a company with just one asset which it considers may be impaired. The details it has are as follows:

- The machine is shown in the balance sheet at a carrying amount of $5,600.
- The machine has a remaining economic life of three years.
- The positive cash flow over the next three years is estimated to be $2,000 each year.
- The fair value of the machine is $4,200.

If we compare the carrying amount of the machine with the fair value, then the machine is impaired, that is, the carrying amount is the higher amount. But we need to calculate the value in use to compare this with the fair value and we will take the higher of the two amounts as the recoverable value.

To calculate the value in use, we need to convert the cash flow into present values. We can explain the concept of present values with a simple example. Imagine a friend asks to borrow $100 and promises to pay back the $100 in one year's time. As much as you like your friend, you should not agree because $100 in one year's time is not as much as $100 now. The reason for this is that you could invest your $100 now and get more than $100 in one year's time because of the interest you would earn. If interest rates are 10%, you would get $110.

The question is what amount would you have to invest now to get $100 in one year's time? This is known as discounting and fortunately there are Discount Tables that give the factor we must use. If interest rates are 10%, the tables show that we would have to discount $100 in one year's time by 0.909 to get the amount that we would have to invest now. Working to the nearest dollar, this means we would have to invest $100 × 0.909 = $91 now to get $100 in one year's time.

This process of discounting future cash flows is known as calculating the present value of those flows. For the example, we are using a discount rate of 10%.

Value in use calculation

Year	Positive cash flow	Discount factor	Present value
1	2,000	0.909	1,818
2	2,000	0.826	1,652
3	2,000	0.751	1,502
Total			4,972

We have taken the discount factor from the tables using a 10% rate. The positive cash flows of $2,000 each year for three years are worth $4,972 in present values.

We can now carry out the full analysis using the figures we have calculated:

Fair value $4,200
Value in use $4,972
Carrying amount $5,600

1. First we compare fair value ($4,200) with the value in use ($4,972). The highest of these two amounts ($4,972) is the recoverable amount.
2. We compare the recoverable amount ($4,972) with the carrying amount ($5,600). As we have the machine at $5,600 and the recoverable amount is only $4,972, the machine is impaired.
3. The amount of the impairment ($628) must be charged to the Income Statement as an expense, and the amount shown in the Balance Sheet will be reduced to $4,972.

In this example we used 10% as our discount rate, but the standard has guidelines. The discount rate to be applied for measuring value in use should be the pre-tax rate based on the current market assessments of the time value of money and the risk specific to the asset. If it is not possible to use a market-determined rate, the entity may use either its own weighted average cost of capital, or its incremental borrowing rate, or other market borrowing rates that are appropriate.

As you can imagine, in a large company the calculations required to conduct an impairment test are complex and time-consuming. The following example of the impact of an impairment test is taken from Unilever's Annual Report 2005:

Extract from Unilever Annual Report 2005

During 2005, *Slim•Fast* maintained its leadership of the weight management sector by refreshing its product range and offering a more personalised diet plan. However, the 2005 impairment review of the global *Slim•Fast* business resulted in an impairment charge of €363 million due to the continued decline of the weight management sector. This charge has been reflected in operating profit for The Americas region.

Value in use of the business was calculated using the present values of projected future cash flows, adjusted to reflect the risk present in the markets in which the business operates. The pre-tax discount rate applied to the business was 11%. As a result of the impairment review, the carrying value of the business was determined to be in excess of the value in use, thereby requiring an impairment loss to be recognised.

6.7 Impairment and CGUs

With many companies it is impossible to identify cash flows with one particular asset. Usually there are several assets working in conjunction to generate a cash flow. Wherever possible, the calculation of the recoverable amounts should be determined for individual assets. If it is impossible to determine the recoverable amount for an individual asset, the recoverable amount for the asset's cash-generating unit (CGU) should be identified and used.

A CGU is the smallest identifiable group of assets that generates cash inflows from continuing use, and that are largely independent of the cash inflows from other assets or groups of assets. Mostly the assets will be tangible, non-current assets such as property, plant and equipment. It is possible that the Cash-Generating Unit will also include goodwill that has been acquired. You will remember that companies can place acquired goodwill on their balance sheet.

Where there is acquired goodwill, it requires specific accounting treatment. The amount of goodwill on the balance sheet should be allocated to each of the CGUs or groups of CGUs that are expected to derive benefit. It may be that the goodwill can only be identified with one CGU.

Having identified the CGU, including goodwill where appropriate, the company must then calculate the fair value and the value in use. So the same procedures as shown in Figures 1 and 2 are followed to establish the recoverable amount, i.e., the higher of the fair value and value in use.

If the recoverable amount of the CGU is higher than the carrying amount of the CGU as shown in the balance sheet, the unit and the goodwill allocated to that unit is not impaired. If the carrying amount exceeds the recoverable amount, the CGU is impaired by the amount of the difference and the company must recognise this impairment loss by writing the loss as an expense in the Income Statement and reducing the carrying amount on the Balance Sheet.

Where acquired goodwill is involved, the procedure is as follows:

1. The loss is first charged against the goodwill allocated to the CGU.
2. If the goodwill is insufficient to absorb the loss, then the loss will be allocated over other assets in proportion to the carrying amount of each asset.

Illustrative example: Impairment of a CGU

A cash-generating unit to which acquired goodwill has been allocated has the following assets:

	$000
Property	120
Machinery	80
Acquired goodwill	40
Carrying amount of CGU	240

An analysis shows that the recoverable amount for the CGU is $180,000. The CGU is therefore impaired and an amount of $60,000 must be charged to the Income Statement, and the carrying amount of the assets reduced in the Balance Sheet by the same amount.

If we did not have goodwill, we would write off the impairment loss in proportion to the carrying amount of the tangible assets. The standard requires that first goodwill must be written off completely, and any remaining impairment loss must be borne by the remaining assets in proportion to their carrying amount. The following table shows these calculations:

Applying impairment loss

	Pre-impairment $000	Amount written off $000	Post-impairment $000
Goodwill	40	40	—
Property	120	12	108
Machinery	80	8	72
	240	60	180

Once the goodwill is written off completely, the remaining impaired amount of $20,000 will be written off against the pre-impairment amounts for property and machinery in proportion to their carrying amount:

$$\text{Property: } \$20,000 \times \frac{\$120,000}{\$200,000} = \$12,000$$

$$\text{Machinery: } \$20,000 \times \frac{\$80,000}{\$200,000} = \$8,000.$$

It is possible that in future years the asset is no longer impaired because of changes in the market or in the economy. In these circumstances a company can reverse the impairment, but there are two rules:

1. Impairment for goodwill cannot be reversed; and
2. The reversal on other assets is limited to their original carrying value. In other words, you cannot increase to a higher value.

We will use the example above to demonstrate the application of these rules if the recoverable amount was found to be $220,000.

Reversing impairment loss

	Pre-impairment $000	Post-impairment $000	Reversal $000	Post-reversal $000
Goodwill	40	—	—	—
Property	120	108	12	120
Machinery	80	72	8	80
	240	180	20	200

Note that the amount of the goodwill has not been reversed. Although the new recoverable amount of the CGU is $220,000, the goodwill is not reversed so the total recoverable amount is now $200,000.

Mini case study

Conthai Tours started its business in 2009 by acquiring another company for $690,000. The values of the assets of the business as at 1 January 2009 based on the fair values less costs to sell were as follows:

	$000
Vehicles (10 vehicles)	360
Intangible assets (licences and permits)	90
Cash	180
Trade payables	(60)
	570

As Conthai has paid more for the business than the fair value of its identifiable assets, it has acquired goodwill of $120,000 which will be shown in its balance sheet.

On 1 February 2009, the premises of Conthai were broken into and four of its vehicles were set on fire and completely destroyed. The value of these four vehicles in the balance sheet was $90,000 and due to an administrative error these particular vehicles had not been insured. As a result of this event, Conthai wishes to recognise an impairment loss of $135,000 (inclusive of the loss of the burnt vehicles) due to the decline in the value in use of its tour business.

Conthai must recognise the impairment to the business by comparing the recoverable amount of the cash-generating unit with its carrying value, which stands at $690,000 in the balance sheet, including goodwill. As the four vehicles have been destroyed, they must be completely written off. An impairment loss of $90,000 is recognised first for the burnt vehicles, and the balance ($45,000) must be attributed to goodwill.

At 1 February 2009

	1 Jan 2009 $000	Impairment Loss $000	1 Feb 2009 $000
Goodwill	120	(45)	75
Intangible assets (licences and permits)	90		90
Vehicles	360	(90)	270
Net assets	120		120
	690	(135)	555

On 1 March 2009 a rival tour company commenced business in the same area. It is anticipated that the business revenue of Conthai will be reduced by 25%, leading to a decline in the present value in use of the business which is now calculated at $450,000. The fair value less costs to sell of the intangible assets has fallen to $75,000 as a result of the impact on the business of the operations of the competitor. The net selling values of the other assets have remained the same as at 1 January 2009 throughout the period.

At 1 March 2009

	1 Feb 2009 $000	Impairment Loss $000	1 Mar 2009 $000
Goodwill	75	(75)	
Intangible assets	90	(15)	75
Vehicles	270	—	270
Net assets	120		120
	555	(90)	465

Usually an impairment loss is allocated to those assets which have the most subjective valuations. Thus, impairment identified in this way should usually be allocated firstly to goodwill and then to other assets on a pro-rata basis. With Conthai, we are told that the fair values of all assets except the intangible assets (the licences and permits) have remained constant.

This position is made very clear in the standard which states that the impairment loss is first allocated to the goodwill of the cash-generating unit and then to the other assets on a pro-rata basis. The standard goes on to say that in allocating the impairment loss, the carrying amount of an asset will not be reduced below the highest of its fair value less costs to sell; its value in use; and zero. The assets for Conthai were originally measured at their fair value. Therefore, it is only the intangible assets and goodwill that can be impaired.

Conthai therefore recognises a further impairment loss of $90,000, although the value in use of the business is now only $450,000.

6.8 Chapter Summary

Intangible Assets

☞ are identifiable non-monetary assets that do not have a physical substance.
☞ must be depreciated over their useful economic life or an annual impairment review must be conducted.
☞ Internally generated goodwill cannot be recognised.
☞ Research costs should not be capitalised.
☞ Development costs may be capitalised if certain criteria are met.

Impairment

☞ applies to all non-current assets, both tangible assets and intangible assets, and to goodwill.
☞ For all assets, assess annually whether there is an indication of impairment.
☞ Annually test for impairment all intangible assets with an indefinite useful life.
☞ Use a CGU if it is impossible to identify cash flows with one particular asset.
☞ Calculate the fair value and the value in use of the asset.
☞ The recoverable amount is the higher of the fair value and the value in use.
☞ If the carrying amount of the asset is higher than the recoverable amount, there has been an impairment.
☞ Impairments can be reversed, except for goodwill.

Progress Test

1. Which of the following statements regarding research and development costs are correct?

   1) Research expenditure should always be capitalised
   2) Development expenditure should be capitalised and amortised over 10 years
   3) Capitalised development expenditure should be shown on the balance sheet as a non-current asset
   4) Research expenditure, if it meets certain criteria, can be capitalised

      a) 1 and 2 only
      b) 4 only
      c) 3 only
      d) 2 and 4 only

2. A company purchased a new machine at a cost of $400,000 on 1 January 2010, which it depreciates over 3 years. It predicted that the future cash flows from using the equipment would be as follows:

$$\text{Year 1} - \$150,000$$
$$\text{Year 2} - \$220,000$$
$$\text{Year 3} - \$230,000$$

   The equipment has no residual value and the company uses a discount rate of 10%. Within a few months of purchasing the machine, the company finds that the manufacturer is now offering it at $350,000 and now that the machine has been used, the company considers that it could only sell it for $300,000. Is the asset impaired?

3. Imperial Bicycles Inc. is conducting a review of its machinery and equipment at the end of the financial year. The present carrying amount in the balance sheet of one machine is $580,000, but it is no longer used to full capacity because of a lack of demand for the product. The company is considering whether to sell the machine and another company has offered to purchase it for $460,000. Imperial Bicycles considers that the machine has a remaining life of 3 years and would generate positive cash flows of $200,000 each year. The company uses a 10% discount rate in its calculations. Is the asset impaired?

4. In conducting an impairment test, you should compare the carrying amount of the asset to:

   a) the recoverable amount of the asset
   b) the values other companies are showing in their balance sheet
   c) what it would cost to replace the asset

5. In accordance with IAS 38 Intangible Assets, an intangible asset with an indefinite useful life should be amortised:

   a) over twenty years as a presumed maximum
   b) over twenty years in all cases
   c) over twenty years as a presumed maximum, or more if subject to annual impairment reviews
   d) not amortised but tested annually for impairment

6. Which of the following statements about research and development expenditure are correct?

   a) Research expenditure, other than capital expenditure on research facilities, should be recognised as an expense as incurred
   b) In deciding whether development expenditure qualifies to be recognised as an asset, it is necessary to consider whether there will be adequate finance available to complete the project
   c) Development expenditure recognised as an asset must be amortised over a period not exceeding five years

7. Which one of the following statements is correct?

   a) Intangible assets cannot be treated as having an indefinite life
   b) Intangible assets with a finite useful economic life should be maintained at cost and tested annually for impairment
   c) Intangible assets with an indefinite useful life should be tested annually for impairment

8. Which one of the following statements is correct?

   a) Expenditure during the research phase of a project may sometimes be capitalised as an intangible asset
   b) Expenditure during the development phase of a project may sometimes be capitalised as an intangible asset
   c) Both research and development expenditure can be capitalised

9. A brand name that was acquired separately from any other asset should initially be recognised at:

   a) cost less depreciation
   b) either cost or fair value at the choice of the acquirer
   c) cost
   d) fair value

10. The recognition criteria for an intangible asset includes which of the following conditions?

    a) It is an integral part of the business
    b) Its cost can be measured reliably
    c) It must be measured at cost
    d) It is probable that future economic benefit will arise from its use

7

Accounting Policies, Errors, Provisions and Contingencies

Learning Objectives

At the end of this chapter you should be able to:

☞ Differentiate amongst accounting policies, changes in accounting estimates and prior period errors
☞ Identify adjusting and non-adjusting events after the financial period end
☞ Explain the criteria for determining a provision
☞ Describe contingent liabilities and contingent assets.

7.1 Introduction

We all know that the world is an uncertain place. We may intend to do one thing but we are prevented for some reason and we have to adjust our strategy. We may also be aware that some things are going to change in the future and we need to make plans now. The same applies to companies and the preparation of financial statements.

When a company reaches the end of a financial year and has to prepare its financial statements, it is confronted with several difficulties. Firstly, the amount of accounting work to be done is significant. Secondly, the company will be required by stock exchange rules to publish its financial statements within a certain period of time. Finally, not all the information it requires will be available so it will have to make some estimates.

This chapter is about those uncertainties and covers the following three standards:

- IAS 8 Accounting Policies, Changes in Accounting Estimates and Errors
- IAS 10 Events After the Reporting Period (this standard was originally titled Events After the Balance Sheet Date, but it was changed in 2005)
- IAS 37 Provisions, Contingent Liabilities and Contingent Assets.

IAS 8 is in three parts. The first part covers accounting policies. We have discussed these in earlier chapters but now we will look in detail at the requirements of the standard. The second part of the standard is concerned with those estimates that the company had to make. The final part explains what action a company must take if it has made a mistake in its financial statements but did not realise it until they had been published.

IAS 10 is a straightforward and very helpful standard. Let us assume that a company has completed its financial statements but, before they are authorised by the board of directors, an event will occur. Something new will have happened that was unexpected or information may become available that causes the company to change its opinion on the circumstances at the actual date of the financial statements. The standard explains the actions to be taken in these situations.

IAS 37 is the most difficult standard in this chapter. The wording of the standard is not always easy to understand and the matters that it deals with are complex. The IASB intends to amend the standard at some time in the future. In this chapter we will explain the most important requirements of the existing standard.

7.2 IAS 8 Accounting Policies, Changes in Accounting Estimates, and Errors

Accounting policies

IAS 8 covers three different topics but all may have an impact on the financial statements. We will discuss accounting policies first as the establishment of accounting policies is critical for the appropriate application of accounting standards. The disclosure of accounting policies is essential to assist the user in understanding financial statements.

Definition — accounting policies

These are the specific principles, bases, conventions, rules and practices applied by an entity in preparing and presenting financial statements.

Below we reproduce the first two Notes from the Accounting Policies of J Sainsbury plc:

1. General information

J Sainsbury plc is a public limited company ("Company") incorporated in the United Kingdom, whose shares are publicly traded on the London Stock Exchange. The Company is domiciled in the United Kingdom and its registered address is 33 Holborn, London EC1N 2HT, United Kingdom.

The financial year represents the 52 weeks to 22 March 2008 (prior financial year 52 weeks to 24 March 2007). The consolidated financial statements for the 52 weeks to 22 March 2008 comprise the financial statements of the Company and its subsidiaries ("Group") and the Group's interests in associates and joint ventures.

The Group's principal activities are grocery and related retailing.

2. Accounting policies

(a) Statement of compliance

The Group's financial statements have been prepared in accordance with International Financial Reporting Standards ("IFRS") as adopted by the European Union and International Financial Reporting Interpretations Committee ("IFRIC") interpretations and with those parts of the Companies Act 1985 applicable to companies reporting under IFRS. The Company's financial statements have been prepared on the same basis and as permitted by Section 230(3) of the Companies Act 1985, no Income Statement is presented for the Company.

(b) Basis of preparation

The financial statements are presented in sterling, rounded to the nearest million (£m) unless otherwise stated. They have been prepared under the historical cost convention, except for derivative financial instruments and available-for-sale financial assets that have been measured at fair value.

The above is only the start of the statement of accounting policies and for many companies the statement of accounting policies will take 5–10 pages. The contents follow to a large extent the issues dealt with by the various standards. The company will explain how it values inventories, its treatment of goodwill, the calculation of pensions, the recognition of revenue and similar matters.

IAS 8 sets out the criteria for selecting and applying accounting policies, and accounting for changes in accounting policies. A company should follow the requirements of standards or interpretations that have been issued in forming its accounting policies. There may be occasions where a standard or interpretation does not address the specific issues. In these circumstances, management must use its own judgment in setting its policy. In doing this, a company should make reference to the following sources:

- any other IASB Standard or Interpretation dealing with relevant matters;
- definitions, recognition criteria and measurement concepts for assets, liabilities, income and expenses contained in the IASB's Framework for the Preparation and Presentation of Financial Statements;
- recent pronouncements by other standard setting bodies that do not conflict with IFRSs and the Framework.

Once having established its policies, a company must be consistent in applying them. This does not mean that there cannot be changes, but there are only two reasons for making a change:

- A standard or interpretation has been issued that requires companies to make the change.
- The company believes that the change improves the reliability and relevancy of information in the financial statements.

Usually a change brought about by a new standard or interpretation will be relatively easy to implement. The standard will include transitional arrangements to guide the company through the change.

If the change is not due to an IFRS but a company decision, it must be applied retrospectively to all periods presented in the financial statements as if the new accounting policy had always been applied. In other words, the financial statements of the current period and each prior period presented are adjusted so that it appears as if the new accounting policy had always been applied.

This requirement for retrospective application is extremely important but could be a huge burden for a company. The standard, therefore, offers some relief. A company need not make retrospective application where it is impracticable and the company has made every reasonable effort to do so. It is impracticable if:

- the effects of the retrospective application cannot be determined;
- the retrospective application requires assumptions about what would have been management's intent at that time;
- the retrospective application requires significant estimates of amounts and it is impossible to distinguish objectively information about those estimates that provides evidence of circumstances that existed on the dates as at which those amounts are to be recognised, measured and disclosed; and would have been available when the financial statements for that prior period were authorised for issue from other information.

Accounting estimates

When a company is preparing its financial statements, it will not have the complete information for some items and must therefore make an estimate. This is a normal part of business life. Companies will make estimates for several items and the following are ones that we have discussed in previous chapters:

- Doubtful debts — this is the amount owing by customers that the company believes it may not be able to collect for various reasons. We discussed this in Chapter 3.
- Depreciation — companies have to estimate both the useful economic life of the asset and the future scrap value of the asset.
- Inventory obsolescence.

Understandably, as time progresses, companies receive new information and this may cause them to change their estimates. The standard explains how these changes are actioned in the financial statements. A change in an estimate will affect the expected future benefits and obligations of the company and therefore the carrying amount in the financial statements must be adjusted.

It is important to note that a change in estimate is not due to an error being made. It is assumed that the best estimate was made on the evidence that was available at that time. There is therefore no need to change the financial statements for previous years as they were prepared on the best evidence at that time. It is necessary to change the financial statements in the present period when the change is made and in future periods if appropriate.

A change in an accounting estimate is different from a change in accounting policies and from accounting errors. A change in an accounting estimate is an adjustment to the financial statements because new information or new developments have taken place. We have explained above what a change in accounting policies is and we consider accounting errors in the next section. This difference between accounting policies and accounting estimates is explained in the illustrative example below.

Illustrative example 1: Accounting policies and accounting estimates

The ability of management to change accounting policies is severely restricted and should not be confused with accounting estimates. For example, a business may change its accounting policy because the new policy provides better information to the users. If an entity determines that it should increase the amount for doubtful debts from 3% to 5% of the accounts receivable because of a poor economy, this is not a change in accounting policy. It is a change in the accounting estimate of the amount that it expects to recover from account receivables.

Illustrative example 2: Change of life in an asset

A company purchases machinery on 1 January 2005 for $50,000. The company considers that the machinery has a useful life of 10 years and no residual value. The annual depreciation charge using the straight-line method is:

$$\text{Annual depreciation charge} = \frac{\$50,000}{10 \text{ years}} = \$5,000.$$

By 31 December 2008, the machinery has a carrying value of $50,000 – ($5,000 × 4 years) = $30,000.

On 1 January 2009 the company decides that the remaining useful life of the machinery is only 4 years and not 6 years. The annual depreciation charge from 1 January 2009 and for the four years following will be:

$$\text{Annual depreciation charge} = \frac{\$30,000}{4 \text{ years}} = \$7,500.$$

Any changes in accounting estimates are not applied retrospectively: they are applied prospectively. This is because the entity has received new information that has encouraged it to change its estimates of future events and transactions.

Prior period errors

Prior period errors are exactly that: they are mistakes that the company has made in the past in its financial statements but has only now realised it. Examples of prior period errors are:

- Mathematical errors
- Fraud
- Mistakes in applying accounting policies
- Misinterpretations or failure to observe facts.

Such errors are not changes in accounting policies or changes in accounting estimates. The company has made a mistake in its financial statements. Errors will frequently be so insignificant that they will have no impact on the financial statements. In this case, the error can be corrected through net profit or loss for the current period.

Definition — materiality

This occurs where omissions or misstatements are material because they could influence the economic decisions of users. Materiality depends on the size and nature of the omission or misstatement judged in the surrounding circumstances.

Where the error is material, the company must correct it retrospectively. There are two possibilities:

- Restating the comparative amounts for the prior periods in which the error occurred;
- Where the error occurred before the earliest prior period presented, restating the opening balances of assets, liabilities and equity for that period.

For example, if a prior period error has occurred, the company must adjust the financial statements for when it occurred and not the present financial statements. Thus, a company preparing its financial statements for 2009 may find an error was made in the 2008 financial statements. The correction should not be made in the 2009 financial statements but in the year when the error took place. To do otherwise would make the 2009 financial statements incorrect.

Prior period errors are fundamental in nature and should only be recognised if it is clear that the original financial statements should not have been issued because of these errors. If the error arises due to a fault in an accounting estimate, but it was the best estimate that could be made at that time with the information available, it is a change in accounting estimates.

As with accounting policies, the standard permits companies to not make the changes if it is impracticable, but various disclosures are required.

7.3 IAS 10 Events After the Reporting Period

Definition — events after the reporting period

Those events, both favourable and unfavourable, that occur between the reporting date and the date on which the financial statements are authorised for issue.

There is always a delay between the date on the financial statements and the date they are authorised by the board of directors. For example, a company's financial statements for the year to 31 December 2009 may not be authorised until the end of February 2010 or even later. There are many reasons for this. First, if the end of the year is 31 December, it will require much work by the accountants to prepare financial statements. Secondly, companies will not have all the information available to them and will have to make some estimates. Finally and most importantly, the financial statements will have to be approved by the auditors before the board of directors authorises that they can be made publicly available.

During this period, some significant events may occur. These events provide information, without which the user of the financial statements may not obtain a full understanding of the position and performance of the business. These events may be favourable or unfavourable as far as the financial performance and position of the company is concerned. Below we give two examples of events that may occur between the date of the financial statements and the date they are authorised. In both cases we assume that the financial statements are dated 31 December but are not authorised until 20 February.

Event 1: The holiday hotel

After preparing its financial statements, a company discovers that one of its holiday hotels that was hit by a storm on 25 December has been revalued on 12 February at an amount less than 50% of the carrying amount in the balance sheet.

Event 2: Fire at the factory

On the day before the board of directors intends to authorise the accounts, the main factory is destroyed by fire and is not insured.

Both of these events are significant but are different in their timing. The hotel is damaged by the storm before the end of the year, although the board of directors did not know the extent of the damage. With the factory, there was no problem at 31 December when the financial statements were dated. The fire did not take place until one day before the financial statements were to be authorised.

We have two similar but, from the point of timing, different situations. In the first situation, the board receives new information about conditions at the balance sheet date. In the second situation, the board receives information about events after the balance sheet date but before the financial statements are authorised. The standard divides these events into adjusting events and non-adjusting events. The accounting treatment of each differs.

Adjusting events

Adjusting events give new evidence on conditions as at the date of the balance sheet. Where we have an adjusting event, the financial statements must be changed to show this new information before they can be authorised. For example, a factory may be shown at a carrying value of $10 million in the balance sheet. Shortly after, an independent valuator informs the company that this valuation is incorrect and the factory is only to be valued at $8 million as at the balance sheet date. Evidence has therefore become available that shows the original valuation to be incorrect and the financial statements must be restated before they can be authorised. Examples of adjusting events are:

- Discovery of fraud or errors
- Information about the value or recoverability of an asset at the year end

- Settlement of an outstanding court case, i.e., a case that was in court before the year end has been settled after the year end.

Illustrative example: An adjusting event

An entity's financial statements for the year ended 31 December 2008 were completed on 31 March 2009 and were authorised for issue on 12 May 2009. In April 2009, it transpired that fraud had been committed at one of the divisions and the figure for revenues was overstated by 20%. This event is treated as an adjusting event because evidence has become available on what the correct revenue figure should have been as at 31 December 2008. Thus, the financial statements should be restated before being authorised.

Non-adjusting events

Non-adjusting events do not provide new evidence on the conditions as at the balance sheet date, but of events that occur after that date. These events have no impact on the balance sheet at the date it was drawn up but are of such significance that the users should be informed. For instance, a factory has been correctly valued at the year end but is later destroyed by fire before the authorisation date. The financial statements are correct as at the year end and do not have to be restated. However, a non-adjusting event has occurred that is of significant importance and disclosure should be made. A company would include this information in its Notes to the Accounts in its Annual Report. Examples of non-adjusting events are:

- Fire after the balance sheet date destroying or damaging non-current assets
- Announcements of a major restructuring plan
- Major purchases of items such as property, plant and equipment
- Purchase of another company
- Major disposal of property, plant and equipment.

We show below a note from the Annual Report of Hugo Boss which gives a "negative" statement, i.e., that there have been no non-adjusting events. This is not required by the standard but is a good communication to the users of the financial statements:

As of March 9, 2006, no material operational changes, structural modifications or business events had occurred in the HUGO BOSS Group that might serve to alter any disclosures contained in the 2005 financial statements.

The following example is the disclosure of a Note taken from the Annual Report of the Swiss company Nestle:

> **Nestle**
>
> *Events occurring after the balance sheet date*
>
> The values of assets and liabilities at the balance sheet date are adjusted if there is evidence that subsequent adjusting events warrant a modification of these values. These adjustments are made up to the date of approval of the Consolidated Financial Statements by the Board of Directors. Other non-adjusting events are disclosed in the Notes.

In determining the appropriate classification of the event, it is essential to take all the surrounding circumstances into account. For example, the reduction in value of a property after the balance sheet date but before the authorisation date would normally be considered a non-adjusting event. However, information received after the balance sheet date that demonstrated that the property had, in fact, lost its value at the balance sheet date is an adjusting event.

A company can have an adjusting event but does not have to disclose this in its financial statements. This is because the financial statements have been corrected.

The standard also requires that an entity should not prepare financial statements on a going concern basis if events occur between the balance sheet date and the date of authorisation which indicate that the entity is not a going concern. Entities should disclose the authorisation date for financial statements. It is essential that users know this date as the financial statements and disclosures will not report any events occurring after the authorisation date.

The critical aspect of this standard is the timing of the event and the date of authorisation of the financial statements. The standard offers the following guidance:

1. An entity may have to submit its financial statements for approval after the financial statements have been issued. It is usual for the board to authorise the financial statements for issue prior to submitting them to the shareholders. The date of issue will be the date of authorisation and not the later date when they are submitted to the shareholders for approval.
2. The management of an entity may have to issue its financial statements to a supervisory board (made up solely of non-executives) for approval. The financial statements are authorised when the board submits them to the supervisory board.

This is an important section and we provide in Figure 1 the main requirements of IAS 10.

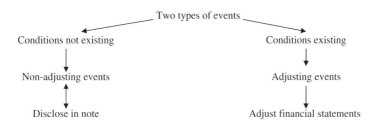

Figure 1. IAS 10 Events after the reporting period

7.4 IAS 37 Provisions

This standard deals with three related topics: provisions, contingent liabilities and contingent assets. We will discuss contingent liabilities and contingent assets in the following section and concentrate on provisions in this section. We have already used the word "provision" when we were discussing doubtful debts. You will also find that some people and companies will refer to "provision for depreciation". Neither of these items are provisions under IAS 37. They are accounting estimates and are dealt with under IAS 8 as explained in the earlier part of the chapter.

IAS 37 attempts to regulate the way that companies account for future uncertainties. In the past, when a company had a very profitable year it would reduce the profit by creating a provision: a type of fund to deal with future uncertainties. If in future years, profits declined for some reason, the company would use these provisions to boost its profits. As far as the users of the financial statements were concerned, the company was reporting a steady profit every year. The true picture may have been that the company had moved from high profits to low profits but was hiding this by the use of provisions.

The abuse of provisions was well-known and they were often referred to as "Big bath provisions" or "Cookie jar provisions" because companies were using them to sweeten their profits and clean up any messes they did not like. The result was that users were being misled. IAS 37 attempts to bring order into a somewhat chaotic practice.

Definition — provision

A provision is a liability of uncertain timing or amount.

The above definition has several criteria that must be met and we have broken them down so that we can focus on each one separately:

- There must be a present obligation (legal or constructive).
- It must have arisen as a result of a past event.

- Payment is probable in order to settle the obligation.
- The amount can be estimated reliably.

Present legal obligation

The standard defines two types of obligations: legal and constructive. A legal obligation is possibly the easiest to identify and could be contractual; or arise due to legislation; or result from some other operation of law.

You can imagine that in a court case there could be some uncertainty whether the company has a present obligation. In such an event the company would seek advice as to whether it is likely to lose the case and thus have a present obligation. Apart from this reservation, a company should be able to determine whether it has a present legal obligation.

Present constructive obligation

This is an obligation arising from a company's own practices or policies in that it has led other people to believe that the company will act in a certain way. This includes those circumstances where past practice leads third parties to reasonably assume that the entity will settle the obligation (e.g., a sale or return policy by a retailer).

Past events

In the standard, the past event is known as an obligating event. The company has taken or not taken some action in the past that results in it having a present obligation now. It is very important under the standard that companies do not make provisions for something they consider may happen in the future. For example, businesses must not make provisions for future operating losses.

Payment is probable

The payment will involve an outflow of economic resources and it is more likely than not that the company will have to make this payment.

Amount can be estimated reliably

Reliably does not mean exactly. If you refer to the definition, it states that a provision is uncertain in amount. The amount recognised as a provision should be the best estimate of the expenditure required to settle the present obligation at the balance sheet date. A business should assess the risks and uncertainties that may operate in reaching the best estimate and any material future cash flows should be discounted to present values.

Examples of provisions include warranty obligations, a retailer's policy on refunds to customers, an obligation to clean up contaminated land, company restructuring and onerous contracts. A company cannot make a provision for future losses. The following is a good example of a legal obligation from a past event where the amount has been estimated reliably.

Detox plc operates in the UK where there is legislation compelling companies to clean up environmental damage that they may cause. In the month of October 2008 the company causes environmental damage and estimates that it will cost approximately $500,000 to remedy. It intends to carry out this work in March 2009. Its year end is 31 December. The work will be carried out in 2009 and Detox must make a provision in its financial statements to 31 December 2008 for the amount of $500,000.

In the following example, although there appears the possibility of making a provision, the circumstances do not fulfill the requirements of the standard.

Inov Inc. is a fast expanding manufacturing company based in India. Its year end is 31 March. In January 2009 the company learns of some new technology emerging in Hong Kong that is likely to present a competitive threat. To meet this competition, it decides that it must invest in the new technology. It calculates that this investment could cost $1.5 million and will be made in August 2009.

In these circumstances the company cannot make a provision in its financial statements to 31 March 2009, although the decision was taken in January. There is not a present obligation because of a past event.

The standard refers specifically to some of the events for which provisions may be made and we will explain the requirements for restructuring and onerous contracts.

Company restructuring

A company may decide that it has to make substantial changes to its organisation. This could be because of an economic downturn and could result in job losses. The company may decide in this financial year that it will restructure, but the actual event and the costs arising from it will take place in the next financial year. If the company can make a reliable estimate of the costs to be incurred, it can make a provision for these, but the standard lays down certain criteria.

The examples given in the standard as restructuring are:

- Sale or termination of a line of business;
- The closure of a business location in a country or region, or the relocation of business activities from one country or region to another;
- Changes in management structure, for example, eliminating a layer of management;
- Fundamental reorganisations that have a material effect on the nature and focus of the business operations.

In the above circumstances a company can make a provision as long as it has a constructive obligation. We observed in the beginning of this section that a company can make a provision for a legal or constructive obligation. Assuming there is no legal reason for the restructuring, a company must demonstrate a constructive obligation by fulfilling two criteria: it must have a detailed formal plan, and it must communicate the plan to those affected.

A detailed formal plan must contain at the minimum the following information:

- the business or part of a business concerned;
- the principal locations affected;
- the location, function and approximate number of employees who will be compensated for terminating their services;
- the expenditure that will be undertaken; and
- when the plan will be implemented.

A restructuring will be planned at a senior management level and will often need board approval. However, that is not sufficient to make the restructuring a constructive obligation. The plan must be communicated to those who are affected. This can either be directly to those affected by the plan, for example employees and suppliers, or a public announcement can be made giving details of the plan. The importance of the timing is demonstrated in the two following scenarios:

Scenario 1

Boardwalk Inc. makes up its annual financial statements to 31 December. The Board approves on 1 December 2009 to close permanently one of its four factories on 1 April 2010. Because of the timing, the Board was unable to communicate its decision before 31 December 2009 to any of those affected. In these circumstances, no provision for the costs to be incurred in 2010 can be made by Boardwalk Inc.

Scenario 2

The details are similar to Scenario 1 but by 16 December 2009, Boardwalk has informed the employees who will be affected at a meeting and has written to all its suppliers and customers. In this case, Boardwalk will be able to make a provision in its financial statements for 2009 for the costs it can reliably estimate that it will incur.

Onerous contracts

Definition — onerous contracts

An onerous contract is where the company has unavoidable costs in meeting its obligations and these exceed the economic benefits that the company expects to receive.

During the course of business, a company will enter into many contracts. Some of these can be cancelled without the company suffering losses, but there are others where the company will have to pay. One example is when a company has entered into a non-cancellable lease to occupy office premises. With three years of the lease remaining, the company decides that it wishes to move to another location. As the lease is non-cancellable, the company will still have to make the lease payments until the end of the contract. In these circumstances, when the company decides to move, it must make a provision for the outstanding amounts to be paid under the lease agreement.

There are several conditions in the standard restricting the use of provisions. An important topic is where a provision is no longer required. A company may have seriously considered that it needed to make a provision for future costs, but events make that provision no longer required. Companies should conduct an annual review of provisions and if the provisions are no longer required, they should be reversed to income. Companies are not able to use a provision made for one eventuality that did not occur as expected for another eventuality that was not predicted. A provision can be applied only to the expenditure for which the provision was originally recognised.

7.5 IAS 37 Contingent Liabilities and Contingent Assets

Definition — contingent liability

A contingent liability is where there is significant uncertainty with a number of aspects regarding the liability.

A contingent liability can take two forms. It can either be a possible obligation (not a present obligation as with a provision) that arises from past events, but confirmation is required to determine whether it is a present obligation. Alternatively, it may be a present obligation but it is uncertain whether the obligation will be settled, or it cannot be measured reliably. It is important to remember that for a provision, a company will adjust its financial statements accordingly, but a contingent liability will only be disclosed as a Note in the Annual Report.

You may find the use of the above terms "possible" and "probable" confusing and it is helpful to consider an example. Let us say that a construction company is threatened with being sued for $1 million by a client for alleged negligence in meeting safety regulations in the construction of an office block.

This cannot be a provision because it is only a threat and there is no evidence that the company will lose, and the amount it would have to pay is not known. If there is a possibility that the court case will go ahead, the company should disclose this as a Note in its Annual Report. If it appears remote that the case will proceed, the company will take no action. To determine what is probable, possible or remote, a company will usually seek legal advice.

Example — provisions and contingencies

Those events leading to a provision or a contingent liability may take many years before they are finally resolved. This means that the particular event may change in the nature of its recognition as time passes. The following example illustrates this.

Bensing Inc. is being sued for damages by one of its major customers who commences legal action in 2008. When preparing the year end 2008 financial statements, the directors' opinion was that the likelihood of any payments being made to the claimant was remote. In accordance with IAS 37, they did not adjust their financial statements or make any disclosures.

In 2009 the court case was still proceeding. The lawyers for Bensing Inc. informed the directors that they considered that it was possible the customer would win the case. The directors therefore disclosed a contingent liability in its financial statements for 2009.

In 2010 the lawyers advise Bensing that it is probable that the customer will win the case and their best estimate is that the damages would be $2.5 million. In this year the directors would make a provision in its financial statements for $2.5 million.

You will find that most disclosures on contingent liabilities refer to court cases. As these cases can take many years to resolve, it is not unusual for a company to disclose a court case as a contingent liability. As the case proceeds and it becomes probable that the company will lose the case, it will make a provision based on the best estimate of the costs it will suffer. An interesting example of a contingent liability is the following extract taken from the Annual Report of Diageo:

> **(ii) Colombian litigation** An action was filed on 8 October 2004 in the United States District Court for the Eastern District of New York by the Republic of Colombia and a number of its local government entities against Diageo and other spirits companies. The complaint alleges several causes of action. Included among the causes of action is a claim that the defendants allegedly violated the Federal RICO Act by facilitating money laundering in Colombia through their supposed involvement in the contraband trade to the detriment of government-owned spirits production and distribution businesses. Diageo intends to defend itself vigorously against this lawsuit.

> **Definition — contingent asset**
>
> A contingent asset is a possible asset that arises from past events and whose existence will be confirmed only by the occurrence or non-occurrence of one or more uncertain future events not wholly within the control of the entity.

The above definition, taken from the standard, is not easy to follow. Fortunately, contingent assets do not often appear in the Annual Reports of companies. When they do, they are likely to be related to court cases. An example is a legal claim that a company is pursuing but is uncertain it will be successful. Contingent assets should not be recognised in the financial statements themselves but are disclosed when an inflow of economic benefits is probable.

Usually in a court case, a company will have to rely on legal advice. If the advice states that it is probable that the company will win the case, a contingent asset would be disclosed in the Notes to the Accounts. If the legal advice states that it is virtually certain that the company will win the case, it is no longer regarded as "contingent" and would appear in the balance sheet as an asset. If it is only possible that the company will win, then nothing will appear in the Annual Report regarding the matter.

IAS 37 is a standard that causes difficulties for companies in its application. The concepts of probable, possible, and remote are not clearly defined in the standard. Additionally, we are dealing with uncertainties and our ability in predicting future events and measuring them in monetary terms is not foolproof.

7.6 Chapter Summary

IAS 8

☞ Changes in accounting policies are not changes in estimates.
☞ A change in accounting policy can be due to a new IFRS or can be voluntary to provide better information.
☞ Changes in accounting estimates are not correction of errors.
☞ A change in estimate is treated prospectively.
☞ Correction of prior period errors should be rare.
☞ Changes in accounting policy and correction of prior period errors are treated retrospectively.

IAS 10

☞ The standard is concerned with events between the date of financial statements and their authorisation.
☞ Events that provide information of conditions at the balance sheet date are adjusting events.
☞ Non-adjusting events are events that occur between the date of the balance sheet and the date of authorisation. If these would affect decisions of users, they should be disclosed.
☞ If the business is likely to cease trading, then accounts should not be prepared on a going concern basis.

IAS 37

☞ With provisions, a company should have a **present** obligation where it is **probable** that there will be a transfer of economic benefits to settle the liability and a reliable estimate can be made. Common examples are restructuring and onerous contracts.

☞ A contingent liability is where there is a **possible** obligation whose existence will be confirmed by future events not wholly within the company's control, or a **present** obligation where it is not probable that economic benefits will be transferred or the amount cannot be estimated. The main examples are court cases and only disclosure is required.

☞ Contingent assets are not frequently seen, and if it is remote that they will occur the company does nothing. If their occurrence is probable, they would be disclosed as a Note.

Progress Test

1. According to IAS 10 Events After the Reporting Period, which events should be disclosed as a Note in the financial statements?

    a) Adjusting events
    b) Non-adjusting events
    c) Both adjusting and non-adjusting events
    d) Neither adjusting nor non-adjusting events

2. For the year ended December 2010, Excel had trades receivable of $47,000. It decides that $2,000 of this represents bad debts and is written off immediately. It decides that a provision of 5% for doubtful debts should be made. What is the amount to be charged to the Income Statement for the provision for doubtful debts?

    a) $5,000
    b) $2,350
    c) $100
    d) $2,250

3. A company has the following events taking place after the end of the reporting period but before the financial statements are approved. Which of these are adjusting events?

    a) Sale of inventory at an amount significantly lower than that shown in the balance sheet
    b) A valuation providing evidence that a property was impaired at the balance sheet date
    c) The insolvency of a major customer with a debt that is shown on the balance sheet

4. Which one of the following statements is correct?

    a) Changes in accounting estimates result from new information or new developments
    b) Changes in accounting estimates are accounted for retrospectively
    c) Changes in accounting estimates are due to mistakes in the past
    d) Changes in accounting estimates are due to fraud

5. Which one of the following should be treated as a change of accounting policy?

    a) A new policy resulting from the requirements of a new IFRS
    b) A company with construction contracts for the first time needs an accounting policy to deal with this
    c) A new accounting policy of capitalising development costs as a project has become eligible for capitalisation for the first time

6. Which, if any, of the following statements are correct according to IAS 8 Accounting Policies, Changes in Accounting Estimates, and Errors?

    a) The correction of fundamental errors relating to a past period should be made in the current period. It is not acceptable to make the correction by adjusting the opening balance of retained earnings
    b) A change in an accounting estimate constitutes a fundamental error and should be accounted for as such
    c) The benchmark treatment for a change of accounting policy is normally to apply it retrospectively, with adjustment to the opening balance of retained earnings

7. Which of the following material events after the balance sheet date and before the financial statements are approved by the directors should be adjusted for in those financial statements?

    a) A valuation of property providing evidence of impairment in value at the balance sheet date
    b) Sale of inventory held at the balance sheet date for less than cost
    c) Discovery of fraud or error affecting the financial statements
    d) The insolvency of a customer with a debt owing at the balance sheet date which is still outstanding

8. Which ONE of the following should be recognised as a provision under IAS 37?

    a) Restructuring costs after a binding sale agreement has been signed
    b) Refurbishment costs due to introduction of a new computer system
    c) Divisional closure costs before a public announcement is made

9. Which of the following is a contingent liability and is disclosed in the financial statements of a company?

    a) The company is involved in a legal case that it may possibly lose, although this is not probable
    b) The company has received a letter from a supplier complaining about an old unpaid invoice
    c) The company has claims outstanding on warranty agreements that it accepts

10. In the year to 31 March 2009, a company is being sued for damages and in its draft financial statements includes a provision for $2 million. On 5 May 2009 when the financial statements had not yet been authorised, the court case was settled and the final total damages payable were $2.5 million. What should the accounting treatment be?

    a) Disclose $2 million
    b) Adjust $500,000
    c) Disclose $2.5 million
    d) Adjust $2 million

8

Leases, Employee Benefits and Taxes

Learning Objectives

At the end of this chapter you should be able to:

☞ Describe the problems with accounting for leases
☞ Explain the two leasing methods available
☞ Identify the different types of employee benefits
☞ Explain the issues of transfer pricing and taxation.

8.1 Introduction

In this chapter we examine three different standards:

- IAS 17 Leases
- IAS 19 Employee Benefits
- IAS 12 Income Taxes.

There is no direct connection between these three standards, but they each deal with an accounting issue that is complex and where accounting regulators have difficulty in finding widely accepted solutions.

Accounting for leases has been a controversial matter for several years. In the business world, it is usual for companies to acquire the use of non-current assets by leasing them rather than purchasing them outright. Leasing is similar to paying a rental to use something, but there are both conceptual problems and practical problems in deciding how to account for the transactions. IAS 17 addresses some of these issues but there are areas where amendments need to be made to the regulations.

IAS 19 is concerned with the entire spectrum of employee benefits. Your first response may be that employee benefits are just wages and salaries and there are no problems. There are, however, different types of benefits from company to company and from country to country. In some companies, employees may be paid a bonus. In some countries, employees receive significant pensions and other benefits such as healthcare when they retire. The standard sets out requirements for these different practices.

Taxes are not set internationally but are determined by each country. The different tax rates in various countries can encourage companies to conduct their operations, or a part of them, in a country where the tax rates are low. This is an economic strategic decision that the standard, IAS 12, does not cover. The matter of taxes set by the government and the relationship with profit set by the IASB does have its own complexities and the standard attempts to resolve these.

With the three standards, we will concentrate on identifying the problems that occur in accounting for the transactions. We will then consider the main requirements relating to the recognition and measurement of these transactions. But the current international accounting standards on these three subjects give rise to arguments and debate, so the IASB is seeking ways to improve them. We can expect changes to be made in the future.

8.2 IAS 17 Leases

> ### Definition — lease
>
> An agreement between the lessor (the owner of an asset) and the lessee allowing the latter to rent or hire the asset for an agreed period of time.

Leasing has become an increasingly popular activity in the business world and represents an important source of funding for companies wishing to acquire or use non-current assets. In some taxation regimes, it has been possible to structure agreements so that either, or both, the lessor and the lessee enjoy significant taxation benefits. Leasing does cause accounting problems, however, and we can demonstrate these by the three following illustrations.

Echo Inc. needs to buy some machinery with a life of 5 years costing $150,000 but has no cash. It therefore has to seek a method for funding the acquisition and there are three options:

Option 1

Echo could borrow $150,000 from the bank. The bank will want repayment of the loan and interest. If we assume five annual repayments of $30,000 for the loan and $6,000 annually for interest, then:

- Balance Sheet has asset of machinery $150,000 and a liability to the bank of the same amount.
- On payment of each installment, the liability to the bank reduces by $30,000 and an interest charge to the Income Statement of $6,000.
- End of each year, an annual depreciation charge to the Income Statement of $30,000.

The important point with Option 1 is that Echo will show a large loan on its Balance Sheet. Echo may not want to inform the users of its financial statements that it has a large loan because they may assume that Echo is financially weak. Echo therefore considers Option 2. We will assume for this option that there is no accounting standard, so Echo has the power to show the transaction how it wishes.

Option 2 — without IAS 17

- Bank buys asset for $150,000 and claims to be the owner.
- The bank charges Echo annual rental installments of $36,000.
- In Echo's accounts, there is only the annual charge to the Income Statement of $36,000.

If you compare Option 2 to Option 1 you will see that the charge to the Income Statement is the same: $36,000. The big difference is that nothing is shown on the Balance Sheet of Echo, so those users who are interested in its financial statements will not realise the true position.

Option 3 — with IAS 17

The standard attempts to ensure that the transactions are properly accounted for and it identifies two situations:

1. When the asset is transferred to the other party (in this case Echo Inc.) and there is a type of loan, this is known as a finance or capital lease. With a finance lease, Echo must show the asset and the loan on its Balance Sheet.
2. When the asset is only rented from the lessor, this is known as an operating lease. With an operating lease, Echo will only show the rental payment on its Income Statement.

The distinction between finance lease and operating lease is clearly very important for companies and the information that is shown on their financial statements. There may also be a temptation for companies to identify an agreement as an operating lease when it is in fact a finance lease.

The standard differentiates the two types of leases. An operating lease is easiest because this is any lease agreement that is not a finance lease. In these cases, the lessee charges the lease payments as a rental to its Income Statement. We will now consider the issues with finance leases.

> **Definition — finance lease**
>
> A finance lease is an agreement between two parties that transfers substantially all risks and rewards of ownership from the lessor to the lessee.

The way companies comply with the standard is illustrated in the following Notes to the Accounts taken from the Annual Report of Kingfisher plc:

> Where assets are financed by leasing agreements which give rights approximating to ownership, the assets are treated as if they had been purchased outright. The amount capitalised is the lower of the fair value or the present value of the minimum lease payments during the lease term at the inception of the lease.... All other leases are operating leases.

With a finance lease, the lessor is the legal owner of the asset. The lessee, the company using the asset, will make periodic payments to the lessor over a period of time. The above definition states that where substantially all risks and rewards are transferred, it is a finance lease. This means that it will fall under point 1 of Option 3 — it is a type of loan. The above definition specifies risks and rewards and it is helpful to clarify what is meant by this. Remember: it is the lessee, the company that is using the asset, that bears substantially all the risks which can be thought of as losses, and rewards which can be thought of as gains. The following table identifies these:

Table of risks and rewards

Risks	Rewards
The asset is idle due to lack of demand	The generation of profit from using the asset
Because of technological obsolescence, the asset loses part of its value	The ability to use the asset for most of its useful life
The costs of maintaining and repairing the asset	The possibility of being able to sell the asset if it increases in value

Lease agreements can be very complex and lengthy documents. They are legal agreements and cover all aspects of the relationship between the lessor and the lessee. In the above table we include the costs of maintaining and repairing the asset as a risk. Lease agreements will normally include a specific requirement relating to this risk. The following extract is taken from a standard Lease Agreement for Equipment:

6. In addition to the rental charges set out in this Agreement, the Lessee shall, at the Lessee's own expense, during the Rental Period, pay the cost of the following:
a. all fuel and lubricants required to operate the Equipment;
b. all repairs required to be made to the Equipment in order to keep it in good repair and running order;
c. replacing broken or worn-out parts as the result of normal use and wear and tear; and
d. any and all local, municipal, provincial and federal taxes, assessments and charges levied upon the Equipment during the Rental Period.

Although the above examples of risks and rewards are helpful, more guidance is required and the standard identifies various events and arrangements that can be used to identify a finance lease. Not all of these need to be present in the one transaction.

Examples of a finance lease

- The ownership of the asset transfers to the lessee at the end of the lease term.
- The lessee can purchase the asset at a bargain price at the end of the lease term.
- The asset is so specialised that only the lessee could use it.
- The present value of the minimum lease payments is substantially equal to the fair value of the asset.
- Any losses to the lessor due to the lessee cancelling the agreement are borne by the lessee.
- Fluctuations in fair value at the end of the lease term are borne by the lessee.
- The lessee can extend the term of the lease for a second term at a rate below the current market rate.

Most of the above are fairly straightforward but we will explain minimum lease payment as it is important. The minimum lease payment is the amount that the lessee must pay over the term of the lease. The lessee may have an option to purchase the asset outright at some future date at below market price. In that case, the minimum lease payments are the payments to the date of the option plus the amount of payment required to purchase the asset at that date.

The minimum lease payment includes not only rental payments but there will be certain costs incurred in negotiating and arranging the lease. These costs incurred by the lessee are known as initial direct costs and can be added to the cost of the asset. There are other costs paid by the lessee which should not be included and one of these is contingent rent. This is the portion of the lease payment that is not fixed in amount but fluctuates due to movements in another factor. For example, a lessee may have to pay a percentage of the sales achieved or an amount based on the actual usage of the asset.

Having established that a company, the lessee, has entered into a finance lease, the question arises as to the amount that should be shown on the balance sheet as a non-current asset, i.e., the amount capitalised. The standard states that it is the lower of the fair value of the asset and the present value of the minimum lease payments.

Definition — fair value

This is the amount for which an asset could be exchanged, or a liability settled, between knowledgeable, willing parties in an arm's-length transaction.

One particular situation is where a company enters into a lease for land and buildings. Land has an indefinite life and, usually, the title for the land will not pass at the end of the lease but will be retained by the lessor. In these circumstances the land will be treated as an operating lease. The buildings may be a finance lease and the minimum lease payments will have to be apportioned between the land and buildings to their relative fair values. The land will not appear on the lessee's balance sheet as it is an operating lease, but the buildings will be capitalised if they are on a finance lease.

For our purposes in this chapter, we can regard fair value as the current market value. The term "present" minimum lease payment is important and needs some explanation. We discussed in an earlier chapter how we discount future cash flows to arrive at the present value. It is that process the standard is referring to and we need not worry about the calculations at this stage, but how we apply the main requirements of the standard. The following example will clarify the requirements.

Example

Axto Inc. takes out a lease for equipment on 1 January 2010. The lease agreement is for 5 years and Axto is responsible for all maintenance and repair charges. The company must pay a rental charge of $26,500 at the end of each year. The market value of the equipment on 1 January 2010 is $100,000. The present value of the minimum lease payments is $99,500.

Comments

This is a finance lease as Axto has the risk of the maintenance and repairs. Also, the present value of the minimum lease payments is approximately equal to the current market value of the equipment. Do not be misled by the actual rental payments that the company must make! The standard states that the amount of the non-current asset to be shown on the balance sheet is the lower of the fair value of the asset and the present minimum lease payments. In the case of Axto, this will be $99,500.

Having determined that a company has entered into a finance lease and therefore must put the asset and liability on its Balance Sheet, the next issue is the amount of depreciation to be charged each year to the Income Statement. The standard states that an asset should be depreciated over the shorter of the lease term and its useful life. If it is reasonably certain that the lessee will gain ownership of the asset, then it would be over the useful life.

If we continue with the example of Axto and assume that the useful life is 6 years and the equipment has no residual value, the shorter life is the lease term of 5 years. As we have already determined that the asset will be capitalised at $99,500, the annual depreciation charge will be $99,500/5 = $19,900.

The following example of the treatment of leases is taken from the Notes to the Accounts in the Annual Report of GlaxoSmithKline:

> ### Leases
>
> Leasing agreements which transfer to the Group substantially all the benefits and risks of ownership of an asset are treated as finance leases, as if the asset had been purchased outright. The assets are included in PP&E or computer software and the capital elements of the leasing commitments are shown as obligations under finance leases. Assets held under finance leases are depreciated on a basis consistent with similar owned assets or the lease term if shorter. The interest element of the lease rental is included in the Income Statement. All other leases are operating leases and the annual rentals are included in the Income Statement on a straight-line basis over the lease term.

Our final comment on accounting for leases is what is known as sale and lease-back transactions. In this arrangement, the owner of an asset sells it to another party and then immediately leases it back again. For example, a government department may own a large building that it occupies. It sells this to a financial institution and receives cash. It then leases back the building and continues to occupy it. The agreement on the selling price and the terms of the lease will together determine what type of lease it is and the accounting treatment.

If it is a finance lease, any apparent profit on the sale must not be recognised as income. Instead, it should be deferred and amortised over the lease term. Essentially, the transaction is regarded as the lessee raising finance secured on an asset that it continues to hold. The sale is not a disposal of the asset as it is leased back to the owner.

Where the transaction is designated as an operating lease, any profit on sale is immediately recognised as long as it was conducted at fair value. If it was not at fair value, the rules are:

1.   Where sale price is lower than fair value, recognise the profit or loss immediately unless the loss is compensated by a rental below market rates. In this case, defer and amortise the loss in proportion to the rental payments over the period the asset is used.
2.   Where the sale price is above fair value, defer and amortise the excess above fair value over the period the asset is used.
3.   Where the fair value is less than the carrying amount, the loss should be recognised immediately.

This is a complex standard and we have considered the main requirements. Lease agreements are very lengthy and contain many specific conditions and responsibilities of the parties. Remember that the lease agreement is a legal document and may be written in such a way as to make the agreement look like an operating lease. In an earlier chapter we explained that international accounting standards are concerned with principles, not rules, and the economic reality of the transaction must be accounted for and not the legal form. It is important that the accountant considers the examples in the standard of finance leases and does not rely solely on the legal agreement.

We will now summarise some of the main points we have discussed above. As far as operating leases are concerned, the requirements of the standard are simple: the lessee treats an operating lease as an expense on a straight-line basis over the term of the lease. With finance leases, the position is more complex and the following applies:

•   A finance lease is recognised as an asset and a liability in the lessee's balance sheet at the lower of the fair value of the item leased and the present value of the minimum lease payments.
•   Finance lease payments should be apportioned between the finance charge and the reduction of the outstanding liability.
•   The finance charge represents a constant periodic rate of interest on the outstanding liability.
•   The leased asset is depreciated in accordance with IAS 16. The same depreciation policy for all assets should be applied to the asset held under the finance lease and, if there is uncertainty over final ownership, the shorter of the lease term and the useful life of the asset should be applied.

Finally, below is an example taken from the Notes to the Accounts of British Airways Annual Report. This shows that it has some aircrafts on operating leases and others on finance leases. You will note that we are looking at extremely large sums of money, with the company having payment commitments of £862 million under operating leases for aircrafts.

The Group has entered into commercial leases on certain properties, equipment and aircraft. These leases have durations ranging from five years for aircraft to 150 years for ground leases. Certain leases contain options for renewal.

a. Fleet

The aggregate payments, for which there are commitments under operating leases as at March 31, fall due as follows:

£ million	Group		Company	
	2009	**2008**	**2009**	**2008**
Within one year	**84**	77	**60**	62
Between one and five years	**334**	169	**309**	143
Over five years	**444**	17	**444**	17
At March 31	**862**	**263**	**813**	**222**

b. Property and equipment

The aggregate payments, for which there are commitments under operating leases as at March 31, fall due as follows:

£ million	Group		Company	
	2009	**2008**	**2009**	**2008**
Within one year	**84**	86	**80**	82
Between one and five years	**249**	244	**238**	229
Over five years, ranging up to the year 2145	**1,562**	1,612	**1,557**	1,603
At March 31	**1,895**	**1,942**	**1,875**	**1,914**

Finance leases (£ million)	Fleet	Property	Equipment	Group
Analysis at March 31, 2009				
Owned	2,535	950	260	**3,745**
Finance leased	2,004			**2,004**

The future for leasing

Discussions are taking place at the international level of bringing about major changes in accounting for leases. There is the belief, supported by evidence, that some companies are abusing the current standards. Essentially, lease agreements are being written that make it appear as if the lease is an operating lease and not a finance lease (called capital leases in some countries). In this way, the asset and, more importantly, the liability do not appear on the lessee's balance sheet.

It can be argued that part of the problem is that some countries use a "rules-based" approach in the standard, whereas the IASB adopts a principles-based approach. You may wish to refresh your memory on the differences in the approaches which were discussed in Chapter 2. The rules-based standard appears to allow companies to exploit its requirements.

Leasing is a regular transaction for several companies, and accounting standards to regulate these agreements have been issued by most countries and also internationally. A cornerstone of all the standards is the classification of leases into either operating or finance leases. The classification as a finance lease determines that the leased item will appear on the balance sheet of a company as an asset and as a liability.

For example, the US standard (SFAS 13) defines a capital lease as one under which any one of the following four conditions is met:

(i)   the present value at the beginning of the lease term of the payments not representing executory costs paid by the lessor equals or exceeds 90% of the fair value of the leased asset;
(ii) the lease transfers ownership of the asset to the lessee by the end of the lease term;
(iii) the lease contains a bargain purchase price;
(iv) the lease is equal to 75% or more of the estimated economic life of the leased asset (FASB, 1976).

You can imagine that a creative company can easily word a lease agreement to ensure that they do not meet the percentage thresholds in the standard. For example, with requirement (i), it would be possible to construct the agreement so that the present value is 89% and not 90%.

As we saw above, the international standard (IAS 17 Leases) avoids setting out quantitative thresholds as in the US, but states that the classification of a lease depends on the substance of the transaction rather than the form.

The debate and discussions on the most appropriate method for accounting for leases and proposals for a new approach have been on the agenda for many years. In 1996, the G4+1 published a special report entitled "Accounting for leases: A new approach". The report advocated a conceptual approach to lease accounting, whereby the distinction between finance leases and operating leases is removed. Lessees would recognise as assets and liabilities all material rights and obligations arising under lease contracts.

The present discussions taking place at the international level are moving in the direction of making all leases finance leases. In other words, these transactions will appear on the balance sheet. This presents some problems as to the treatment for short-term leases or leases that are not material. It is likely to be a long time before final agreement is reached, but we could see a substantial change in the way we account for leases.

8.3 IAS 19 Employee Benefits

Definition — employee benefits

All forms of consideration given to an employee in exchange for the employee's services. Examples are: cash bonuses, retirement benefits and private healthcare.

The standard on employee benefits includes all forms of consideration, and accounting for employee benefits raises a number of issues. When studying this standard we are considering all forms of consideration given by a business in exchange for services provided by its employees in a financial period. These include:

- Short-term benefits that fall due within 12 months of services being given, e.g., wages, salaries, bonuses, non-monetary benefits;
- Post-employment benefits, e.g., pensions and continued private medical healthcare;
- Other long-term benefits, e.g., long-term disability benefits and paid sabbaticals;
- Termination benefits, i.e., when employee leaves.

In this section we are going to concentrate on short-term benefits, post-employment benefits and termination benefits. With all types of benefits, the general principle is that the cost of providing employee benefits should be recognised in the period when the employee earns the benefit, rather than when it is paid or payable.

Short-term employee benefits are regarded as those payable within 12 months after service is provided and should be recognised as an expense in the period that service is provided. This includes vacations and paid sick leave to other acceptable absences where the benefits are still payable.

The company should charge the benefit to the Income Statement. If the benefit remains unpaid at the end of the financial period, it would be treated as a current liability on the Balance Sheet. When it is finally paid, the amount of cash held by the company will decline by the amount of the payment and the liability will be removed from the Balance Sheet. This situation can be demonstrated in the following example:

Short-term benefit example

A company has 20 employees. They are all paid the same rate of $150 per day and are entitled to 10 days holiday on full pay. The expense to the company in its Income Statement for 2010 for the vacation pay is $20 \times \$1,500 = \$30,000$. One employee decides that she will take only 8 days holiday and the remaining 2 days she will take in 2011. The company agrees to this plan. The amount of $30,000 in the Income Statement is correct, but the company will not have paid the 2 days holiday to the employee as they have not yet been taken. The amount of $2 \times \$150$ will be a current liability on the Balance Sheet.

Retirement benefits, also known as post-employment benefits, cause the greatest accounting problems. There are two types: the defined contribution plan and the defined benefit plan. For defined contribution plans, contributions are recognised as an expense in the period that the employee provides service. In many schemes, the employee and the employer both agree to contribute to the plan.

The amount paid into the defined contribution plan is fixed and the payments are invested to build up a "fund" for the particular employee. The amount of the contributions and the income that the investment has generated should be a substantial amount by the date the employee retires and can be used to provide regular pension payments.

The disadvantage of the defined contribution plan is that the amount of the final fund relies heavily on the success of the investments. If we have been through a very poor economic period, the fund will be much smaller than the employee hoped for and the pension will be correspondingly less. With the defined contribution plan, the risk lies with the employee: they may not receive the pension they anticipated. There is no risk to the employer and the only commitment is the agreed amount of contribution.

Defined benefit plans do not work on the basis of contributions but define the amount of pension a person will receive on retirement. This is usually calculated by using a formula that takes into account the employee's length of service and salary. For example, an employee may be in a scheme that pays one-sixtieth for each year of service multiplied by the employee's average salary for the last three years of his or her employment. An employee with 40 years' service and an average annual salary of $120,000 will receive a pension of $40/60 \times \$120,000 = \$80,000$ each year.

Employers will want to know the amount of contribution that they must make each year to pay for the final pension. Imagine that a company has an employee starting on 1 January 2010 who will retire in 2050. The company will have several questions it needs to answer so that it can calculate the annual contributions to the pension plan it must make between 2010 and 2050. Answers are needed to:

- Will the employee leave or die before he or she is due to retire?
- How many years' service will the employee actually have?
- What will the employee's final salary be?
- What will be the investment return on the contributions made each year?
- How long will the employee live after retirement because the pension will have to be paid until the employee dies?

There are many other variations and possibilities that the company has to resolve and it is normal to rely on the expert judgement of actuaries when calculating the contribution payments. These are professional people who deal with probabilities and will be able to provide the required information.

The above is only a brief description and companies often have several types of pension schemes for different groups of employees. There are also hybrid plans that are part defined benefit and part defined contribution. Pension plans are really a task for the experts and accounting for them relies on the experts' professional opinions.

The main issue for companies is that with defined benefit plans, they have an obligation to make up any shortfall if there are insufficient funds to pay out the promised benefits. The risk lies with the employer and not the employee.

Our discussion on pension plans has concentrated on the accounting issues. The actual operation and regulation of pension plans for employees are conducted by companies and must comply with the laws of the countries in which they operate. We demonstrate these differences with three examples from companies in different countries.

The first example is taken from the Notes to the Accounts of the Annual Report of Intercontinental Hotels and the wording is not very different from that in the standard:

Pensions

Defined contribution plans — Payments to defined contribution schemes are charged to the Income Statement as they fall due.

Defined benefit plans — Plan assets are measured at fair value and plan liabilities are measured on an actuarial basis, using the projected unit credit method and discounting at an interest rate equivalent to the current rate of return on a high-quality corporate bond of equivalent currency and term to the plan liabilities. The service cost of providing pension benefits to employees for the year is charged to the Income Statement.

The cost of making improvements to pensions is recognised in the Income Statement on a straight-line basis over the period during which any increase in benefits vests. To the extent that improvements in benefits vest immediately, the cost is recognised immediately as an expense. Actuarial gains and losses may result from: differences between the expected return and the actual return on plan assets; differences between the actuarial assumptions underlying the plan liabilities and actual experience during the year; or changes in the actuarial assumptions used in the valuation of the plan liabilities.

Actuarial gains and losses, and taxation thereon, are recognised in the Group statement of recognised income and expense.

Actuarial valuations are normally carried out every three years.

As a comparison, the following extract is taken from the 2008 Annual Report of China Telecom Corporation ltd. This is a statement of their accounting policy and it makes reference to the lengthy notes that give full details of the pension plans. The plans are administered by the PRC government.

Employee benefits

The Group's contributions to defined contribution retirement plans administered by the PRC government are recognised as an expense in the Consolidated Income Statement as incurred. Further information is set out in Note 36. Compensation expense in respect of the stock appreciation rights granted is accrued as a charge to the Consolidated Income Statement over the applicable vesting period based on the fair value of the stock appreciation rights. The liability of the accrued compensation expense is re-measured to fair value at each balance sheet date with the effect of changes in the fair value of the liability charged or credited to the Consolidated Income Statement. Further details of the Group's stock appreciation rights scheme are set out in Note 37.

The third example is taken from the Annual Report of the French company, Total, and refers not only to pension plans but also to employee incentives and profit-sharing schemes. The first note demonstrates the complexity and scope of some employee incentive and profit-sharing plans. The second note on pension plans illustrates the impact of government legislation and also that, in some instances, agreement must be made with the trade unions.

Employee incentives and profit-sharing

On June 30, 2006, an incentive agreement and a profit-sharing agreement were signed for 2006, 2007 and 2008, concerning TOTAL S.A., CDF Énergie, Elf Exploration

Production, Total E&P France, Total Raffinage Marketing (formerly Total France), Total Infrastructures Gaz France, Total Lubrifiants, Total Additifs et Carburants Spéciaux, Total Fluides and Totalgaz. A new incentive agreement and a new profit-sharing agreement are expected to be signed in 2009.

The amount of the special profit-sharing and incentive reserve to be distributed by all of the companies that signed the Group agreements for fiscal year 2008 would total 116 M€.

Company savings plans give employees of the Group's companies covered by these plans the ability to make discretionary contributions (which the Company may, under certain conditions, supplement) to the plans invested in the shares of the Company (see pages 128 and 129 of this Registration Document). In order to reaffirm the Group's commitment in favour of sustainable development, the fund TOTAL DIVERSIFIÉ À DOMINANTES ACTIONS was transformed, on September 2006, into a Socially responsible investment fund (*Fonds à investissement socialement responsable*). The Group made additional contributions to various savings plans that totaled 48.7 M€ in 2008.

Pension savings plan

Pursuant to French law 2003-775 of August 21, 2003 reforming pensions, an agreement was signed with the unions on September 29, 2004 to set up, as of January 1, 2005, a Collective Retirement Savings Plan (PERCO) replacing the Voluntary Partnerships Plan for Employee Savings (PPESV) created in the agreement of March 15, 2002. An amendment to this agreement signed on December 20, 2005, allows for an increase in France of the employee and Company contributions and for contribution of bonuses and/or profit-sharing.

The final part of IAS 19 deals with termination benefits. Companies may decide to reduce the size of their workforce and either identify workpeople who must leave the company or ask for volunteers. Countries use different terms to describe this occurrence, the most common being redundancies or lay-offs. Depending on the circumstances, the employees who are made redundant will receive a payment on the termination of their employment.

For termination benefits, the standard specifies that amounts payable should be recognised when the enterprise is demonstrably committed to either:

- terminating the employment of an employee or group of employees before their normal retirement date; or
- providing termination benefits as a result of an offer made in order to encourage voluntary redundancy.

A company has demonstrated that it is committed to this course of action when it has a detailed plan for the termination and cannot withdraw from it. The detailed plan must show:

- the location, function and approximate number of employees whose services are to be terminated;
- the termination benefits for each job classification or function;
- the time at which the plan will be implemented. Implementation should begin as soon as possible and the period of time to complete implementation should be such that material changes to the plan are not likely.

8.4 IAS 12 Income Taxes

In a country which has adopted International Accounting Standards, the reported profits of the company will be based on accounting standards and not on tax laws. Each country will have its own tax laws even if companies are using international standards. It would be misleading for companies to deduct the tax to be paid that has been calculated on national tax laws from a profit calculated on a different basis.

A country-by-country examination of tax systems is beyond the scope of this chapter, but there are two basic national philosophies of taxation: the territorial principle and the worldwide principle. The territorial principle implies that income earned outside a home country's territory is not taxable. This is, in fact, a kind of governmental subsidy to encourage a home country's businesses to sell their products outside their borders. The worldwide principle implies that a country has the right to collect taxes on income earned outside the home country by a company domiciled in the home country. The worldwide principle results in double taxation, since income earned outside a country is taxed by the foreign tax authorities and then taxed by the home tax authorities.

Understandably, multinational companies wish to minimise the taxes they pay worldwide and to avoid double taxation. They produce the product in one location, and sell it in another, resulting in an ability to choose the tax jurisdictions in which they perform various operations. One method for reducing worldwide taxes is through judicious use of transfer prices.

A transfer price is the price charged between organisational units of the same company. Internationally, the transfer price is the price paid for the transfer of goods and/or services between two subsidiaries of the same multinational corporation. These transfer prices can occur for both goods and services. Many multinationals produce a product in one country, and sell it in a second country, or charge a subsidiary for some type of service the multinational may provide. Thus, transfer prices occur even if no actual goods cross borders. Since there are different tax rates from one country to another, the issue of transfer prices gives multinationals an incentive to shift taxable profit to low tax rate jurisdictions using transfer prices as a mechanism.

The standard, IAS 12, is not specifically directed at multinationals and transfer pricing, but attempts to ensure that financial statements provide a reasonable picture of the tax position and the reported profits. Adjustments are made to the current tax expense so that the reported tax charge is consistent with the reported profit for the period. The difference between the current tax expense and the adjusted figure is known as deferred tax. IAS 12 explains the requirement for the recognition and measurement of deferred tax.

It also deals with transactions and other events of the current period that are recognised in the financial statements; recognition of deferred tax assets arising from unused tax losses or unused tax credits; the presentation of income taxes in the financial statements; and the disclosure of information relating to income taxes. The standard uses some very specific terms and the main definitions are as follows:

- Temporary difference: A difference between the carrying amount of an asset or liability and its tax base.
- Taxable temporary difference: A temporary difference that will result in taxable amounts in the future when the carrying amount of the asset is recovered or when the liability is settled.
- Deductible temporary difference: A temporary difference that will result in amounts that are tax deductible in the future when the carrying amount of the asset is recovered or when the liability is settled.

The main requirement of IAS 12 is that businesses should recognise current taxes that are payable with respect to profits or current taxes that are recoverable with respect to losses. The amounts should be calculated using the rates available in the relevant regulations at the balance sheet date.

The tax charge for a period may not be calculable from a company's reported profit for a year shown on its financial statements. This is because the tax payable will be determined by the tax laws of the country and this will involve adjusting the profit figure as calculated using international accounting standards. To make the financial statements internally consistent, the current tax is adjusted so that the total tax charge is based on the company's reported financial profits. The difference is known as deferred tax.

The main differences between the tax "profit" and the international accounting standard profit are:

- The depreciation calculated under IAS 16 for reporting purposes differs from the allowances accepted by the tax authorities.
- Employee expenditure is recognised when incurred for accounting purposes and when paid for tax purposes.

- Costs of research and development are charged in the Income Statement in one period for accounting purposes, but are allowed for tax purposes in another period.

The following is a simple example of deferred tax arising. A company acquires a non-current asset for $60,000. It depreciates it over three years and in year 1 it charges $20,000 to the Income Statement. The carrying value shown in the Balance Sheet at the year end is $40,000. In the country where the company operates, the tax legislation allows the full cost in year 1, so the tax base is nil. The temporary difference is $40,000 because the company has reduced its tax liability by $60,000 under tax legislation, although only $20,000 is shown as an expense in the Income Statement in the current year. The current tax expense is lower than that calculated on the reported profits in the Income Statement. The deferred tax liability shows the liability of the company in future years. Of course, if the company is growing and each year is acquiring non-current assets, it could be several years before the company has to pay the tax.

An entity must recognise the deferred tax because the reported profit may be misinterpreted unless the user is informed of the deferred tax, and a deferred tax liability will become an actual tax liability in future periods. A deferred tax liability should usually be recognised in full for all tax differences unless it arises from:

- goodwill for which amortisation is not deductible for tax purposes;
- the initial recognition of an asset/liability that is not part of a business combination and affects neither the accounting nor the taxable profit at the time of the transaction;
- investments where the enterprise is able to control the timing of reversal of the tax difference and it is probable that the reversal will not occur in the foreseeable future.

Deferred tax is measured at tax rates expected to apply when the deferred tax asset is realised or when a deferred tax liability is settled. The tax rates used must have been enacted or substantially enacted by the balance sheet date. A deferred tax asset or liability is not discounted. The deferred tax is calculated using the balance sheet liability method. An assessment is made of the temporary difference between the carrying amount of an asset or liability and the amount of that item for tax purposes (known as "tax base").

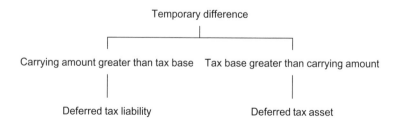

We complete this section with the following extract from the Annual Report of Pearson:

n. *Taxation*

Current tax is recognised on the amounts expected to be paid or recovered under the tax rates and laws that have been enacted or substantively enacted at the balance sheet date. Deferred income tax is provided, using the liability method on temporary differences arising between the tax bases of assets and liabilities and their carrying amounts in the consolidated financial statements. Deferred income tax is determined using tax rates (and laws) that have been enacted or substantively enacted by the balance sheet date and are expected to apply when the related deferred tax asset is realised or when the deferred income tax liability is settled. Deferred tax assets are recognised to the extent that it is probable that future taxable profit will be available against which the temporary differences can be utilised. Deferred income tax is provided in respect of the undistributed earnings of subsidiaries other than where it is intended that those undistributed earnings will not be remitted in the foreseeable future. Current and deferred tax are recognised in the Income Statement, except when the tax relates to items charged or credited directly to equity, in which case the tax is also recognised in equity.

8.5 Chapter Summary

This is a difficult chapter but the three standards we have examined are very important. Transactions involving leases, employee benefits and taxes are conducted by all companies and you need to know what the transactions involve and what the main requirements of the standards are. The issues are made more complex because the practices vary from country to country and we have seen this in the extracts from the Annual Reports which we have included. Taking the three standards in turn order, the main points are:

IAS 17 Leases

☞ For operating leases, the lessee treats an operating lease as an expense on a straight-line basis over the term of the lease.

☞ A finance lease is recognised as an asset and as a liability in the lessee's balance sheet at the lower of the fair value of the asset and the present value of the minimum lease payments.

☞ Finance lease payments should be apportioned between the finance charge and the reduction of the outstanding liability.

☞ The finance charge represents a constant periodic rate of interest on the outstanding liability.

☞ The leased asset is depreciated in accordance with IAS 16. The same depreciation policy for all assets should be applied to the asset held under the finance lease and, if there is uncertainty over final ownership, the shorter of the lease term and the useful life of the asset should be applied.

IAS 19 Employee Benefits

☞ Short-term benefits fall due within 12 months of services being given. They should be shown in the Income Statement of the relevant financial period. Any payments that are not made by the end of the financial period should be shown as a liability.

☞ Post-employment benefits require different accounting treatments depending on the nature of the scheme. Defined contribution plans are accounted for in the financial period concerned, but defined benefit plans will need the services of an actuary to determine the correct accounting treatment.

☞ Termination benefits should be accounted for in the financial period concerned. A company must demonstrate with a detailed plan that it is committed to the terminations.

IAS 12 Income Taxes

☞ The problem arises with taxes because tax authorities do not use the financial reporting profit to calculate the tax payable.

☞ Users of financial statements would be misled if an explanation was not provided of the differences between the tax payable and the financial reporting profit.

☞ The main difference for most companies in the tax payable is that the depreciation charged for financial reporting purposes is different from the amount allowed by tax authorities.

☞ Deferred tax is calculated by using the balance sheet liability method.

Progress Test

1. Which of the following terms best describes benefits which are payable as a result of an entity's decision to end an employee's employment before the normal retirement date?

   a) Termination benefits
   b) Post-employment benefits
   c) Defined contribution plans
   d) Defined benefit plans

2. Which ONE of the following is included in the definition of minimum lease payment?

   a) Required payments over the lease term
   b) Contingent rent
   c) Costs for services and taxes to be paid by and reimbursed to the lessor

3. A company takes out a lease for machinery on 1 January 2009 for 5 years. The company is responsible for all maintenance costs over the term of the lease. The asset has a fair value of $110,000 and the company will pay rentals of $26,000 at the end of each year for five years. The present value of the minimum lease payments is $99,000. What amount should the company capitalise on 1 January 2009?

   a) $110,000
   b) $130,000
   c) $99,000
   d) It should not be capitalised

4. A company leases a machine with a fair value of $250,000 for a period of 5 years. Initial direct costs in negotiating the lease were $10,500. The present value of minimum lease payments is $235,000. What amount should be capitalised in the balance sheet?

   a) $250,000
   b) $245,500
   c) $235,000
   d) $260,500

5. A company takes out a lease for machinery for 5 years. The company is responsible for all maintenance costs over the term of the lease. The asset has a fair value of $20,000 and the company will pay rentals of $5,300 at the end of each year for five years. The present value of the minimum lease payments is $19,500. What amount should the company capitalise on the balance sheet?

   a) $20,000
   b) $26,500
   c) $19,500
   d) Nil

6. A company has a finance lease on an asset of which the fair value is $420,000. The present value of the minimum lease payments is $400,000. The asset has a useful life of 8 years and the lease is for a period of 6 years after which the asset

can be acquired for a near zero cost, which is substantially below the expected value of the asset at that date. Straight-line depreciation is used. What is the annual depreciation charge?

a) $52,500
b) $66,667
c) $70,000
d) $50,000

7. A company has leased a factory with adjoining land that it will use for parking its vehicles. The lease of the factory is for 30 years. The fair value of the land is $750,000 and the fair value of the factory is $315,000. The land has an indefinite economic life but the expected useful life of the factory is 30 years. The title of land will not pass at the end of the lease. What is the value of the assets to be capitalised in the balance sheet?

a) $315,000
b) Nil
c) $1,065,000
d) $750,000

8. On 1 January 2010 a company enters into a four-year lease for a motor vehicle. The fair value of the vehicle is $66,000 and the present value of minimum lease payments is $63,000. The estimated useful life of the vehicle is 5 years and it has no residual value. The company has a policy of using straight-line depreciation. What is the annual depreciation charge in 2010?

a) $15,750
b) $12,600
c) $13,200
d) $16,500

9. A company purchased a building in January 2008 for $450,000. The accounting depreciation charge is 5% straight-line and this is used in its Income Statement. For tax purposes, depreciation of 2% straight-line is allowed. The tax rate is 25%. What should be the deferred tax balance at 31 December 2008?

a) Zero
b) $13,500 deferred tax asset
c) $9,000 deferred tax liability
d) $22,500 deferred tax asset

10. A company has a machine which had a carrying amount in the financial statements of $36,000 at 31 December 2009. Its tax written down value (the tax base) at that date was $18,000. The tax rate is 30%. In accordance with IAS 12, what is the deferred tax balance in respect of this asset at 31 December 2009?

    a) $9,000 asset
    b) $5,400 liability
    c) $10,800 asset
    d) Zero

9

Financial Instruments
and Share-Based Payments

Learning Objectives

At the end of this chapter you should be able to:

☞ List and explain different types of financial instruments
☞ Give examples of financial assets and financial liabilities
☞ List the classifications for financial assets and liabilities
☞ Explain the appropriate accounting treatment for financial instruments
☞ Describe share-based payments.

9.1 Introduction

> **Definition — financial instruments**
>
> Any contract that gives rise to a financial asset of one entity and a financial liability or equity instrument of another entity.

We will look more closely at the above definition as we work through this chapter. The main points to note are that there must be a contract and this will give one party to the contract a financial asset and the other party a financial liability. Accounting for financial instruments is the most difficult area in accounting and revisions are constantly being considered to improve the regulations. The world economic crisis in

2008/2009 has been blamed by some on the use and abuse of financial instruments, particularly derivatives.

The appropriate accounting treatment is influential on how banks, other financial institutions and the entire economy operate. The International Accounting Standards Board will be given advice by governments, banks, investors and many others. Some of that advice will be well-meaning, but some will be from people who want the regulations to fit in with their own needs. The IASB has to somehow balance all of these competing demands.

The following standards and interpretations relating to financial instruments have been issued, and some have been amended a few times and other amendments are proposed:

- IAS 32 *Financial Instruments: Presentation*
- IAS 39 *Financial Instruments: Recognition and Measurement*
- IFRS 7 *Financial Instruments: Disclosures*
- IFRIC 2 *Members' Shares in Co-operative Entities and Similar Instruments*
- IFRIC 9 *Reassessment of Embedded Derivatives*
- IFRIC 10 *Interim Financial Reporting and Impairment*
- IFRIC 16 *Hedges of a Net Investment in a Foreign Operation.*

This list demonstrates the complexity of the topic. We cannot cover all these documents in depth, so we are going to concentrate on the main requirements. At the end of the chapter we will add some comments on share-based payments, IFRS 2. Although this does not fall under the heading of financial instruments, it is relevant to some of the topics we discuss in this chapter.

We will start this chapter by explaining some important aspects of the world of finance. Students who have already taken a finance course will be familiar with the terms and operations of the markets. Students without this knowledge will find the next section most helpful in understanding this background.

9.2 The Financial Environment

A market is a mechanism bringing buyers and sellers together, so they can perform transactions in the marketplace to obtain goods and services to satisfy their needs. At one time, markets were physical places where buyers and sellers might meet, negotiate prices, and goods could change hands. As society became more complex and technology became more advanced, the market was not necessarily a physical place, but simply some mechanism by which buyers and sellers could search for each other efficiently and exchange products, cash, or services.

Markets can exist for just about anything individuals desire: products, services, or even finance. Financial markets exist to provide a source of cash to people with a need for cash. If financial markets work well, those with good business projects can obtain cash to set those projects into motion. In a small market with face-to-face contact, a provider of financing could judge whether a project was worthy of financing, assess the risk of the proposal, and charge a price based on the assessment of the risk.

Markets for financing, like markets for products and services, evolved from face-to-face meetings to remote contacts on a local and international basis. Regulations and financial information are necessary to support these activities and to minimise risk.

Companies and investors face all types of risks. There are those that are associated with the conduct of the business itself and the manufacturing, trading and retailing operations. Other types of risk arise because of the financial transactions that take place in the normal course of business. Companies and individuals will attempt to reduce or eliminate this risk.

Companies can raise capital either internally, through their own operations, or externally, through transactions in various financial markets. External financial markets can be considered short-term (less than a year) or long-term. Short-term financial markets are often called money markets. Long-term financial markets are called capital markets, and include the equity market, the debt market that includes borrowing from other firms, and the bank market. Multinational companies that used to raise equity capital solely from sources within their own country now look to other countries for potential shareholders and this is known as cross-border financing.

Companies engage in cross-border financing for a variety of reasons. Financial reasons include the fact that a company might be able to obtain cheaper financing outside its own borders, lowering its overall cost of capital. In addition, a company might find it convenient to obtain external financing in countries where it has significant operations.

Non-financial reasons to engage in cross-border financing include the objective to be a world-class company maintaining financial relationships in many countries. A company might wish to broaden its shareholder base to include citizens and other institutions from many countries in addition to its home base. A company might find it politically expedient to maintain financial relationships inside a particular country in order to obtain additional business contacts both inside and outside of a foreign government, or simply to be regarded with favour by a local government. In any case, cross-border financial activity is increasingly compatible with the cross-border movement of goods and services.

Whenever and wherever a company engages in financial markets, it encounters risk. The types of financial risk that companies face are interest rate risk from making investments or taking out loans, or exchange rate risk through international trade. It is impossible to eliminate risk completely, but companies can attempt to reduce it by hedging the risk. The following extract is taken from the Annual Report of Carphone Warehouse and illustrates their approach to risk:

> **Financial risk** Exchange rates
> **Why** Reported profits distorted by exchange rate movements; value of assets and liabilities similarly affected
> **Action** Exchange rate exposures are primarily to the Euro and Swiss Franc, which are historically stable currencies. Exposures to exchange rate movements are continuously monitored and hedging of specific transactions is undertaken where the risks are considered material

In Chapter 13 we will examine the regulations concerning accounting for changes in exchange rates. In this chapter, we will continue our examination of financial instruments. As we can see from the above extract, Carphone Warehouse attempts to reduce its risks by hedging.

> **Definition — hedging**
>
> Hedging is reducing risk by taking action now to reduce the possibility of future losses, usually with the possibility of not enjoying any future gains.

An example of hedging is where a company knows that it has to purchase supplies of materials in six months' time. It is concerned that the price will rise before it needs the materials. It can enter into an agreement now to purchase the goods in six months' time, but at a price that is current. The following example is taken from Rolls Royce Annual Report:

> We manage our exposure to the US dollar by long-term hedging. Today we have the benefit of a hedge book of approximately US$10 billion, which means that we have clear visibility of the exchange rate we can achieve over the next three years.

By this action, the company avoids the risk of the prices increasing in six months' time when it requires the materials. It also loses the opportunity to make a gain if the price decreases in six months' time.

In the above example, the company has entered into a contract. There are several types of these contracts and the terms "complex financial instruments" and "derivatives" are used.

> **Definition — derivatives**
>
> A derivative is a complex financial instrument whose value depends on (or is derived from) the value of another basic underlying variable or asset.

Derivatives are commonly traded among financial institutions, individual investors, fund managers, corporations, and private companies. The trades are conducted at either a physical location such as an Exchange, or remotely in what is termed an over-the-counter market. New, interesting, non-standard derivatives to meet these needs are constantly being designed. Some of these are very complex and, it is argued, led to the economic meltdown in 2009.

Definition — over-the-counter market

A market that trades in financial instruments outside the jurisdiction of a recognised stock exchange.

The four main types of derivatives we will discuss are: forward contracts, futures contracts, options and swaps.

Forward contract

A forward contract is an agreement to buy or sell an asset at a certain future time for a certain price. It is the simplest form of derivative and is traded in the over-the-counter market. One of the parties in a forward contract agrees to buy the underlying asset on a future specified date for a certain specified price. The other party agrees to sell the asset on the agreed date for the agreed price. The price at which the parties agree to transact in the future is called the delivery price. No money changes hands at the time the parties enter into a forward contract.

Once forward contracts are agreed, they can be traded between investors, typically on the over-the-counter market. For example, a banker in Hong Kong believes that the US dollar is going to increase in value against the Italian Lira. She wants to benefit from her prediction. At the same time, a company in the US expects a large payment in Italian Lira in six months' time. The company will need to convert this payment in Italian Lira into US dollars and is concerned about the exchange rate in six months' time. The company will therefore attempt to hedge this exchange risk by entering into a forward contract with the Hong Kong banker.

Futures contract

A futures contract is very similar to a forward contract. The main difference is that futures contracts are traded on an Exchange, which sets rules for trading. This simplifies the trading process and helps the market achieve higher liquidity. Futures contracts are traded on a variety of commodities, including live cattle, sugar, wool, lumber, copper, gold, tin and aluminium. They are also traded on a wide array of financial assets, including stock indices, currencies, and Treasury bonds.

Options

There are two types of options. In contrast to forwards and futures, options give the owner the right, but not the obligation, to transact. The owner therefore will only transact if it is profitable to do so. The price at which the parties transact in the future is called the strike price. When the transaction takes place, the owner of the option exercises the option.

Swaps

A swap is simply an agreement between two parties to exchange cash flows in the future. The agreement defines the dates when the cash flows are exchanged and the manner in which amounts are calculated. Swaps typically lead to cash flow exchanges on several future dates. There are interest rate swaps where a floating-rate loan is exchanged for a fixed-rate loan by agreeing to pay a fixed payment in return for a variable payment. Similarly, currency swaps can be used to transform borrowings in one currency to borrowings in another currency, by agreeing to make a payment in one currency in return for a payment in another currency.

Having had a brief review of the financial environment, you can imagine that there are difficulties in accounting for these complex financial instruments. The situation is made even more difficult for the standard setters because new derivatives are being designed that are not dealt with adequately in the existing regulations. In the next section we will examine what the standard requires on accounting for financial instruments.

9.3 Financial Instruments

The definition of financial instruments states that there must be a contract and this gives rise to financial assets, financial liabilities and equity. This means that non-contractual obligations, for example those relating to taxation, are not financial instruments. The definition of a financial instrument is also two-sided: the contract must always give rise to a financial asset of one party, with a corresponding financial liability or equity instrument of another party.

If we look in detail by what is meant by equity, financial assets and financial liabilities, it will help to explain the types of transactions that are taking place.

Equity

An equity is a contract that evidences a residual interest in the assets of an entity after deducting all of its liabilities. If we put this in terms of the accounting equation we discussed in an earlier chapter, then

$$\text{Assets} - \text{Liabilities} = \text{Capital (Equity)}.$$

Examples of equity are:

- Ordinary shares
- Preference shares (non-redeemable and discretionary dividend)
- Warrants or written call options (allow the holder to purchase ordinary shares for a fixed amount of cash).

Financial assets

This is possibly the easiest of the financial instruments to understand and we can explain financial assets by listing some examples:

- Cash
- Equity instrument of another entity (e.g., investment in another entity's shares)
- Receivables and loans to another entity
- Investments in bonds and other debt instruments issued by another entity
- Derivative financial assets.

The following assets are NOT financial assets, and we have examined them and the particular standards that set out their accounting treatment in earlier chapters:

- Inventories
- Property, plant and equipment
- Leased assets
- Intangible assets
- Prepaid expenses.

Financial liabilities

Financial liabilities are slightly more complex and include a contractual obligation to deliver cash or another financial asset to another entity, or to exchange financial assets or financial liabilities with another entity under conditions that are potentially unfavourable to the entity; or a contract that will or may be settled in the entity's own equity instruments and is not classified as an equity instrument of the entity. Examples of financial liabilities are:

- Trades payable
- Loans from other entities
- Bonds and other debt instruments issued by the entity
- Derivative financial liabilities
- Preference shares that are redeemable at a specified date and for a specified amount
- Obligations to issue own shares worth a fixed amount of cash.

Care must be taken with the last example as it emphasises shares worth a fixed amount. Normally shares fluctuate in price, so if you enter into a contract that specifies the number of shares, the price will not be known until the contract is completed. You can enter into a contract where the amount is known but not the number of shares. For example, a company enters into a contract in 2010 that entails issuing its own shares in January 2015 to the value of $500,000. This is a financial liability as the number of shares are variable but the amount is fixed.

The following examples are NOT financial liabilities:

- Warranty obligations
- Income tax liabilities
- Constructive obligations.

At this stage it is useful to summarise the nature of the transactions that involve financial instruments. Derivative financial instruments create rights and obligations between two parties. For example, if a company enters into a futures contract where it promises to purchase US$2 million on 31 December 2012 at the price of CDN$2.20 million, both parties (the entity and the counterparty to the futures contract) have a neutral position at the date of making the agreement. This is because the price is the market value of the USD on the futures market when the agreement is made. This means that at the date of the agreement, no party has "favourable" or "unfavourable" conditions.

As time progresses, so the USD on the futures market price will change and may increase or decrease. In that case, the futures contract will represent a financial asset for one party, because it will give the right to exchange financial assets or financial liabilities with another party under conditions that are potentially favourable. The other party will have a financial liability because it will have a contractual obligation to exchange under potentially unfavourable conditions.

9.4 Classification of Financial Instruments

Having examined equity, financial assets and financial liabilities, we can now discuss the accounting requirements of IAS 39. The critical part of the standard is classifying the assets based on the purpose for entering into the contract. That classification must be carried out when the financial instruments are first recognised, i.e., entered into the financial statements of the company. The classification will determine how the company will subsequently account for the financial instruments, including accounting for any gains or losses.

All financial assets and liabilities within the scope of IAS 39 must be classified into one of the following categories. For financial assets there are four categories, and for financial liabilities there are two.

Classification of financial assets under IAS 39:

- fair value through profit or loss;
- available for sale;
- held to maturity; and
- loans and receivables.

Classification of financial liabilities under IAS 39:

- fair value through profit or loss;
- at amortised cost.

Classification is based on facts, circumstances and the intent of management at the date they became the party to the contract. A look at examples of the different classifications will clarify the types of financial instruments we are considering.

Fair value through profit or loss

A financial asset at fair value through profit or loss is one that is acquired principally for the purpose of selling it in the near future. Examples of trading financial assets that would require fair value through profit or loss are:

- debt and equity securities that are actively traded by the company;
- loans and receivables acquired by the company with the intention of making a short-term profit from fluctuation in price or dealer's margin;
- securities held under repurchase agreements;
- derivatives other than those used in hedging.

Available-for-sale financial assets

Available for sale can be considered as a residuary category. Those financial assets that do not fall under any of the other three categories come under this heading, or the company has decided to put them under this heading.

Held-to-maturity financial assets

Held-to-maturity investments are financial assets with fixed or determinable payments and fixed maturity that an entity has the positive intention and ability to hold to maturity. Fixed or determinable payments and fixed maturity means a contractual arrangement that defines the amounts and dates of payments to the holder, such as interest and principal payments on debt. The asset must be quoted in an active market. As shares do not usually have a maturity date, such financial assets cannot be put under this category.

Held-to-maturity is an exception from the general requirement to measure financial assets at fair value. For this reason, there are strict criteria that an asset and the company must meet before assets can be categorised as held-to-maturity. IFRS requires a positive intent and ability to hold a financial asset to maturity. The intent and ability must be assessed when an asset is acquired and at each subsequent statement of financial position date.

Loans and receivables

Loans and receivables are financial assets with fixed or determinable payments that are not quoted in an active market, that are not intended for trading, and that are not initially designated as available for sale. Financial assets such as loans, accounts receivable, investments in debt instruments and deposits held in banks can be classified in this category, provided they are not quoted in an active market.

Initial recognition

An entity recognises a financial asset or a financial liability on the Statement of Financial Position when it first becomes a party to the contract. Under IAS 39, all financial instruments are measured initially by reference to their fair value, which in most cases (though not always) is the amount an entity receives or pays.

When a financial asset or financial liability is initially recognised, an entity measures it at its fair value plus (in the case of a financial asset or financial liability not at fair value through profit or loss) transaction costs that are directly attributable to the acquisition or issue of the financial asset or financial liability.

9.5 Measurement of Financial Instruments

There are three measurement "stages":

1. Initial measurement — when the instrument is first recognised
2. Subsequent measurement
3. Impairment — adjustments due to incurred losses.

Initial measurement

When the financial instrument is first recognised, it is usually measured at fair value. This is the amount at which an asset could be exchanged or a liability settled between knowledgeable, willing parties in an arm's-length transaction, i.e., the actual or estimated price when the transaction takes place. This approach is exemplified in the following extract from the Annual Report of Morrisons:

Financial instruments

Financial assets and liabilities are recognised on the Group's balance sheet when the Group becomes a party to the contractual provisions of the instrument. Derivative financial instruments are initially measured at fair value, which normally equates to cost, and are remeasured at fair value.

Subsequent measurement

On initial recognition of the financial instrument, it is measured at fair value. In subsequent years, there are three types of measurement that can be made. The measurement used depends on which of the four categories for financial assets and two categories for financial liabilities the instrument is placed. The three methods of subsequent measurement are:

1. Cost, which is the amount at which an asset was acquired or a liability incurred, including transaction costs. Only investments in unquoted equity instruments for which there is no fair value can be measured at cost.
2. Amortised cost, which is the cost of an asset or liability adjusted to achieve a constant effective interest rate over the life of the asset or liability. Only the following can be measured at amortised cost:

    I. Held-to-maturity investments
    II. Loans and receivables
    III. Financial liabilities not measured at fair value through profit or loss.

3. Fair value, which is a published price quotation in an active market. Where there is no active market, valuation techniques such as discounted cash flow models or option pricing models can be used. The following categories of financial assets and financial liabilities are normally measured at fair value in the balance sheet:

    I. Financial assets at fair value through profit or loss
    II. Available-for-sale financial assets
    III. Financial liabilities at fair value through profit or loss.

This is a complicated series of regulations and the following table gives the measurement method for the main types of instruments:

Financial instrument	Method of measurement
Held-to-maturity investments	Amortised cost
Available-for-sale financial assets	Fair value
Financial liabilities at fair value through profit or loss	Fair value
Loans and receivables	Amortised cost
Investments in unquoted equity instruments	Cost
Financial assets at fair value through profit or loss	Fair value
Financial liabilities not measured at fair value through profit or loss	Amortised cost

Fair value measurement

Fair value measurement has caused the greatest amount of controversy because of its impact on profit and loss. Fair value is not the amount that an entity would receive or pay in a forced transaction, involuntary liquidation or distress sale. Where there are movements in the fair value, the profit or loss will go through the Income Statement. All assets classified at fair value through profit or loss (including all derivatives) and many available-for-sale financial assets are measured at fair value.

The standard has the belief that fair value can be measured reliably for all financial instruments. IAS 39 provides the following hierarchy for determining an instrument's fair value:

- *Active market — quoted market price:* The existence of published price quotations in an active market is the best evidence of fair value and, when they are available, they must be used to measure fair value. The phrase "quoted in an active market" means that quoted prices are readily and regularly available from an Exchange, dealer, broker, industry group, pricing service or regulatory agency. Those prices represent actual and regularly occurring market transactions on an arm's-length basis. The price can be taken from the most favourable market readily available to the entity even if it was not the market in which a transaction would occur.
- *No active market — valuation techniques:* If the market for a financial instrument is not active, fair value is established by using a valuation technique. The objective of a valuation technique is to establish what the transaction price would have been on the measurement date in an arm's-length transaction motivated by

normal business considerations. Valuation techniques that are well-established in financial markets include reference to a transaction that is substantially the same with adjustment for the differences, discounted cash flows and option pricing models. An acceptable valuation technique incorporates all factors that market participants would consider in setting a price, and should be consistent with accepted economic methodologies for pricing financial instruments.

- *No active market — equity instruments:* Normally it is possible to estimate the fair value of an equity instrument acquired from an outside party. However, if the range of reasonable fair value estimates is significant, and no reliable estimate can be made, a company is permitted to measure the instrument at cost less impairment. This method can also be used for derivative financial instruments that can be settled only by physical delivery of such unquoted equity instruments.

9.6 Convertibles and Treasury Shares

Two financial instruments that we have not considered and which are reasonably common are compound instruments, sometimes known as convertibles and Treasury shares. Convertibles contain both a financial liability and an equity element. Treasury shares are those that have been reacquired by the company.

Compound instruments must be treated according to their substance and the component parts of equity and liability accounted for and treated separately. For example, to raise funds, a company may issue a bond on which it has to pay interest. However, the holder of the bond has a call option (the right) to convert the bond into a fixed number of ordinary shares at sometime in the future. The holder of the bond is likely to do this if the sell price is increasing.

For convertibles, the company must use split accounting. The two components are separated for accounting purposes by deducting from the fair value of the instrument the amount separately calculated for the liability. The residual will represent the amount attributable to equity. The following steps are used by the company:

1. Calculate the fair value of the convertible — this is usually the proceeds received from the holder when it is issued.
2. Calculate the fair value of the liability component.
3. Deduct 2 from 1 and the difference is the residual amount — the equity component.

Treasury shares are a company's own equity instruments which it has reacquired. These must be deducted from the amount of equity shown on the balance sheet. When a company reacquires shares, the consideration paid is deducted from equity.

No gain or loss is recognised. If the company resells the Treasury shares, no gain or loss is shown in profit or loss. The following extract from the Annual Report of Enterprise Inns explains their accounting policy for Treasury Shares:

The directors' present intention is that shares purchased pursuant to this authority will be cancelled immediately on purchase. Alternatively, the shares may be held in Treasury (provided any Treasury shares held do not exceed 10% of the Company's issued share capital), sold for cash or (provided Listing Rule requirements are met) transferred to an employee share scheme. The effect of any cancellation would be to reduce the number of shares in issue. For most purposes, while held in Treasury, shares are treated as if they have been cancelled (for example, they carry no voting rights and do not rank for dividends).

9.7 Financial Instruments: IAS 32 Presentation and IFRS 7 Disclosures

These two standards are closely related and IAS 32 was amended and some of its requirements moved to IFRS 7. Both standards contain many technical terms and address sophisticated financial transactions. In this section we will briefly introduce the scope and objectives of both standards.

IAS 32 establishes principles for presenting financial instruments as liabilities or equity and for offsetting financial assets and financial liabilities. The stance that it adopts for the classification is that of the issuer of the financial instruments. The standard relates to and fits in with the principles for recognising and measuring financial assets and financial liabilities in IAS 39 and for disclosing information about them in IFRS 7.

The standard contains a long list of circumstances where IAS 32 does not apply. This is usually because certain entities and types of financial instruments are dealt with under other standards. What the standard does apply to are contracts to buy or sell a non-financial item that can be settled net in cash or another financial instrument, or by exchanging financial instruments, as if the contracts were financial instruments, with the exception of contracts that were entered into and continue to be held for the purpose of the receipt or delivery of a non-financial item in accordance with the entity's expected purchase, sale or usage requirements.

IFRS 7 was issued to bring disclosure requirements up-to-date with what has been happening in practice. The techniques for managing exposure to risks arising from financial instruments have developed in recent years. Entities have developed new approaches, and the IASB decided that a standard was required to deal with these developments. Users need information about risk exposure and how the entity manages it.

The IFRS is wide in scope and includes a list of the financial instruments that are affected by the standard. The standard applies to all entities — those with only a few financial instruments and those with many. The amount of disclosure required depends on the range and number of financial instruments held.

In general terms, the standard requires disclosure of the significance of financial instruments for an entity's financial position and performance, and qualitative and quantitative information about exposure to risks arising from financial instruments, including specified minimum disclosures about credit risk, liquidity risk and market risk. The qualitative disclosures describe management's objectives, policies and processes for managing those risks. The quantitative disclosures provide information about the extent to which the entity is exposed to risk, based on information provided internally to the entity's key management personnel.

9.8 The Future of Financial Instruments

The financial crisis in 2009 raised many concerns about the complexity of the standards dealing with financial instruments. There were even arguments that the standards contributed to the crisis as they forced some companies to record substantial losses which were not representative of what was really happening.

One difficulty identified was the many different classifications of financial instruments and the different accounting treatments associated with them. This meant that in similar situations, impairment losses on certain financial instruments could be very high depending on how they were classified.

Many discussions were held at the international level on the financial crisis and accounting requirements. The response of the IASB was to issue proposals in the middle of 2009 to replace the existing classification categories. The new classifications and measurement requirements were intended to form the basis of subsequent proposals for impairment treatments and hedge accounting. At the time of writing this book, those proposals had not been released.

The new proposals are for two measurement categories: amortised cost and fair value.

Amortised cost

The Board identified two criteria to determine which financial assets or financial liabilities would be accounted for at amortised cost. The Board believed that this would ensure that amortised cost provides decision-useful information about the amounts, timing and uncertainty of future cash flows.

Financial assets measured at amortised cost would not have the deficiencies that exist in IAS 39, and would be subject to a single impairment model.

Fair value

The IASB proposed a fair value option for financial instruments otherwise measured at amortised cost. A financial instrument could be measured at fair value through profit or loss if such designation eliminates or significantly reduces a measurement or recognition inconsistency (sometimes referred to as an "accounting mismatch").

The Board made additional proposals at the same time all aimed at simplifying accounting for financial instruments and addressing the criticisms that had been made in respect of the complexity of the standards and their adverse effect during the global financial crisis.

It will take some years before we see the impact of any changes and it is uncertain whether they will bring about the desired improvements. There is an argument put forward that the main problem is not the complexity of the accounting standards but the complexity of the financial instruments themselves, and the inability of some financial institutions dealing in them to predict their effect.

9.9 IFRS 2 Share-Based Payments

Definition — share-based payments

A transaction where the entity transfers equity instruments (e.g., shares or share options) in exchange for goods or services supplied by employees or third parties.

There are three types of share-based payments:

- *Share-based payment transactions,* where payment may be made in cash on a value based on the entity's share price **or** in shares;
- *Equity-settled share-based payment transactions,* where the entity issues shares in exchange for goods or services;
- *Cash-settled share-based payment transactions,* where the entity pays cash to a value based on the entity's share price.

The basic principle for accounting for share-based payments is that an expense is recognised in the Income Statement in the period in which a share-based transaction is entered into. The corresponding entry will either be a liability or an increase in equity, depending on whether the transaction is settled in cash or shares. Where there is a choice in payment, the entity will recognise a liability if it determines that it will pay in cash. If the entity finally settles by issuing shares rather than paying cash, the value of the liability should be transferred to equity.

It is the practice in many companies that an employee will receive shares or share options for services rendered. This is particularly applicable for senior managers and directors. The reason for this is the belief that the employee will be motivated to perform better by the share option. To understand the reason for motivation, we will explain how share options work.

A stock option gives the owner (the employee) the right to buy shares (stock) from the company at a fixed price (the strike price) at a future date. For example, a company gives a director the stock option to purchase shares at a future date at the price when the share option is granted. Let us say that the director pays $5 for the option and the price of the share at that time is $40. If the share price increases in value, the director will purchase shares in six months' time at the current price which is $40. If in six months' time the share price drops to $30 (under-the-water), the director does not exercise the option and loses the $5. If in six months' time the share price is $60, he purchases the share for $40 and makes a profit. This is a clear incentive for the director to ensure that the share price increases.

The following example from the Annual Report of the Royal Bank of Scotland shows the performance measures that must be met for share options to be granted:

> For executive share options granted in 2007 and 2008, the performance condition is based on the average annual growth in the company's adjusted EPS over the three-year performance period commencing with the year of grant. The calibration of the EPS growth measure is agreed by the Remuneration Committee at the time of each grant having regard to the business plan, prevailing economic conditions and analysts' forecasts. In respect of the grant of options in 2008, options will only be exercisable if, over the three-year period, the growth in the company's adjusted EPS has been at least 5% per annum (the "threshold level"). The percentage of options that vest is then determined on a straight-line basis between 30% at the threshold level and 100% at the maximum level for growth in adjusted EPS of 9% per annum. The market price of the company's ordinary shares at 31 December 2008 was 49.4p, and the range during the year ended 31 December 2008 was 41.4p to 370.5p.

It can be argued that share options do not act as an incentive for the following reasons:

1. Directors might forego increasing dividends to shareholders in favor of using the cash to try to increase the stock price.
2. Directors may have a tendency to pick a higher-risk business strategy which may not be in the best long-term interests of the company.
3. Stock options may be too far underwater (below exercise price) to motivate the manager effectively.
4. Directors may try to manipulate share price movements of the company on the stock market to match the time horizons of their stock options.
5. Share prices are affected not just by company performance but also by other factors beyond the company's control.

Unfortunately, there were several abuses of the practice with some directors becoming very rich. IFRS 2 attempts to remove these abuses by determining and recognising the compensation costs over the period in which the employees'/ directors' services are rendered. Compensation may be for past services or for future services (often to entice the employee to stay with the company for a set period of time).

Where the agreement is in respect of future services, the agreement between the company and the director will have "vesting conditions", e.g., the director will stay for two years; the profit will improve annually by 5% over the next three years. In this situation, the recognition of future services must be spread over the entire period.

For the normal agreement whereby an employee will receive the options as long as he or she meets specified conditions such as remaining an employee with the company for a set period of years, the requirements are:

1. Calculate fair value of options when they are granted.
2. Charge fair value equally to the Income Statement over specified number of years.
3. Increase shareholders' equity by an amount equal to the Income Statement charge.

9.10 Chapter Summary

☞ Accounting for financial instruments is one of the most complex areas and is subject to changes.

☞ Financial instruments can be classified into financial assets, financial liabilities and equity.

☞ A financial instrument arises from a contract where one party will hold a financial asset and the other party a financial liability.

☞ Financial assets are classified into four categories and financial liabilities into two.

☞ Financial instruments must be classified on initial recognition as this determines their subsequent accounting treatment.

☞ There are three stages in measuring financial instruments: initial measurement, subsequent measurement and impairment.

☞ Fair value measurement causes the greatest controversy.

☞ Convertible instruments (convertibles) must be accounted for by their component parts of debt and equity.

☞ Share option payments are a normal business practice but the granting of share options has been abused.

Progress Test

1. In 2008 a company issues several share options to its senior managers. What type of share-based transaction does this represent?

   a) Liability settled
   b) Cash settled
   c) Equity settled
   d) Asset settled

2. A company enters into contract with a firm of consultants for a range of services. Payment is in cash and is based upon the price of ordinary shares on completion of the contract. What type of share-based contract does this represent?

   a) Liability settled
   b) Equity settled
   c) Asset settled
   d) Cash settled

3. Which of the following is not a financial asset?

   a) Cash
   b) An equity instrument of another entity
   c) Loans to another entity
   d) Prepaid expense

4. Which of the following statements best describes the principle for classifying a financial instrument as a financial liability or equity?

   a) They are classified in accordance with the substance of the contractual arrangements and the definitions of a financial liability or equity
   b) Issued instruments are classified as liabilities or equity in accordance with the legal form of the contractual arrangements and the definitions of a financial liability or equity
   c) Issued instruments are classified as liabilities or equity in accordance with the directors' decision
   d) Issued instruments are classified as liabilities in accordance with the risks and rewards of the contractual arrangement

5. Which of the following is NOT a financial asset?

   a) Cash
   b) Inventories
   c) Investments in another entity's shares
   d) Investments in debt instruments issued by another entity

6. Which ONE of the following is not a financial liability?

   a) Trades payable
   b) Loans from other entities
   c) Income tax liabilities
   d) Bonds and other debt instruments issued by the entity

7. What is the principle of accounting for a compound instrument (a convertible)?

   a) It is classified as either a liability or an equity depending on its predetermined characteristics
   b) It is classified according to the separate components of financial liability and equity
   c) It is classified as a liability until it is converted into equity
   d) None of these

8. At what amount is a financial asset or financial liability measured on initial recognition?

   a) Zero
   b) The consideration paid
   c) Fair value
   d) Any of these

9. What is the best evidence of the fair value of a financial instrument?

   a) Its cost
   b) The value using discounted cash flow techniques
   c) Its quoted price in an active market
   d) The present value of future cash flows less impairment

10. For which ONE of the following would you use cost for measurement?

    a) Held-to-maturity investments
    b) Investments in unquoted equities
    c) Available-for-sale financial assets
    d) Financial liabilities not measured at fair value through profit or loss

10

Business Combinations and Consolidated Financial Statements

Learning Objectives

At the end of this chapter you should be able to:

☞ Differentiate between the different types of corporate relationships and the accounting treatments required

☞ Define "control" and explain the procedures for consolidated financial statements

☞ Explain the main requirements of a business combination

☞ Explain the nature and accounting treatment for goodwill

☞ Define "subsidiary" and the procedures for preparing consolidated accounts

☞ Define "significant influence" and the procedures for accounting for Associates

☞ Define "joint control" and describe the three different types of joint ventures and the appropriate accounting treatment for each

☞ Explain related party transactions.

10.1 Introduction

There are many types of relationships in the business world. One company may own another company completely or to a large extent. Two or more companies may act together on a particular joint venture. For good operational reasons, a company may invest in another company.

These relationships have to be accounted for and the main standards are:

- IAS 27 Consolidated and Separate Financial Statements
- IFRS 3 Business Combinations
- IAS 28 Investments in Associates
- IAS 31 Interests in Joint Ventures
- IAS 24 Related Party Disclosures.

The above standards identify the nature of the relationship and determine what the accounting requirements should be. The nature of the relationship depends on how involved the companies are, and the table below provides an indication of the types of relationships:

Standard	Content of standard	Relationship
IAS 27 and IFRS 3	Combination and consolidation	Control
IAS 28	Associates	Significant influence
IAS 31	Joint ventures	Operational activities
IAS 24	Related Parties	Connections

A most important part of each of the standards is the explanation of the types of relationship and how they may be identified. Possibly the most complex arrangements are where there is control in the relationship and consolidated financial statements are required. This topic will take up the major part of this chapter.

Associates and joint ventures are frequent occurrences in business life and we will cover both of these topics. IAS 24 Related Parties is mostly concerned with the disclosure of certain information.

Before starting this chapter, you may wish to return to Chapter 4 and refresh your memory on the Statement of Financial Position. The key points are:

- The Statement of Financial Position is based on the accounting equation which must always balance. It can be written as Assets – Liabilities = Share Capital.
- Assets include both non-current assets and current assets but not goodwill unless it has been purchased.
- Share capital is also known as equity and will include the shares original investment by the owner plus any profits (earnings) that have been made and retained in the business.

10.2 IFRS 3 Business Combinations

There is clearly a relationship between all of these standards, but we will start by focusing on IFRS 3 Business Combinations, with comments on the others in this section as the issues arise. In the following sections we will examine the other standards in detail, finishing with IAS 24 Related Party Disclosures.

IFRS 3 was revised in 2007 and only came into effect on 1 January 2009, so company practices based on the new standard may take some years to become established. The main changes that you need to be aware of are:

- new restrictions on the expenses that can form part of the acquisition costs;
- revisions of the treatment of contingent consideration;
- measurement of non-controlling interests (previously known as minority interests);
- the methods for measuring consolidated goodwill.

We will now look at the requirements of IFRS 3, discussing the importance of these changes.

Definition — business combination

The bringing together of separate entities or businesses into one reporting entity.

Determining an acquisition

The standard states that a business is an integrated set of activities and assets that is capable of being conducted and managed for the purpose of providing a return in the form of dividends, lower costs or other economic benefits directly to investors or other owners, members or participants.

In general terms, we would consider a business is where there are activities being conducted to convert inputs into outputs. There are processes, employees, plans to produce outputs, and there is the prospect of customers willing to purchase a business.

The usual event is that one business will acquire another business either by offering shares or a combination of both. This will give the acquirer (parent) control of the other company (subsidiary). This may be a 100% acquisition where the subsidiary is wholly owned, or the subsidiary may only be partially owned but sufficient to give control. In a partial ownership, there will be other owners and these are called non-controlling interests, previously known as minority interests.

When one entity acquires control over another entity, the purchase method of accounting must be used. The basic principle is that there will always be an acquirer and an acquiree and it is possible to identify the acquirer. You will see references in business newspapers from time to time about the "merger" of two companies. From an accounting perspective, this is more likely than not an acquisition and has to be accounted for by using the purchase method.

The above assumes that it is always possible to identify the acquirer and the main indicator will be whether the acquirer has obtained control of the other entity. In most instances this should be relatively easy to establish, and in the next section on IAS 27 we discuss the various characteristics of control.

Where control is not easy to demonstrate, the standard offers the following guidance to identify the acquirer:

- the larger entity is likely to be the acquirer and this is where the fair value of one entity is significantly greater than that of the other;
- the entity that has undertaken a share issue for cash for the acquisition is likely to be the acquirer;
- the entity that has the ability to select the management team of the combined entity is likely to be the acquirer.

The cost of the acquisition

The general principle is that the cost of a business combination is the total of the fair values of the consideration given by the acquirer plus any directly attributable costs of the business combination. Expenses such as fees of lawyers and accountants acting as advisers must be charged to the Income Statement and cannot be considered as part of the consideration.

Fair value is the amount which an entity will pay for an exchange between unrelated and willing parties (i.e., not in a forced sale). Fair value should be measured at the date that the exchange takes place, which in most instances is the date on which the acquirer gains control of the other entity.

The consideration paid may be:

- cash or other assets transferred to the acquiree;
- liabilities assumed by the acquirer, for example, taking on the liability for a bank loan of the acquiree;
- the issue of equity instruments, such as ordinary shares.

There are instances where only a provisional fair value is measured at the acquisition date. If there are adjustments arising within 12 months of the acquisition date, they can be set back to the acquisition date and the goodwill recalculated.

For example, a company may have made an acquisition of 100% of another company on 1 January 2009 for the sum of $320,000. A provisional fair value of the net assets at that time was $260,000. The goodwill would be $60,000 at that stage. On 1 June, a final fair value is set at $270,000, so the goodwill is recalculated to $50,000

($320,000 – $270,000). These would be the amounts reported in the parent's financial statements at the year end. If there were any further adjustments to the fair value after the year end, i.e., 12 months, these would have to be recognised under profit or loss.

Definition — contingent consideration

An obligation of the acquirer to transfer additional assets or equity interests to the former owners of an acquiree as part of the exchange for control of the acquiree if specified future events occur or conditions are met.

There are instances where the acquirer has the right to have some of the previous consideration returned when specific conditions are met, but we will concentrate on the circumstances in the definition of contingent consideration given in the text box above.

Where an acquisition is made, the acquirer believes that the acquired business will continue to make profits in the future and even increase those profits. In some businesses, for example in the advertising industry, the value of the business acquired is mostly the creative abilities of the employees and the clients the business has. To ensure that these do not leave when the acquirer takes control, there will often be a clause in the agreement that specifies the future profits to be achieved over the next 3–5 years. If these are achieved or surpassed, the acquirer agrees to pay further consideration.

Such agreements are sometimes referred to as earn-outs and will include clauses on the previous owners continuing to work in and promote the business to obtain those profits. The advantage of such agreements to acquirers is that they have some reassurances on the future success of the business, but the future payment they make is contingent on that success. For the previous owners, they have the possibility of receiving a much higher consideration in total than if they had settled for one amount at the time of the acquisition.

The revised standard requires the acquirer to recognise at the date of acquisition the fair value of the contingent consideration (which may be paid in 3–5 years' time) as part of the consideration for the acquiree. Applying this definition to contingent consideration is not easy and could give rise to problems for some companies.

Example

World Promotions Inc. wholly acquires European Advertising Inc. The acquisition agreement states that there is a contingent consideration to be paid of 90 million shares in two years' time if European Advertising Inc. achieves certain levels of profit, and it is believed that these are achievable. At the acquisition date, the published share price of World Promotions Inc. quoted shares is $1.00 per share. As it is believed the profit levels will be met, World Promotions Inc. will include the cost of the 90 million shares as part of the consideration.

Having looked at the consideration, we need to examine what the acquirer obtains for its money. At the acquisition date, the acquirer must recognise the acquiree's assets, liabilities and contingent liabilities at their fair value if they meet the following criteria:

- assets, other than intangible assets, should be recognised where it is probable that the associated future economic benefits generated by the use of the assets will flow to the acquirer and their fair value can be measured reliably;
- liabilities, other than contingent liabilities, should be recognised where it is probable that an outflow of economic benefits will be required to settle the obligation and their fair value can be measured reliably;
- intangible assets or contingent liabilities should only be recognised in an acquisition where they meet the definition of an Intangible Asset as per IAS 38 *Intangible Assets* and their fair value is capable of being measured reliably.

As you can imagine, the above is a lengthy exercise and the standard, in its Appendices, offers guidance for the fair value measurement of specific assets and liabilities.

Having gone through the exercise of determining the value of the consideration it is paying and the cost of the identifiable net assets (assets – liabilities) it is acquiring, the acquirer is likely to find that the amount it is paying is higher than the value of the net assets it is acquiring.

The critical factor in the calculation is that only identifiable assets are included. But acquiring companies means, in all probability, acquiring the reputation of the business, loyal customers, procedures and processes that are established. These characteristics all contribute to the future economic benefits the acquirer hopes to enjoy, but they are not specifically and individually identified. They come under the general description of "Goodwill". This is a complex and controversial topic and we need to explore it in detail in the next section.

10.3 Goodwill and Non-Controlling Interests

The accounting treatment of goodwill is so important and critical in the acquisition of another business that we need to look at it separately before continuing our examination of consolidated financial statements.

> **Definition — goodwill**
>
> Future economic benefits arising from assets that are not capable of being individually identified and separately recognised.

When one company acquires another, it will expect to pay for all the tangible non-current assets such as property, plant and equipment. It will also expect to pay for the intangible assets that it acquires and we discussed these in an earlier chapter. There may be other adjustments but we can leave those to later. The fact is that even if the value of the tangible assets and intangible assets are added together, the acquiring company will usually pay more than this amount. The reason for this is that it wishes to acquire an operating and, possibly, a profitable business. It is not just acquiring assets but all those other ingredients that make up that business. These include such things as reputation of the business, experience and knowledge of the workforce, contacts with suppliers, customer base, and established systems and procedures.

All of these ingredients fall under the heading of "goodwill". This is defined in IFRS 3 as future economic benefits arising from assets that are not capable of being individually identified and separately recognised. Goodwill is therefore an integrated part of the business that cannot be separated from it. The following example from AstraZeneca's Annual Report illustrates an acquisition where goodwill is involved:

MedImmune, Inc.

On 1 June 2007, AstraZeneca announced the successful tender offer for all the outstanding shares of common stock of MedImmune, Inc., a world-leading biotechnology company with proven biologics discovery and development strength, pipeline and leading biomanufacturing capability. At that date, approximately 96.0% of the outstanding shares were successfully tendered; the remaining shares were acquired by 18 June 2007. The financial results of MedImmune, Inc. have been consolidated into the Group's results from 1 June 2007. Cash consideration of $13.9 bn was paid for the outstanding shares. After taking account of the cash and investments acquired, together with the settlement of MedImmune's convertible debt and outstanding share options, the total cash paid to acquire MedImmune was $15.6 bn. In most business acquisitions, there is a part of the cost that is not capable of being attributed in accounting terms to identifiable assets and liabilities acquired and is therefore recognised as goodwill. In the case of the acquisition of MedImmune, this goodwill is underpinned by a number of elements, which individually cannot be quantified. Most significant amongst these is the premium attributable to a pre-existing, well-positioned business in the innovation-intensive, high-growth biologics market with a highly skilled workforce and established reputation. Other important elements include buyer-specific synergies, potential additional indications for identified products and the core technological capabilities and knowledge base of the company.

If goodwill is so difficult to identify, the question arises as to how one places a value on it at the acquisition of another business. We will work through a simple example to demonstrate this by using horizontal balance sheets:

Acquirer Inc.
Balance sheet before acquisition

	$		$
Non-current assets	1,500	Equity	1,200
Cash	1,000	Liabilities	1,300
	2,500		2,500

Acquirer agrees to pay $900 cash to acquire Dulldog. Having made the acquisition, Acquirer calculates the fair value of the assets it has acquired. Normally there would be an extensive list of assets and liabilities, but in this example we will just consider the assets. Acquirer's calculations are as follows:

	$	$
Purchase price		900
Fair value of tangible assets		
Premises	600	
Machinery	100	700
Difference		200

As Acquirer paid more than the fair value of the tangible assets, the difference of $200 is goodwill. If we add the non-current assets of $700 to the $1,500 of non-current assets that Acquirer already owns, deduct the $900 paid for Dulldog from the cash that Acquirer had and insert goodwill into the balance sheet, it will balance:

Acquirer Inc.
Balance sheet after acquisition

	$		$
Non-current assets	2,200	Equity	1,200
Goodwill	200		
Cash	100	Liabilities	1,300
	2,500		2,500

The above is a simplified example of the process of acquisition and the treatment of goodwill. There are several complications and IFRS 3 has been revised and there are now two different methods for measuring goodwill. We will examine these later, but let us first look at the main requirements of IFRS 3:

- The acquirer recognises separately the acquiree's identifiable assets, liabilities and contingent liabilities at their fair value at the date of acquisition.
- Intangible assets of the acquiree at the acquisition date can only be recognised if they meet the definition requirements and can be measured reliably.
- Goodwill is the residual acquisition cost. It is recognised by the acquirer as an asset from the acquisition date and is initially measured as the excess of the cost of the business combination over the acquirer's share of the net fair values of the acquiree's identifiable assets, liabilities and contingent liabilities.

You can see from the above regulations that goodwill is a balancing figure and some would argue that it is so vague and unreliably identified that it should be written off by the company immediately as an expense. The counter-argument is that the company has paid for it and it will last a long time and should bring future economic benefits.

Some would accept the argument that it should be recognised in the balance sheet but contend that goodwill should be amortised over a number of years. At one time various countries used this approach, but they all used different periods of time as nobody can predict how long goodwill will last.

The regulation now with purchased goodwill under IFRS 3 is:

- Goodwill should be tested for impairment at least annually.
- Goodwill cannot be systematically amortised.
- Goodwill should not be revalued.

If you refer to our earlier chapter on impairment, you will see that where there is an impairment of a cash-generating unit, any goodwill must be written off immediately and cannot be reinstated in the financial statements. This procedure for impairment is illustrated in the following extract from the Annual Report of CarPhone Warehouse:

Goodwill is reviewed at least annually for impairment, or more frequently where there is an indication that goodwill may be impaired. Impairment is determined by assessing the future cash flows of the CGUs to which the goodwill relates.

Where the future cash flows are less than the carrying value of goodwill, an impairment charge is recognised in the Income Statement.

On disposal of a subsidiary undertaking, the relevant goodwill is included.

You will have noticed that in this section we have referred to goodwill that has been acquired and to purchased goodwill. The reason for this is that internally generated goodwill cannot be recognised by a company.

Many successful companies have, over the years, built up excellent reputations, have good procedures, loyal employees and all the other ingredients that one connects with purchased goodwill. They cannot place this internally generated goodwill on their balance sheet. IAS 38 Intangible Assets states that internally generated goodwill cannot be recognised as an asset because it is not an identifiable resource controlled by the company that can be measured reliably at cost.

It is this criterion of being able to measure reliably that is critical. When a company purchases goodwill through the acquisition of another company, we can calculate the amount it has paid. With internally generated goodwill, however, a company would never be able to demonstrate how much it had cost. If you look at the Annual Reports of famous companies, the only goodwill that they will show on their balance sheet is the goodwill they have purchased.

In this section on goodwill we have demonstrated how goodwill is calculated but also illustrated the uncertain nature of goodwill. The accounting standards are very cautious and you are required to test goodwill at least annually for impairment. If a cash-generating unit is impaired, goodwill is the first asset to be written off and you cannot revalue goodwill.

This caution over the nature of goodwill has been expressed by many learned judges over the years, in particular to the loyalty of a customer to a business. In Whiteman Smith Motor Co Ltd v Chaplin [1934] 2 KB 35, the Court identified four types of customers:

- the dog, who stays faithful to the person and not the location;
- the cat, who stays faithful to the location and not the person;
- the rabbit, who comes because it is close and for no other reason;
- the rat, who is casual and is attracted to neither person nor location.

The moral is that when you acquire another business and purchase the goodwill, you do not know what you are really getting. If you hope that the goodwill includes customers loyal to that business, it may well depend on what type of animal they are.

Negative goodwill or bargain purchases

An acquiring company may make a bargain purchase where the cost of acquiring the company is less than the fair value of the identifiable net assets acquired. In these circumstances, there is a "negative" goodwill and the acquirer has made a gain which will be shown as such in the Income Statement. However, prior to the recognition of a gain from a bargain purchase, the company must reassess the identification and measurement of:

- the identifiable assets acquired and liabilities assumed;
- the non-controlling interest in the acquiree, if any;
- for a business combination achieved in stages, the acquirer's previously held equity interest in the acquiree.

Non-controlling interests (NCI)

If less than a full acquisition is made, there will be some owners of the company who hold the minority of shares and therefore do not have control. These were previously called minority interests and, before IFRS 3 was revised, only one method of accounting for goodwill was permitted. The standard now allows the acquirer (parent) to measure any goodwill in one of two ways:

1. at the Group's proportionate share of the acquiree's (subsidiary's) identifiable net assets (this is the "old" method);
2. at fair value (the "new" method).

The "old" method concentrated on the parent's ownership interest and therefore only calculated the amount of goodwill acquired by the parent. This was calculated as the difference between the consideration paid by the parent and its share of the fair value of the subsidiary's net identifiable assets. This method did not refer to the NCI because it was only intended to recognise the parent's share of goodwill. The part of goodwill owned by the non-controlling interests is not recognised.

It is argued that the new method gives a full view of the goodwill of the subsidiary including non-controlling interests. It views the entire group as an economic entity with all equity holders, including non-controlling interests, as shareholders of the group even if they are not shareholders in the parent.

Example

In this example we will use the same basic figures for calculating goodwill but show the amount if there is a 100% acquisition, the old method using an 80% acquisition, and the new method using an 80% acquisition.

Bigone Corp acquires 100% ownership of Smallone Corp for $250,000. The fair value of the assets acquired is $150,000. Therefore:

	$000
Consideration	250
Net assets acquired at fair value	150
Goodwill (100%)	100

Now let us assume that Bigone Corp only acquires 80% ownership. The consideration is $200,000. This is calculated by the proportion of the full consideration for 100%, i.e., 80% of $250,000. In the following calculation we are going to calculate the goodwill by using the old method — that is, only taking the Group's share of goodwill into account. Note that the goodwill is only 80% of the goodwill if there had been a 100% acquisition:

	$000
Consideration	200
Net assets acquired (80% of $150)	120
Goodwill	80

Companies can use the old method if they wish, or they can adopt the new (economic entity) method. This will show the full value of goodwill including that owned by the non-controlling interests:

	GROUP $000			NCI $000
Consideration transferred for 80%	200	Net value (20% of $250)		50
Fair value of net assets (80%)	(120)	Net assets (20% of $150)		(30)
Goodwill	80			20

The goodwill of $100,000 is higher using the new method rather than the old method ($80,000) because the goodwill attributable to the non-controlling interests is included.

Where an entity decides to use the new method to value non-controlling interests, it can only be applied at the date of acquisition. Where this method is used, the goodwill shown on the balance sheet will include the goodwill attributable to the non-controlling interests. The opposite side of the balance sheet will show the non-controlling interests including their share of goodwill.

Definition — retained earnings

Net profits retained in the company after dividends and any other distributions have been made to investors.

Before we demonstrate some of these points with a worked example, we need to consider retained earnings. When a company acquires another company, the acquiree will have been in operation for a number of years. It would have been earning profits.

A part of these profits will have been distributed to shareholders and a part will be retained in the business to finance future growth.

When the business is acquired, the acquirer purchases these retained profits. The rule is that any pre-acquisition retained earnings of a subsidiary are not aggregated with the parent company's retained earnings, only the post-acquisition retained earnings. Any pre-acquisition retained earnings must be cancelled against the investment by the parent company in the subsidiary company. A simple example will demonstrate this.

Example — retained earnings

HighCorp acquires LowCorp on 1 January 2009. It pays $40m for 60% of LowCorp. At the date of acquisition, the share capital of LowCorp was $10m and it had retained earnings of $30m. By the end of the year LowCorp had retained earnings of $50m.

The share capital and retained earnings of LowCorp will be eliminated against the cost of the investment in the consolidated financial statements. We will explain this in the next section, but at this point we are interested in calculating goodwill and we are going to use the old method:

	$m	$m
Cost of investment		40
Less share of assets acquired		
Share capital	10	
Retained earnings	30	
	40	
60% share of assets acquired		24
Goodwill		16

Note that the pre-acquisition earnings have been included in our calculation. The post-acquisition earnings, i.e., LowCorp's profit retained after the acquisition date, will be included in HighCorp's retained earnings when the consolidated financial statements are prepared.

10.4 IAS 27 Consolidated and Separate Financial Statements

IAS 27 Consolidated and Separate Financial Statements and IFRS 3 Business Combinations are closely connected. In this explanation of consolidations we will assume that you have understood the issues of goodwill and non-controlling interests.

Definition — consolidation

Consolidation is the replacement in the parent's accounts of the cost of its investment in the subsidiary by what it actually represents, i.e., the parent company's share of the net assets of the subsidiary and the element of goodwill paid for at the acquisition date.

The above definition uses some terms with which you may not be familiar. A parent company is one which controls another company, known as the subsidiary. A parent company may have several subsidiaries to make a group of companies. Generally, where there is a parent with one or more subsidiaries, the parent will have to publish consolidated financial statements. These are the financial statements of a group of companies presented as those of a single company.

In the above paragraph we stated that a parent company exists where the parent **controls** the subsidiary. There are several measures of control as shown in the following list:

- Where one entity has more than half the voting rights in another entity (either directly or indirectly);
- Where the parent has the power to control more than 50% of voting rights (e.g., by exercising share conversion rights);
- Where the parent has the power to appoint or remove the majority of the board of directors that control the entity;
- Where the parent has the power to cast the majority of votes at a board meeting of the entity.

Quite frequently, control is measured by the percentage of the ordinary shares of one company held in another, as this is a measure of the voting rights. This control can exist even where it is held through another subsidiary. For example, Parent company owns 100% of Subsidiary 1. This means that Subsidiary 1 is a wholly-owned subsidiary. Parent company owns 33% of Company 2 which, on this basis, would not become a subsidiary. However, Subsidiary 1 owns 20% of Company 2. This means that Company 2 is a subsidiary because Parent company owns 33% directly and an additional 20% through its wholly-owned Subsidiary 1.

This is a simple relationship and in practice there are even more complicated examples. IAS 27 states that *control* is presumed to exist if the parent owns, directly or indirectly through subsidiaries, more than half of the voting power of an entity unless, in exceptional circumstances, it can be clearly demonstrated that such ownership does not constitute control.

IAS 27 emphasises that the reference to *power* in the above definition of *control* means the ability to do or affect something. Consequently, an entity has control over another entity when it currently has the ability to exercise that power, regardless of whether control is actively demonstrated or is passive in nature. This example of the power to affect matters is demonstrated in the following extract from the Annual Report of Baosteel:

> Consolidation has been prepared for subsidiaries in which the Group holds more than half of the issued shares of capital, or over which it can exert significant controlling powers to govern financial and operating policies.

The objective of IAS 27 is to enhance the relevance, reliability and comparability of the information that a parent company provides in both its separate financial statements and its consolidated financial statements for a group of entities under its control. Every parent must prepare a set of consolidated financial statements, except where shareholders of the parent gain limited benefit; for example, where the parent is itself a wholly-owned subsidiary, or a partially-owned subsidiary where non-controlling interests have agreed to no consolidated financial statements.

Special purpose entities (SPE)

A special purpose entity (SPE) is described as an entity created to accomplish a narrow and well-defined objective (e.g., to effect a lease, research and development activities or a securitisation of financial assets). An SPE may take the form of a corporation, trust, partnership or incorporated entity. SPEs are often created with legal arrangements that impose strict and sometimes permanent limits on the decision-making powers of their governing board, trustee or management. It is argued that they operate on "auto-pilot" as these powers cannot usually be changed other than by the entity that established the SPE.

The entity which established the SPE may transfer assets to the SPE, obtain the right to use assets held by the SPE or perform services for the SPE. For all intents and purposes, the entity that established the SPE also controls it, although it may not report it as such. The criticism is that companies have used SPEs to avoid placing liabilities on their Statement of Financial Position and/or to mislead users as to the full extent of the group's operations and relationships with other companies.

These transactions were referred to as "off-balance sheet transactions" and many of the major financial frauds that have taken place involved SPEs. To prevent further abuses, the Standards Interpretation Committee issued SIC 12 in December 1998. There have been subsequent amendments but the Interpretation is clear. SIC 12 requires consolidation where the substance of the relationship is that the SPE is controlled by another entity, e.g., predetermines activities, enjoys the majority of benefits. The following extract from the Notes of Unilever's Annual Report demonstrates how companies recognise this requirement:

> IFRS interpretation SIC 12 and US GAAP FIN 46R require that entities with which we have relationships are considered for consolidation in the consolidated accounts based on relative sharing of economic risks and rewards rather than based solely on share ownership and voting rights.

10.5 Consolidation Procedures

In the previous sections we looked at the mechanics of business combinations and the problem of goodwill. We will now summarise the main requirements of IAS 27 and IFRS 3. The latter standard has been recently revised.

The main steps in an acquisition are:

1. Identify acquirer which obtains control of acquiree.
2. Determine acquisition date when control acquired.
3. Recognise and measure assets, liabilities and minority interests (NCIs now).
4. Recognise goodwill or bargain purchases.

In subsequent years following the acquisition, the parent company will have to bring all the separate financial statements of the individual subsidiaries together to prepare consolidated financial statements. These involve several adjustments and we will examine briefly the guidance under IAS 27.

Non-current asset transfers

During the normal course of business operations, non-current assets such as machinery may have been transferred from one group company to another and a profit may have been made. Using the single entity concept, the non-current asset should be stated in group accounts at the amount as if the transfer had not been made. In other words, you must remove the profit element as a profit cannot be made between two members of the same group of companies. This removal of the profit element will also involve an adjustment to depreciation.

Example

On 1 January a subsidiary sells equipment that had cost $20,000 to its parent for $25,000. The parent depreciates equipment at 10% each year. For the group accounts at the year end, the profit of $5,000 must be eliminated and the additional depreciation of $500 ($2,500 – $2,000) must be eliminated.

Inter-company balances

Members of a group usually trade with each other. An accounts receivable in the set of financial statements of one subsidiary will be matched by an equal accounts payable in the financial statements of another group company. For the individual companies that is correct, but it is misleading to show the group owing cash to and from itself. On consolidation, the inter-company amounts must be cancelled.

Unrealised profit

If a member of a group holds inventory at year end purchased from another member, the company making the sale will show a profit in its accounts — but the group has not made a profit. The member company that bought the goods will record the inventory at the cost to itself, but this is not the actual cost to the group. For the consolidated accounts, the inventory in the Balance Sheet and the closing inventory in the Income Statement must be reduced to the cost without the "internal" profit.

Example

At the year end the parent has $250,000 of inventory that it purchased from its wholly-owned subsidiary. The cost to the subsidiary of manufacturing these goods was $220,000 and it correctly shows in its own accounts a profit of $30,000. For the group accounts, the "profit" on the inventory must be eliminated by showing the inventory in the Balance Sheet and the Income Statement at its cost of $220,000.

Non-controlling interests

Non-controlling interests used to be known as minority interests. There are occasions when the acquiring company obtains sufficient shares to be able to claim control, but there are a percentage of other shareholders. These interests must be presented in the Consolidated Statement of Financial Position within equity, separately from the equity of the owners of the parent. Profit or loss and each component of other comprehensive income are attributed to the owners of the parent and to the non-controlling interests. Total comprehensive income is attributed to the owners of the parent and to the non-controlling interests, even if this results in the non-controlling interests having a deficit balance.

We will explain some of these transactions by looking at a simple example of a consolidated balance sheet with a wholly-owned subsidiary.

Example — The consolidated balance sheet

Luscent Manufacturing Company has a fully-owned subsidiary, Sulphur Trading Company, which it has owned since Sulphur's incorporation. All of the output of Luscent is sold to Sulphur. Below are the two balance sheets of the companies at 31 December 2009. We have drawn them up as tables, instead of the regular format, to simplify our explanation. In practice, all the necessary headings would be inserted.

	Luscent $000	Sulphur $000
Tangible assets	350	450
Investment in Sulphur (shares at cost)	400	
Inventories	160	120
Accounts receivable	80	90
Cash at bank	10	—
Total assets	**1,000**	**660**
Equity	700	400
Retained earnings	150	200
Accounts payable	150	60
Total equity and liabilities	**1,000**	**660**

$50,000 in Luscent's accounts receivable is due from Sulphur and is shown in that company's accounts payable.

To prepare the Consolidated Statement of Financial Position, we cancel items that appear as assets in one Statement of Financial Position and as a liability in the other Statement of Financial Position. In this example there are two such items. The first is the shares held by Luscent in Sulphur which is matched by Sulphur's equity of $400,000. The second is the accounts receivable in Luscent's Statement of Financial Position matched by the accounts payable that Sulphur shows.

Consolidated Statement of Financial Position at 31 December 2009 (wholly-owned subsidiary)

	$000	$000
Non-current assets		800
Current assets		
Inventories	280	
Accounts receivable	120	
Cash	10	410
Total assets		1,210
Equity		700
Retained earnings		350
Accounts payable		160
Total equity and liabilities		1,210

In the above example, the subsidiary is wholly-owned. We will take the same figures but assume that Luscent owns 80% of Sulphur's shares that it bought at cost. The adjustment has to be made for the minority interests. We will have to adjust for Luscent's ownership of the shares, but this time it will be only 80%. We repeat the above table, but we have reduced Luscent's investment to $320,000 (80%) and we have merely increased Luscent's inventory by $80,000 so that we retain consistency and comparability between the two examples.

We will assume, once again, that $50,000 in Luscent's accounts receivable is due from Sulphur and shown in that company's accounts payable.

	Luscent $000	Sulphur $000
Tangible assets	350	450
Investment in Sulphur (80% shares at cost)	320	
Inventories	240	120
Accounts receivable	80	90
Cash at bank	10	—
Total assets	**1,000**	**660**

Equity	700	400
Retained earnings	150	200
Accounts payable	150	60
Total equity and liabilities	**1,000**	**660**

Before we construct the consolidated statement, we will calculate the non-controlling interests. The NCIs own 20% of Sulphur's capital ($80,000) and 20% of its retained earnings ($40,000). The total for non-controlling interests is therefore $120,000 and in the following statement we show it after retained earnings:

**Consolidated Statement of Financial Position at 31 December 2009
(80% owned subsidiary)**

	$000	$000
Non-current assets		800
Current assets		
Inventories	360	
Accounts receivable	120	
Cash	10	490
Total assets		1,290
Equity	700	
Retained earnings ($150,000 + 80% of $200,000)	310	1,010
Non-controlling interests		120
Accounts payable		160
Total equity and liabilities		1,290

Example — the consolidated income statement

Our final topic in this section on consolidated accounts is the Income Statement. We will use the example of Luscent, the parent, having an 80% investment in Sulphur. You may have realised at this point that of the consolidated profit, 80% will belong to Luscent and 20% will belong to the non-controlling interests.

The only complication we will include is that Sulphur made $12,000 sales to Luscent during the year. These goods had been purchased from an outside supplier for $8,000. You will remember from our earlier discussions in this chapter that a group cannot make a profit by member companies trading with one another. We will assume taxation is 50%.

	Luscent	Sulphur	Adjustment	Consolidated
	$000	$000	$000	$000
Sales	150	76	(12)	214
Cost of sales	60	40		
Gross profit	90	36	(4)	122
Admin expenses	30	6		36
Profit before taxation	60	30		86
Tax	20	10		30
Profit after taxation	40	20		56
Non-controlling interest				4

Comments

1. The sales figure is reduced by $12,000, the amount of the sales that Sulphur made to Luscent.
2. Gross profit must be reduced by $4,000, the amount that Sulphur would have taken in its own Income Statement. The cost of sales figure can be calculated by deducting the consolidated gross profit from the consolidated sales.
3. The non-controlling interest share of the profit is calculated at 20% of Sulphur's profit after tax because it is in that company that the shares are held.

10.6 IAS 28 Investments in Associates

Definition — associate company

An enterprise where the investor has significant influence but not control/joint control.

An investor may have a significant influence in another company that is neither a subsidiary nor a joint venture and, therefore, it does not appear in the consolidated financial statements under the provisions of IAS 27. It is important that the user is made aware of the nature and implications of this investment. The standard therefore defines what is meant by an associate company.

IAS 28 establishes the concept of significant influence and the criteria to establish significant influence. It provides guidance on accounting for associates in the consolidated financial statements under the equity method and the disclosures required.

Definition — significant influence

The power to participate in the financial and operating policy decisions of another business but not control them.

The presence of significant influence in a business normally arises where the investor has 20% or more of the voting power. There are exceptions to this rule. For example, an investor may hold more than 20% of the voting rights, but is unable to exercise significant influence because another investor holds the remaining voting rights. The reverse situation can occur where the investor has less than 20% of the voting rights, but circumstances permit significant influence to be applied. This fluctuating nature of significant influence is reflected in the Annual Report of British Airways:

On June 9, 2006, the Group's shareholding in Comair Ltd was reduced from 18.3% to 12.9%. Due to the Group's ability to exercise significant influence, the investment in Comair Ltd was accounted for by the equity method. In September 2006, the Group's shareholding in Comair Ltd decreased to 10.92% and the Group no longer had the ability to exercise significant influence over the investment.

Where there is significant influence, the equity method of accounting for investments in associates should be used in the consolidated financial statements. The main requirements for the equity method are:

- Investment is initially recognised at cost.
- Subsequent periods are adjusted for changes in the investor's share of net assets of the associate.
- Profit/loss should be eliminated from any inter-entity transactions (sales-purchases).
- Investor's interest should be shown in its balance sheet as a single-line item under non-current assets.

The investor should use the financial statements of the associate with the same financial date as the financial statements of the investor unless it is impracticable to do so. In these circumstances, the most recent financial statements should be used as long as the difference is no greater than three months. Adjustments must be made for any significant transactions or events occurring between the different accounting period-ends of the associate and the investor.

The following extract is from the balance sheet of Scottish and Newcastle Breweries. It shows not only the Investment in Associates, but also the Investment in Joint Ventures which is the next topic in this chapter:

Non-current assets:			
Property, plant and equipment	15	883	999
Intangible assets	16	2,999	2,711
Investment in joint ventures	17	1,346	1,268
Investment in associates	**18**	**38**	**40**
Financial assets	20	270	230

10.7 IAS 31 Interests in Joint Ventures

Definition — joint venture

A contractual arrangement where two or more parties (venturers, NOT investors) have joint control of an economic activity.

Two or more parties may enter into an agreement to carry out an economic activity that is subject to joint control. This presents particular problems as to the appropriate accounting treatments and the disclosures that should be made. Joint ventures may take many different forms and structures and IAS 31 describes three main types.

It is important to note that in the above definition, the term "control" is used. The standard defines control as *the power to govern the financial and operating policies of an activity so as to obtain benefits*. Joint ventures are therefore different from Associates where there is only significant influence. What differs IAS 31 from the regulations on consolidation is that there must be joint control.

Definition — joint control

The contractual agreed sharing of control so that no individual contracting party has control.

Joint control exists only when the strategic financial and operating decisions relating to the economic activity require the unanimous consent of the parties sharing control.

The standard identifies three types of joint ventures, namely jointly controlled operations, jointly controlled assets, and jointly controlled entities. For each of these types, there is a different accounting treatment.

Jointly controlled operations

These type of arrangements involve the use of assets and other resources of the venturers rather than the establishment of a separate company. Each venturer uses its own assets, incurs its own expenses and liabilities, and raises its own finance. In these cases, the venturer must recognise in its financial statements the assets that it controls, the liabilities and expenses that it incurs, and its share of the income from the sale of goods or services. An example of a jointly controlled operation is where several specialist tradespeople and independent builders agree to provide materials and labour to construct a new housing development. Each venturer will receive a pre-agreed percentage of the revenue from sales and include this in its financial statements.

Jointly controlled assets

These arrangements involve the joint control, and often the joint ownership, of assets dedicated to the joint venture. Each venturer may take a share of the output from the assets and each bears a share of the expenses incurred. In these cases, the venturer must recognise its interest in the assets on a proportional basis. The venturer also recognises liabilities or expenses incurred by it or its share of those jointly incurred. The income from the sale or its share of output from the joint venture is also recognised. A common example of this type of joint venture is an oil pipeline controlled and operated by several oil companies.

Jointly controlled entities

These are corporations, partnerships, or other entities where two or more venturers have an interest, under a contractual arrangement that establishes joint control. In these cases, the venturer uses proportionate consolidation (IAS 27) or the equity method in compliance with IAS 28. These methods are not used when the asset is held for sale in compliance with IFRS 5. They are also not used if the venturer is itself a subsidiary and the owners do not object to either method being applied and the debt and equity securities are not publicly traded.

Proportionate consolidation

In the above explanation we have stated that with jointly controlled entities, two different methods may be used — proportionate consolidation or the equity method — and we have already explained the latter. With the proportionate consolidation method, the venturer includes its share of the assets and liabilities on the Balance Sheet. On the Income Statement the venturer includes its share of income and expenses. One of two formats may be used. Either the share can be combined line by line with similar items in its financial statements, or the items can be shown separately line by line.

The following Note from the Annual Report of Diageo shows the use of the proportionate consolidation method and how the company changed when it moved to IFRSs from UK accounting standards:

> *IAS 31 – Interests in joint ventures* defines a jointly controlled entity as an entity where all parties enter into a contractual arrangement that specifies joint control, by unanimous consent, of all strategic financial and operating decisions. IFRS allows the group to adopt either proportionate consolidation or the equity method when consolidating jointly controlled entities. Diageo has adopted proportionate consolidation as its group policy. This has resulted in some group entities, previously equity accounted under UK GAAP, being proportionately consolidated under IFRS.

If a venturer ceases to have joint control, it should cease using whichever of the two methods it has adopted. If it obtains complete control, it should account for it in accordance with IAS 27.

10.8 Related Party Transactions

When we read the financial statements of a company, we assume that all the transactions have been carried out at arm's length. In other words, normal business practices have been followed and there are no relationships with other companies, groups or individuals that may mean transactions were not conducted independently.

> **Definition — related party transaction**
>
> A transfer of resources, services or obligations between related parties regardless of whether a price is charged.

IAS 24 is a disclosure standard with the objective of ensuring that financial statements draw the users' attention to the possibility that the existence of related parties and material transactions with them have affected the reported financial results. The standard lists the parties that are related to an entity and uses the definitions given in IAS 28 and IAS 31 to specify the relationship.

The standard states that a party is related to an entity if:

(a) Directly, or indirectly through one or more intermediaries (persons or entities), the party:

 (i) Controls, is controlled by, or is under common control with, the entity (this includes parents, subsidiaries and fellow subsidiaries);
 (ii) Has an ownership interest in the entity that gives it significant influence over the entity; or
 (iii) Has joint control (control shared between two or more entities) over the entity;

(b) The party is an associate (as defined in IAS 28 Investments in Associates) of the entity;

(c) The party is a joint venture in which the entity is a venturer (see IAS 31 Interests in Joint Ventures);

(d) The party is a member of the key management personnel of the entity or its parent;

(e) The party is a close member of the family of any individual referred to in (a) or (d);

(f)   The party is an entity that is controlled, jointly controlled, or significantly influenced by, or for which significant voting power in such entity resides with, directly or indirectly, any individual referred to in (d) or (e); or

(g)   The party is a post-employment benefit plan for the benefit of employees of the entity, or of any entity that is a related party of the entity.

Close members of the family of an individual are those family members who may be expected to influence, or be influenced by, that individual in their dealings with the entity. They may include:

(a)   The individual's domestic partner and children;
(b)   Children of the individual's domestic partner; and
(c)   Dependants of the individual or the individual's domestic partner.

The standard gives examples of transactions that should be disclosed if they are with a related party. Relationships between parents and subsidiaries must be disclosed irrespective of whether any transactions have taken place between them. An entity must disclose the name of its parent and, if different, the ultimate controlling party.

10.9 Chapter Summary

☞ In this chapter we have considered different types of corporate relationships.
☞ IAS 27 is concerned with ensuring the relevance, reliability and comparability of consolidated financial statements.
☞ Consolidated financial statements are required where one company has control over another.
☞ IFRS 3 is concerned with the process of combining companies.
☞ There must always be an acquirer in a business combination.
☞ The acquirer will deduct the cost of the net assets acquired from the purchase price to calculate the value of goodwill.
☞ Only purchased goodwill can be shown on the balance sheet.
☞ Purchased goodwill cannot be amortised but must be tested for impairment annually.
☞ Purchased goodwill cannot be revalued.
☞ IAS 28 is concerned with Associates where there is significant influence.
☞ Accounting for associates uses the equity method.
☞ IAS 31 is concerned with joint ventures where the parties exercise joint control.
☞ There are three types of joint ventures, each requiring a different accounting treatment.

Progress Test

1. Jacobs Company acquires 100% of the equity share capital of Crackers Company by issuing 600,000 new $1 ordinary shares which had a fair value of $10 each at the acquisition date. In addition, the acquisition resulted in Jacobs incurring fees payable to external advisers of $500,000. What is the amount of the consideration?

   a) $6,000,000
   b) $6,500,000
   c) $5,500,000
   d) $600,000

2. In a business combination, which of the following statements is correct?

   a) Goodwill is always a positive amount
   b) Goodwill is always 10% of the consideration
   c) Goodwill is always a negative amount
   d) Goodwill can be either a negative or a positive amount

3. A company makes a 100% acquisition for $120 million. At the acquisition date, the fair value of the assets acquired was $130 million. How should the difference between the consideration transferred and the net assets acquired be shown in the acquiring company's financial statements?

   a) Gain on bargain purchase of $10 million recognised in the Statement of Financial Position
   b) Gain on bargain purchase of $10 million deducted from other intangible assets
   c) Gain on bargain purchase of $10 million recognised in profit or loss
   d) Loss on goodwill in the Income Statement

4. Entow Company acquires a 75% interest in Kendle Company when the retained earnings are $600,000. When Entow is drawing up its financial statements at the year end, the retained earnings of Kendle are $1,600,000. What figure in respect of retained earnings should Entow include in the Consolidated Statement of Financial Position?

   a) $600,000
   b) $750,000
   c) $1,200,000
   d) $1,600,000

5. On 1 January 2009 a subsidiary sells equipment that had cost $40,000 to its parent for $50,000. The parent depreciates equipment at 10% each year. What adjustment should be made to the consolidated accounts at the end of 2009?

   a) Eliminate profit on transfer of $10,000 and the additional depreciation of $1,000
   b) Eliminate cost of equipment and all depreciation charged
   c) No action is required
   d) Eliminate the profit of $10,000 but do not adjust depreciation

6. The acquirer of another company must measure goodwill at:

   a) the NCI's proportionate share of the acquiree's identifiable net assets only
   b) fair value only
   c) the NCI's proportionate share of the acquiree's identifiable net assets **or** at fair value
   d) the NCI's proportionate share of the acquiree's identifiable net assets **and** at fair value

7. An associate company is where the investor has:

   a) significant influence
   b) controlling interest
   c) joint control
   d) related party relationship

8. Where several companies jointly control and operate a pipeline, this is an example of:

   a) jointly controlled operations
   b) related party relationship
   c) jointly controlled assets
   d) jointly controlled entity

9. Where several specialist tradespeople and independent builders agree to provide materials and labour to construct a new housing development, this is an example of:

   a) jointly controlled operations
   b) related party relationship
   c) jointly controlled assets
   d) jointly controlled entity

10. Dash owns 100% of Line. Line sells goods to Dash for $80,000 on which it makes a profit of $10,000 and Line still has these in inventory at the year end. During the year, the total revenue for Dash is $920,000 and for Line it is $240,000. What should the amount of revenue be in the Consolidated Income Statement?

    a) $920,000
    b) $1,160,000
    c) $1,080,000
    d) $1,120,000

11

Specific Industries and Practices

Learning Objectives

At the end of this chapter you should be able to:

☞ Explain the accounting treatment for construction contracts
☞ Apply the percentage of completion method
☞ Differentiate investment properties from other tangible types of property
☞ Explain the measurement method used for investment properties
☞ Identify the change of standard when there is a change in use of a property
☞ Describe biological transformation and biological assets
☞ Explain the accounting treatment for biological assets
☞ Discuss the issues regarding the exploration and evaluation of mineral resources
☞ Explain the accounting treatment for exploration and evaluation of mineral resources
☞ Present the criteria for identifying a non-current asset held for sale.

11.1 Introduction

In this chapter we consider standards that are specific to certain industries. There are certain business industries that have particular activities and operations that require a standard. The ones we examine are:

- IAS 11 Construction Contracts
- IAS 40 Investment Property

- IAS 41 Agriculture
- IFRS 5 Non-Current Assets Held for Sale and Discontinued Operations
- IFRS 6 Exploration for and Evaluation of Mineral Resources.

IAS 11 does not cover speculative building where a property developer builds a large number of residential homes and sells them to individual buyers. The standard covers construction contracts for buildings such as hospitals, carparks, bridges and similar long-term construction projects. The problem is that the date that construction activity commences and the date it is completed fall into different accounting periods.

IAS 40 looks at those business activities that invest in properties either to rent them to others to provide an income or those properties that can be sold at a gain. With such businesses, the main assets are the properties and the standard provides guidance on their valuation. It also clarifies an issue in respect of IAS 8 Accounting Policies, Changes in Accounting Estimates and Errors that we examined in Chapter 7.

IAS 41 is concerned with the agriculture industry. This presents the challenge of how we account for items that are growing and maturing. In some countries, agriculture is a main industry and the standard is extremely important for them.

IFRS 5 requires that assets that are held for sale should be presented separately in the Statement of Financial Position. Discontinued operations should be shown separately in the Statement of Comprehensive Income. These requirements ensure that users will be better able to make projections about the core activities and performance of the company.

IFRS 6 goes only part of the way to establish accounting practices in the mining industry. Explorations for gas and oil are significant activities and are very expensive. Over the years, different accounting practices have developed in several countries and the standard aims for comparability in accounting treatment.

Each of these industries, practices and accounting standards use terms and expressions that are specific to the industry and highly technical. We will explain the most important ones so that you can understand the main aspects of the standards.

11.2 IAS 11 Construction Contracts

Normally with construction contracts, the date that construction activity commences and the date it is completed fall into different accounting periods. The problem arises on determining the allocation of revenue and costs to the accounting periods when the construction activity is carried out. The standard uses the recognition criteria as set out in the Framework for the Preparation and Presentation of Financial Statements and gives guidance on the application of these criteria.

Where a builder constructs several buildings, such as residential houses, and hopes to sell them, any properties that remain unsold at the end of the financial period will be valued using IAS 2 Inventories. IAS 11 applies where there is a contract to construct a building or a group of buildings for a client. The client may be a private concern, a local authority or the government.

There are some key terms in these types of activities and they are:

- A **construction contract** is specifically negotiated between the client and the contractor.
- A **fixed price contract** is where the final price is agreed at the beginning and will be stated in the contract.
- A **cost plus contract** is where the contractor is reimbursed for all fees plus a percentage profit.
- **Escalation clauses** in an agreement allow the contractor to charge more for certain reasons. These reasons are usually events that have occurred outside the contractor's control.
- **Rectification costs** are mistakes by the contractor who must pay for them.
- **Retention monies** is an agreed amount held back by the client for a period of time. This is to ensure that the building is satisfactory and that faults do not appear after a few months.

A contract may contain an agreement to construct an additional asset, or the contract may be amended subsequently to permit this. The construction of the additional asset should be treated as a separate contract if the price is negotiated separately or if the addition is distinct from the original asset.

You must keep in mind that contracts can be very big and very expensive. The contractor will have had to submit a tender to the prospective client, usually in competition with other contractors. The tender will give a complete schedule and timing of the work to be completed and the price the contractor will charge which is referred to as the contract revenue.

To illustrate the size and scope of construction companies and the projects they undertake, we include two extracts from the Annual Report of Balfour Beatty. The first one is a project in the UK, and the second a project in Singapore. These are only two of the various activities they are involved in currently:

Transport for London chose Balfour Beatty's integrated approach for the project management and delivery of the Northern Ticket Hall to the required quality standards.

Already one of the busiest interchanges on the London Underground network, King's Cross St Pancras is set to become busier still. The relocation of Eurostar services to St Pancras, which adjoins the Underground, together with the forthcoming introduction of fast commuter services from Kent and anticipated local regeneration, is expected to drive up passenger numbers by some 33%. This figure will be further increased during the 2012 Olympic Games. The new underground Northern Ticket Hall, being built by Balfour Beatty to a demanding schedule, will help to ensure that the station can handle this huge surge in passenger volumes.

Long-term project

The Northern Ticket Hall is the second phase of the £774m King's Cross St Pancras CTRL works programme and follows Balfour Beatty's successful involvement in the first phase. Balfour Beatty's current role is to create a capacious new main access into the Underground station. Significant earthworks are involved, with excavations reaching a depth of four storeys below ground. A roof slab installed above the ticket hall will seal what is in effect a giant concrete box.

The rapid growth in demand for technical education in Singapore creates a pressing need to develop high-quality, sustainable educational facilities. Using the PPP model developed in the UK, the Institute of Technical Education (ITE) in Singapore chose Balfour Beatty's Groupwide experience in designing and delivering privately-financed educational facilities to ensure the best outcome.

Innovation is the hallmark of the new CollegeWest campus currently being constructed for the Institute of Technical Education, the principal provider of technical education in Singapore. The building, which features a stunning walkway and a transparent design, is being built and managed through the first Public-Private Partnership (PPP) of its kind in South-East Asia. This S$270m (Singapore dollars) contract, which has a duration of 27 years, is one of the first on the continent to resemble PPP projects familiar in the UK. Through our joint venture businesses Gammon Capital and Gammon Construction, all of the Group's PPP experience has been utilised to create a project-winning proposition. The ground-breaking nature of the project has been recognised by its award as Project Finance International's Asia Pacific PPP Deal of the Year 2008.

In some countries, no profit is taken on the construction contract until it is completed. It can therefore be several years before the company shows the profit it has made on the project. The international standard takes a different approach and there are two methods of accounting permitted.

The first method is known as the percentage of completion method. This can only be used where the outcome of the contract can be estimated reliably. In this case, revenues and costs are recognised by reference to the stage of the completion of the contract activity, and the profit for a financial period is shown in the Income Statement for that year. At the end of this section we provide an illustrative example which shows the calculation.

The second method is used when the outcome of a construction contract cannot be estimated reliably. In this case, revenue is only recognised in relation to those costs that are incurred and considered to be recoverable. All contract costs are expensed when incurred. If there is an indication of a probable loss on a contract, it must be expensed immediately.

Contract revenue is the amount agreed in the contract. This will include any variations, claims and incentives that will probably result in revenue and can be measured reliably. Contract costs include costs that are directly attributable, for example, site labour costs, construction materials, and rent of plant and equipment used on the contract. Costs such as insurance, design, and technical assistance that can be allocated to the specific contract can be included in the costs.

Illustrative example: The percentage of completion method

The aim of this method is to match contract costs to contract revenues for the stage of completion. This will allow the profit that can be attributed to the stage of completion at the end of a financial period to be reported. The standard does not specify whether the percentage of completion should be calculated on revenues or costs, so it is assumed that either method is acceptable.

	$ million	Total Contract $ million
Revenue		10.0
Costs incurred to date	5.0	
Future expected costs	3.0	8.0
Expected profit		2.0

The amount of work certified as being complete at the end of the financial period is valued at $5.8m. An independent architect, valuer, or surveyor will carry out this certification.

Percentage completion:

Sales Basis	Cost Basis
$5.8m/$10.0m	$5.0m/$8.0m
= 58%	= 62.5%

Profit for the financial period:

	Sales Basis $ million	Cost Basis $ million
Revenue	$10.0 × 58% = 5.8	$10.0 × 62.5% = 6.3
Costs	$8.0 × 58% = 4.6	$8.0 × 62.5% = 5.0
Profit	1.2	1.3

The following extract from the Annual Report 2008 of Balfour Beatty plc illustrates how they comply with the standard:

(c) Contracting work

Where the outcome of a construction contract can be estimated reliably, revenue and costs are recognised by reference to the stage of completion of the contract activity at the balance sheet date. This is normally measured by surveys of work performed to date. Variations in contract work, claims and incentive payments are included to the extent that it is probable that they will result in revenue and they are capable of being reliably measured.

Where the outcome of a construction contract cannot be estimated reliably, contract revenue is recognised to the extent of contract costs incurred that it is probable will be recoverable. Contract costs are recognised as expenses in the period in which they are incurred. When it is probable that total contract costs will exceed total contract revenue, the expected loss is recognised as an expense immediately.

11.3 IAS 40 Investment Property

There is a clear distinction between a property that is acquired for use by an entity in its own operation and one that is acquired for investment purposes. Investment properties (land, buildings or part of a building or both) are held to earn rentals or for capital appreciation or both. Capital appreciation is when the value of the asset that you have purchased increases, if it is a favourable economic environment.

The standard sets out the appropriate accounting treatment and disclosures are required so that users can gain a better understanding of the financial statements. IAS 40 addresses these issues and this is the first standard to be issued by the IASB that incorporates a fair value model for non-financial assets.

If you refer to previous chapters you will see that we have referred to various types of properties. The one that you may immediately recall is property, plant and equipment which comes under IAS 16. Below we show the types of property that is NOT investment property and is regulated by another standard:

Type of non-investment property	Accounting standard
Intended for sale in ordinary course of business	IAS 2 Inventories
Property being constructed on behalf of others	IAS 11 Construction Contracts
Owner-occupied property	IAS 16 Property, Plant and Equipment
Property being constructed/developed as an investment property	IAS 16 until ready then under IAS 40 as investment property, **BUT** from 1 January 2009 counted as IAS 40

Investment property should be recognised as an asset when it is probable that the future economic benefits that are associated with the property will flow to the business, and the cost of the property can be reliably measured. There are different regulations for the initial and subsequent measurements.

The initial measurement should be at cost including transaction costs such as professional fees, but excluding start-up costs, abnormal waste, or initial operating losses incurred before the planned level of occupancy.

Subsequently, investment property may be carried either at:

- fair value: this is the amount at which the property could be exchanged between knowledgeable and willing parties in an arm's-length transaction; or
- cost less accumulated depreciation and any accumulated impairment losses as prescribed by IAS 16.

If a company selects the cost model, it must also disclose the fair value of the properties, usually in the Notes to the Accounts. If the company cannot determine the fair value, then it must give:

1. a description of the investment property;
2. an explanation why fair value cannot be determined reliably;
3. if possible, a range of estimates for fair value.

If an investment company selects the fair value model, there are certain conditions attached:

- All investment property held must be at fair value.
- Gain or loss due to change in fair value must be charged to the Income Statement.
- Fair value must reflect market conditions at balance sheet date.
- Transfers to and from Investment Property are only recognised when there is a change in use.

The following diagram illustrates these points (BS refers to Balance Sheet and IS to Income Statement):

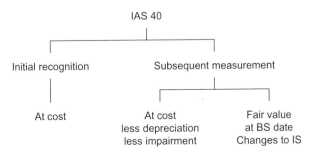

If a company is using the cost model, it can under IAS 8 change its accounting policy and use the fair value model. If you review the chapter on IAS 8 you will see that a company can change its accounting policy to provide more relevant and reliable information. The standard does not permit a company using the fair value model to change to the cost model because the information would not be relevant and reliable.

Of course, a company may have an investment property but then decide to use the premises itself. On the other hand, it may own and use a property then decide to vacate it and rent it out. If such a change in use takes place, there is usually a change in the standard that must be used for accounting purposes. Below are three fairly common scenarios demonstrating the change of use and the change in standard:

1. A company has been renting office space to a third party but now intends to occupy the space itself. This is a change from IAS 40 to IAS 16.
2. A company originally had a building for sale but has decided to rent it to a third party. The building now to be rented will come under IAS 40.
3. A company has been occupying a building but has decided to vacate it and let it to a third party. This would have been under IAS 16 but now comes under IAS 40.

On disposal or permanent withdrawal from use, a property should be derecognised. The gain or loss on derecognition should be calculated as the difference between the net disposal proceeds and the carrying amount of the asset. The gain or loss should be recognised in the Income Statement.

When companies move from their national GAAP to IFRSs, they can expect to see differences in their financial statements and in Chapter 12 we will discuss the transition procedures from national to international standards.

Some companies may find that they experience very few differences in the way that they recognise and measure financial transactions and events. This could be because their own national standards are very similar to international standards. Another reason may be that the type of business they conduct does not give rise to substantial changes in accounting.

IAS 40 is one standard where investment property companies will, most likely, experience a substantial change. We have direct evidence of this. Homburg, a Canadian company, has voluntarily been issuing financial statements that comply with both IFRSs and Canadian GAAP. We show the summary of its first quarter results for 2009 issued in a recent press release. You can see that moving to international standards will affect the financial results of several companies. For the first quarter of 2009, Homburg's net income under IFRS is a 3.7% increase compared to 2008. Under Canadian GAAP the increase is 4.4%.

FINANCIAL HIGHLIGHTS — IFRS
FIRST QUARTER ENDED MARCH 31, 2009 (000's)

	Three Months Ended March 31, 2009	Three Months Ended March 31, 2008	Increase
Property revenue	$80,640	$74,813	7.8%
Property net operating income	$57,268	$55,240	3.7%
Funds from operations	$10,980	$30,256	
Funds from operations per share — basic and diluted	$0.55/$0.55	$1.57/$1.53	

FINANCIAL HIGHLIGHTS — Canadian GAAP
FIRST QUARTER ENDED MARCH 31, 2009 (000's)

	Three Months Ended March 31, 2009	Three Months Ended March 31, 2008	Increase
Property revenue	$80,032	$74,362	7.6%
Property net operating income	$57,195	$54,789	4.4%
Funds from operations	$13,203	$33,634	
Funds from operations per share — basic and diluted	$0.66/$0.66	$1.74/$1.70	

11.4 IAS 41 Agriculture

Definition — agricultural activity

The management by a business of the biological transformation of biological assets for sale, into agricultural produce, or into additional biological assets.

Agricultural activity, particularly in some countries and regions, is a significant part of the economy. This standard sets out the accounting treatment, financial statement presentation, and disclosures for agricultural activity. The standard applies to biological assets and agricultural produce only. It does not deal with the process of turning agricultural produce into products, e.g., grapes into wine, as this process comes under other standards.

The standard differentiates between:

- Biological assets, which are living plants and animals;
- Agricultural produce, which is the harvested product of the biological assets at the time of harvest;

- Products after the point of harvesting where processing has taken place, e.g., sausages, cheese, wine.

We can put this formal definition into an everyday perspective by looking at the products we eat and drink. Calves, cows, pigs, sheep, vines and fruit trees are all examples of biological assets as they are living animals and plants. The agricultural produce is the wool from the sheep, the milk from the cows and the fruit from the trees. Some produce will need processing after the harvest and examples are cheese from the milk, clothes from the wool and wine from the grape.

As far as recognition of biological assets is concerned, the standard uses the standard definition and they should be recognised only where there is control of the asset as a result of past events, it is probable that future economic benefits will flow to the entity, and the fair value or cost of the asset can be measured reliably.

The standard contains the presumption that a biological asset can be measured reliably by using fair value. On initial recognition and subsequently, biological assets should be recognised at fair value less estimated point-of-sale costs, unless fair value cannot be reliably measured. Agricultural produce should be measured at fair value less estimated point-of-sale costs at the point of harvest. Point-of-sale costs include commissions, levies and transfer duties and taxes.

The gain on initial recognition of biological assets at fair value, and changes in fair value of biological assets during a period, are reported in the Income Statement for that period. A gain on initial recognition of agricultural produce at fair value should be included in the Income Statement for the period in which it arises.

IAS 41 presumes that fair value can be measured reliably for most biological assets. If the determination of fair value of a biological asset is not possible at the time it is initially recognised, it is measured at cost less accumulated depreciation and impairment losses. All other biological assets should be measured at fair value. If circumstances change and fair value can be measured reliably, the adoption to fair value less point-of-sale costs should be made.

11.5 IFRS 5 Non-Current Assets Held for Sale and Discontinued Operations

Non-current assets held-for-sale

In general, an asset is held-for-sale when an entity does not intend to use it for its ongoing business but wishes to sell it. The entity will make this decision if it believes that the asset's carrying amount will be recovered principally through a sale transaction rather than through continuing use. As a result, once certain criteria have been met, an entity shall then classify a non-current asset (or disposal group) as held-for-sale.

Definition — disposal group

A group of assets to be disposed of, by sale or otherwise, together as a group in a single transaction, and liabilities directly associated with those assets that will be transferred in a transaction.

The following are the criteria required for an asset or disposal group to be considered held-for-sale:

1. The asset is available for immediate sale in its present condition. The terms of the sale should be usual for sales of such assets (or disposal groups); and
2. The sale must be highly probable. To be highly probable:

   (a) management must be committed to a plan to sell the asset (or disposal group);
   (b) there must be an active programme to locate a buyer and complete the plan;
   (c) the asset (or disposal group) must be actively marketed for sale at a reasonable price;
   (d) the sale should be expected to be completed within one year from the date of classification unless events or circumstances beyond the entity's control delay it;
   (e) it is unlikely that significant changes to the plan will be made or that the plan will be withdrawn.

All of these criteria must be met for the asset to be classified as held-for-sale. For example, if it is evident that what the entity considers is a reasonable price is much too high to attract buyers, it may decide not to continue with the plan. It may decide to keep using the asset itself and the asset will remain on the balance sheet similar to other assets. If an entity has a disposal group and, being unable to sell it, decides to abandon it, the disposal group will be classified as a discontinued operation which we will discuss later.

The following is an excerpt taken from the Annual Report for 2008 for Sinopec:

(10) *Non-current assets held for sale*

A non-current asset is classified as held for sale when the Group has made a decision and signed a non-cancellable agreement on the transfer of the asset with the transferee, and the transfer is expected to be completed within one year. Such non-current assets may be fixed assets, intangible assets, investment property subsequently measured using the cost model, long-term equity investment, etc., but not include deferred tax assets. Non-current assets held for sale are stated at the lower of carrying amount and net realisable value. Any excess of the carrying amount over the net realisable value is recognised as impairment loss.

Criteria for classification as a held-for-sale asset must be met at the end of the reporting period. If the criteria are met after the end of the reporting period but before the authorisation of the financial statements, the classification held-for-sale cannot be used.

Once a non-current asset or disposal group has been correctly classified as held-for-sale, it must be measured at the lower of its carrying amount and the fair value less costs to sell. Costs to sell are the incremental costs that the entity will incur because of the disposal of the assets. Examples may include costs to advertise the assets, costs to transport the assets and costs to uninstall the assets from their present location. Any depreciation on the asset should cease.

Any difference between the carrying value and the fair value less costs to sell is recognised in the Income Statement as an impairment loss. This is an exception to IAS 36 Impairment of Assets which requires the carrying amount to be compared to the recoverable amount. You may wish to refer back to Chapter 6 to refresh your memory on this point. By applying this exception under IFRS 5, the entity recognises immediately any anticipated losses from the sale of the assets as soon as the decision to sell the assets has taken place.

A non-current asset or disposal group where the decision has been made to reverse the classification held-for-sale is measured at the lower of:

- its carrying amount before it was classified as held-for-sale, adjusted for any depreciation that would have been charged if the asset had not been held-for-sale;
- its recoverable amount at the date of the decision not to sell.

This regulation means that an entity cannot write-up an asset past its original carrying value prior to the decision to sell the asset or disposal group.

An example will clarify some of these requirements. A company with the year end 31 December 2008 has an asset it wishes to sell with a carrying amount of $75,000. It was classified as held-for-sale in September 2008. Its fair value less costs to sell at that time was considered to be $50,000. In the Statement of Financial Position the asset would be recorded at $50,000 on a separate line item from ordinary assets held-for-use. Therefore, an impairment loss is required of $25,000 in profit or loss to record the asset at its new value of $50,000. Impairment losses are recorded as part of income from continuing operations in profit or loss unless the specific criteria for discontinued operations are also met.

If the company decided not to sell the asset, the measurement of $50,000 would be reversed to the lower of its carrying amount before it was classified as held-for-sale less any subsequent depreciation, and its recoverable amount at the date of the decision not to sell.

Discontinued operations

A discontinued operation is a disposal group that has been disposed of or is classified as held-for-sale. Discontinued operations are a subset of disposal groups that are measured in the same way as disposal groups but have different presentation and disclosure requirements.

A discontinued operation is a component of an entity that has been disposed of or is classified as held-for-sale, and:

(a) Represents a separate major line of business or geographical area of operations;
(b) Is part of a single coordinated plan to dispose of a separate major line of business or geographical area of operations; or
(c) Is a subsidiary acquired exclusively with a view to resale.

Definition — component of an entity

Part of an entity where the operations and cash flows can be clearly distinguished, operationally and for financial reporting purposes, from the rest of the entity. They are a cash-generating unit or a group of cash-generating units while being held-for-use.

The objective of the standard is to require disclosure of discontinued operations so that the user of financial statements can evaluate their effects on the entire entity. The entity should disclose:

1. The net cash flows, classified as operating, investing and financing, attributable to a discontinued operation for the current and comparative period on the face of the Statement of Cash Flows or in the Notes;
2. A single amount on the Statement of Comprehensive Income that shows the total of:
    (a) after-tax profit or loss from discontinued operations;
    (b) the after-tax gain or loss recognised on the re-measurement to fair value less costs to sell or on disposal.

The entity should also disclose on the face of the Income Statement or in the Notes the revenue, expenses, pre-tax profit or loss and the related income tax expense of the discontinued operation.

11.6 IFRS 6 Exploration for and Evaluation of Mineral Resources

The oil and gas industry is large and complex. Looking at the entire process, we have companies involved in finding, extracting, refining and selling oil and gas. There are also the refined products and related products.

These operations require substantial capital investment and long lead times. Exploration, development and production often take place in joint ventures or joint activities to share the substantial capital costs. We referred to the different types of joint ventures in Chapter 10.

Exploration costs are incurred to discover oil and gas resources. Exploration, as defined in IFRS 6, starts when the legal rights to explore have been obtained. Evaluation costs are incurred to assess the technical feasibility and commercial viability of the resources found. The accounting treatment of exploration and evaluation expenditures can have a significant impact on the financial statements and reported financial results, particularly for entities at the exploration stage with no production activities.

The critical issue is which costs should be shown on the Balance Sheet (capitalised) and which costs should be shown on the Income Statement (expensed).

In the past, companies have used a wide variety of accounting policies in the exploration for and evaluation of mineral resources. As these practices have been so different, it is difficult for the standard setters to introduce a completely new method. IFRS 6 allows companies to continue to use their existing accounting policies. The standard does not require or prohibit any specific accounting policies for the recognition and measurement of exploration and evaluation assets.

There is one provision on this flexibility. The company policies must comply with the requirements of IAS 8 which we examined in Chapter 7. In other words, the accounting policies must provide information that is relevant to the economic decision-making needs of users, and that is reliable. Companies can, if they choose, change their accounting policies for exploration and evaluation expenditures if the change makes the financial statements more relevant and reliable.

As with other standards, we have two times for measurement of assets: the initial measurement and the subsequent measurement. When they are first recognised in the balance sheet, exploration and evaluation assets are required to be measured at cost. Companies can set their own consistent policies on what should be included in cost and IFRS 6 lists the following as examples of expenditures that might be included in the initial measurement of exploration and evaluation assets (the list is not exhaustive):

- acquisition of rights to explore; topographical, geological, geochemical and geophysical studies;
- exploratory drilling; trenching; sampling; and activities in relation to evaluating the technical feasibility and commercial viability of extracting a mineral resource;
- where an entity incurs obligations for removal and restoration as a consequence of having undertaken the exploration for and evaluation of mineral resources, those obligations are recognised under IAS 37 Provisions, Contingent Liabilities and Contingent Assets which we examined in Chapter 7.

After the initial recognition, companies can apply either the cost model or the revaluation model to exploration and evaluation assets. Companies will have both tangible and intangible assets which means that they will use the requirements of IAS 16 Property, Plant and Equipment and IAS 38 Intangible Assets.

Identifying impaired assets can cause problems because of the difficulty in obtaining the information necessary to estimate future cash flows from exploration and evaluation assets. IFRS 6 modifies the rules of IAS 36 to make it more practicable to identify where impairment has taken place. A detailed impairment test is required in two circumstances:

1. When the technical feasibility and commercial viability of extracting a mineral resource become demonstrable, at which point the asset falls outside the scope of IFRS 6 and is reclassified in the financial statements;
2. When facts and circumstances suggest that the asset's carrying amount may exceed its recoverable amount.

The reference to facts and circumstances seems vague, but the standard offers some examples:

- the period for the right to explore in the specific area has expired during the period or will expire in the near future, and is not expected to be renewed;
- substantive expenditure on further exploration for and evaluation of mineral resources in the specific area is neither budgeted nor planned;
- exploration for and evaluation of mineral resources in the specific area have not led to the discovery of commercially viable quantities of mineral resources, and the entity has decided to discontinue such activities in the specific area; and
- sufficient data exist to indicate that, although a development in the specific area is likely to proceed, the carrying amount of the exploration and evaluation asset is unlikely to be recovered in full from successful development or by sale.

The following extract is taken from the Annual Report 2008 of BHP Billiton and gives a comprehensive explanation of their policies:

Exploration and evaluation expenditure

Exploration and evaluation activity involves the search for mineral and petroleum resources, the determination of technical feasibility and the assessment of commercial viability of an identified resource. Exploration and evaluation activity includes:

- researching and analysing historical exploration data
- gathering exploration data through topographical, geochemical and geophysical studies
- exploratory drilling, trenching and sampling
- determining and examining the volume and grade of the resource
- surveying transportation and infrastructure requirements
- conducting market and finance studies.

Administration costs that are not directly attributable to a specific exploration area are charged to the Income Statement. Licence costs paid in connection with a right to explore in an existing exploration area are capitalised and amortised over the term of the permit. Exploration and evaluation expenditure (including amortisation of capitalised licence costs) is charged to the

Income Statement as incurred except in the following circumstances, in which case the expenditure may be capitalised:

- In respect of minerals activities:
  - the exploration and evaluation activity is within an area of interest which was previously acquired in a business combination and measured at fair value on acquisition, or where the existence of a commercially viable mineral deposit has been established.

- In respect of petroleum activities:
  - the exploration and evaluation activity is within an area of interest for which it is expected that the expenditure will be recouped by future exploitation or sale; or
  - at the balance sheet date, exploration and evaluation activity has not reached a stage which permits a reasonable assessment of the existence of commercially recoverable reserves.

Capitalised exploration and evaluation expenditure considered to be tangible is recorded as a component of property, plant and equipment at cost less impairment charges. Otherwise, it is recorded as an intangible asset (such as licences). As the asset is not available for use, it is not depreciated. All capitalised exploration and evaluation expenditure is monitored for indications of impairment. Where a potential impairment is indicated, assessment is performed for each area of interest in conjunction with the group of operating assets (representing a cash-generating unit) to which the exploration is attributed. Exploration areas at which reserves have been discovered but that require major capital expenditure before production can begin are continually evaluated to ensure that commercial quantities of reserves exist or to ensure that additional exploration work is underway or planned. To the extent that capitalised expenditure is not expected to be recovered, it is charged to the Income Statement.

Cash flows associated with exploration and evaluation expenditure (comprising both amounts expensed and amounts capitalised) are classified as investing activities in the Cash Flow Statement.

Development expenditure

When proved reserves are determined and development is sanctioned, capitalised exploration and evaluation expenditure is reclassified as 'Assets under construction', and is disclosed as a component of property, plant and equipment. All subsequent development expenditure is capitalised and classified as 'Assets under construction'. Development expenditure is net of proceeds from the sale of ore extracted during the development phase. On completion of development, all assets included in 'Assets under construction' are reclassified as either 'Plant and equipment' or 'Other mineral assets'.

11.7 Chapter Summary

IAS 11 Construction Contracts

☞ Contracts can be fixed price or cost plus.
☞ The problem is how to identify costs and revenue for a particular period.
☞ Use the stage of completion approach.
☞ One method is to calculate the costs incurred as a percentage of the expected total costs.
☞ Recognise any losses immediately.

IAS 40 Investment Property

☞ Initial recognition at cost.
☞ Subsequently, measure at cost (less depreciation/amortisation) or at fair value.
☞ If at fair value, then value at BS date and changes to Income Statement.
☞ Changes in use of property lead to changes in the applicable standard.

IAS 41 Agriculture

☞ Deals with the biological transformation of a biological asset.
☞ Assumes that biological assets can be measured at fair value.
☞ Differentiates between biological assets, agricultural produce at the point of harvesting and products that have been processed after the point of harvesting.
☞ Gain on initial recognition goes to the Income Statement.
☞ Changes in fair value go to the Income Statement.

IFRS 5 Non-Current Assets Held-for-Sale and Discontinued Operations

☞ Assets held-for-sale must meet strict criteria.
☞ Assets held-for-sale must be shown separately in the Statement of Financial Position.
☞ Discontinued operations should be presented in the Statement of Comprehensive Income.

IFRS 6 Exploration for and Evaluation of Mineral Resources

☞ In the past, companies have followed a variety of practices.
☞ The standard aims to establish criteria of relevant and reliable information.
☞ Initial measurement is at cost.
☞ Subsequent measurement uses either the cost model or the revaluation model.
☞ Impairment is required, but rules of IAS 36 are modified.

Progress Test

1. Under IAS 11 Construction Contracts, which of the following bases should be used for the costs and revenue to go to the Income Statement where the outcome of the contract can be estimated reliably?

   a) Total contract revenue/costs incurred to date
   b) Contract revenue received/costs incurred to date
   c) Contract revenue/costs based on the stage of completion
   d) Total contract revenue

2. Which one of the following projects undertaken by an entity should be accounted for as a construction contract?

   a) An item of plant and machinery being constructed and to be sold as inventory
   b) An office block being constructed as an investment property
   c) A large boat being built for a third party under a specifically negotiated contract
   d) A warehouse being constructed for the entity's own use

3. Which ONE of the following is applicable to a cost plus contract?

   a) The contract may be subject to cost escalation clauses
   b) The contractor agrees the sales price at the outset
   c) The contractor is reimbursed for allowable or otherwise defined costs

4. A company has just completed a two-year contract for the construction of a school. A summary of the details is as follows:

	$000
Labour and materials	20,000
Heavy equipment costs	12,000
Initial design costs	1,500
Disposal proceeds of equipment	1,000

   What are the total contract costs?

   a) $32,000,000
   b) $33,500,000
   c) $31,000,000
   d) $32,500,000

5. Under IAS 40, which ONE of the following additional disclosures must be made when an entity chooses the cost model as its accounting policy for investment property?

   a) The fair value of the property
   b) The value of the property in a bankruptcy
   c) The value in use of the property
   d) No additional disclosures

6. Which TWO of the following properties fall under the definition of investment property and therefore within the scope of IAS 40?

   a) Land held for long-term capital appreciation
   b) Property occupied for own use

c) Property being constructed on behalf of third parties

d) A building owned by an entity and leased out under an operating lease

7. A company purchased an investment property on 1 January 2006 for a cost of $500,000. The property had a useful life of 25 years and on 31 December 2008 it had a fair value of $600,000. The company uses the cost model for investment properties. On 1 January 2009 the property was sold for net proceeds of $480,000. What is the gain or loss to be recognised in profit or loss for the year regarding the disposal of the property, according to IAS 40?

a) $100,000 gain

b) $20,000 loss

c) $40,000 gain

d) $120,000 loss

8. According to IAS 41, which ONE of the following would be classified as a product that is the result of processing after harvest?

a) Grapes

b) Wool

c) Bananas

d) Cheese

9. According to IAS 41, which TWO of the following items would be classified as biological assets?

a) Oranges

b) Chickens

c) Eggs

d) Fruit trees

10. In October 2008 a parts supplier to the truck industry declares that it intends to close a part of its operations as engineering changes have made that particular part obsolete. There will be a phased shutdown with closure finally taking place in July 2009 at the earliest. The year end of the company is 31 December. How should this be treated in the financial statements at 31 December 2008?

a) It should be shown as held-for-sale

b) It should be shown as a discontinued operation

c) It should not appear in the financial statements

12

Presentational Issues

Learning Objectives

At the end of this chapter you should be able to:

☞ Explain the requirements of IAS 1 *Presentation of Financial Statements* and identify its effect
☞ Describe the purpose and content of the main financial statements, including the Statement of Changes in Equity
☞ Calculate the basic earnings per share and diluted earnings per share according to the requirements of IAS 33
☞ Describe the weakness and requirements of IAS 34 *Interim Financial Reporting*.

12.1 Introduction

So far in this book we have concentrated on recognition and measurement issues. Each international accounting standard contains a detailed list of the information to be disclosed by a company. In this chapter we will take a broader view and instead of examining the detailed information to be provided by a company, we will look at the significant presentational issues and the communication of certain types of information. The standards we will study are:

• IAS 1 (Revised). This standard is critical because it lays down the structure and main content of the separate financial statements. You should now be at the stage where you understand the information and its purpose, and you need to refine your knowledge of the actual presentation itself.

- IAS 34 Interim Financial Reporting. This standard is concerned with the frequency of information. Companies produce annual financial statements, but users may find that 12 months is too long to wait before they can make their decisions. To resolve this issue, stock exchanges in different countries require companies to provide summary information either on a quarterly or half-yearly basis. IAS 34 aims to bring comparability in these interim reports.
- IAS 33. This standard is connected to our final chapter as it establishes the requirements for the calculation of the earnings per share of a company. As we will see in Chapter 14, this is an important piece of information for shareholders.

12.2 IAS 1 Presentation of Financial Statements

International Accounting Standard 1 *Presentation of Financial Statements* is a very old standard and has been amended in the past. The latest and most significant revision was issued in 2007 and became effective from 1 January 2009. The revised standard sets overall requirements for the presentation of financial statements, guidelines for their structure and minimum requirements for their content.

The standard states that the objective of financial statements is to provide information about the financial position, financial performance and cash flows of an entity that is useful to a wide range of users in making economic decisions. It also considers that the financial statements show the results of the management's stewardship of the resources entrusted to it. Financial statements continue, therefore, as general purpose documents with a potentially wide range of users.

The standard is very important in its effect on the appearance of the financial statements. It also results in some adjustments in other standards because of changes in wording and requirements. One of the significant requirements of IAS 1 (Revised) is concerned with changes in equity and the presentation of changes relating to owner changes in equity and non-owner changes in equity. This is a topic we have not so far discussed and we will examine these requirements in this chapter. Before we look at some of the details, the main features of IAS 1 are:

- Recognition, measurement, or specific disclosure requirements contained in other standards are not changed.
- All owner changes in equity must be presented in a Statement of Changes in Equity.
- All non-owner changes in equity, being comprehensive income, must be presented in one Statement of Comprehensive Income or in two statements. These are a separate Income Statement, which we examined in Chapter 3, and a Statement of Comprehensive Income.

- If a company makes a change in accounting policy or a retrospective restatement under IAS 8 (see Chapter 7), it must present a Statement of Financial Position as at the beginning of the earliest comparative period.
- Where a company reclassifies to profit and loss items that were previously recognised in comprehensive income, it must disclose this.
- Dividends are distributions to owners and should be included in the Statement of Equity.

A complete set of financial statements comprise:

(a) a Statement of Financial Position as at the end of the period;
(b) a Statement of Comprehensive Income for the period;
(c) a Statement of Changes in Equity for the period;
(d) a Statement of Cash Flows for the period;
(e) Notes, comprising a summary of significant accounting policies and other explanatory information; and
(f) a Statement of Financial Position as at the beginning of the earliest comparative period when a reclassification is made under IAS 8 as we mentioned above.

Although new titles have been introduced for the financial statements, companies may use other titles for the statements. This means that we will see the above titles in any new or amended standards issued, although some companies may continue to use titles such as Balance Sheet.

Having listed the complete set of financial statements, we will list the types of information that they contain. You should be familiar with all of these terms:

(a) assets;
(b) liabilities;
(c) equity;
(d) income and expenses, including gains and losses;
(e) contributions by and distributions to owners in their capacity as owners; and
(f) cash flows.

Fair presentation and compliance

Definition — fair presentation

Fair presentation is the faithful representation of the effects of transactions, other events and conditions for assets, liabilities, income and expenses as set out in the Conceptual Framework.

Companies must present fairly the financial position, financial performance and cash flows. The Conceptual Framework provides the definitions and recognition criteria for the various elements of the financial statements. If a company complies with all IFRSs, with additional disclosure where necessary, it is presumed that the financial statements achieve a fair presentation.

Note that the word "presumed" suggests a degree of caution. Although a company must make an explicit and unreserved statement that its financial statements comply with IFRSs, the company must provide additional disclosures when compliance with the specific requirements in IFRSs is insufficient to enable users to understand the impact of particular transactions, other events and conditions on the entity's financial position and financial performance.

To ensure that the financial statements achieve a fair presentation, a company must select, apply and disclose accounting policies in accordance with IAS 8 and present information that is relevant, reliable, comparable and understandable. In Chapter 1 we discussed the problems in balancing the informational characteristics of relevance and reliability. IAS 1 offers no direct guidance in this area but it does recognise that, in extremely rare circumstances, absolute compliance with a requirement of an IFRS could result in misleading information.

Where management believes that compliance with an IFRS, in certain rare circumstances, leads to misleading information, it may depart from the requirements of the IFRS but must disclose:

- that the financial statements in the form offered present fairly the entity's financial position, financial performance and cash flows;
- that there is compliance with applicable IFRSs, except that there is departure from a particular requirement to achieve a fair presentation;
- the title of the IFRS that has not been complied with and the nature of the departure. The particular requirements of the standard should be explained, together with the reason why that treatment would be so misleading and the treatment adopted instead;
- for each period presented, the financial effect of the departure on each item in the financial statements that would have been reported in complying with the requirement.

This is an extremely important part of IAS 1 and emphasises that the standards are principles-based. It is a recognition that blindly following rules may not always provide information that is relevant, reliable, comparable and understandable. In rare circumstances, management may decide that it must depart from the requirements to ensure that the objectives of the Conceptual Framework are satisfied.

This notion of being able to depart from the requirements as set out, has been present in the UK for many years and is known as the "true and fair" view. There has never been a legal decision on this phrase but it is understood that there are times when the preparers of the financial statements, and the auditors, may have to use judgement to determine the most appropriate method for accounting for and disclosing certain transactions.

This approach can be compared to other accounting regimes where strict adherence to the accounting standards of that country is required. If there is any dispute regarding the information, the defence of the preparers and the auditors of the financial statements is that they complied fully with the "rules". Of course, this defence can be stretched by claiming that the existing rules, even if they are incomplete, were not broken. With a principles-based approach, such a defence could not be used.

The circumstances allowing a company to depart from the requirements of a standard must be rare. But there is always the remote possibility that the relevant regulatory framework prohibits departure from the requirements. In such a case, the management must, as far as possible, reduce the misleading nature of the information by disclosing the title of the IFRS and the nature of the requirement in that standard. Management must also give the reason why compliance would be misleading and, for each period presented, the adjustments to each item in the financial statements necessary to achieve a fair presentation.

Having carefully explained what is meant by fair presentation, the standard looks at each of the financial statements in detail, except for Statement of Cash Flows as the requirements for this are already provided in IAS 7. There is also considerable guidance given to the types of disclosures that should be made in the Notes to the Accounts. In this chapter we will restrict our discussions to the Balance Sheet, Statement of Income and Statement of Changes in Equity.

12.3 Statement of Financial Position

Normally a company is required to present not only the balance sheet for the present financial period, but also the one for the previous period. The information it should contain line by line as a minimum is:

(a) property, plant and equipment;
(b) investment property;
(c) intangible assets;
(d) financial assets (excluding amounts shown under (e), (h) and (i));
(e) investments accounted for using the equity method;
(f) biological assets;
(g) inventories;
(h) trade and other receivables;
(i) cash and cash equivalents;
(j) the total of assets classified as held for sale and assets included in disposal groups classified as held for sale in accordance with IFRS 5 *Non-Current Assets Held for Sale and Discontinued Operations*;

(k) trade and other payables;

(l) provisions;

(m) financial liabilities (excluding amounts shown under (k) and (l));

(n) liabilities and assets for current tax, as defined in IAS 12 *Income Taxes*;

(o) deferred tax liabilities and deferred tax assets, as defined in IAS 12;

(p) liabilities included in disposal groups classified as held for sale in accordance with IFRS 5;

(q) minority interests, presented within equity; and

(r) issued capital and reserves attributable to owners of the parent.

In addition, the balance sheet should include additional line items, headings and subtotals when such presentation is relevant to an understanding of the entity's financial position.

The above list should be presented by the company into the classification of current and non-current assets, and current and non-current liabilities. This is the usual approach, but the standard does allow a company to present all assets and liabilities based on liquidity as long as it is more reliable and more relevant. For example, land is the most illiquid of assets and cash is the most liquid.

An illustration of the layout for a balance sheet is given in the standard and we give below the line titles. For each item, a company is required to give not only the amounts for the current year, but also the amounts for the previous year. You will also find that the published balance sheets of companies give a note number next to each item. This refers to the accompanying notes that provide substantially more detail.

A Company
Statement of Financial Position as at 31 December 2010

	31 December 2010	31 December 2009
ASSETS		
Non-current assets		
Property, plant and equipment		
Goodwill		
Other intangible assets		
Investments in Associates		
Available-for-sale financial assets	———	———
	———	———
Current assets		
Inventories		
Trades receivables		
Other current assets		

Cash and cash equivalents

Total assets

EQUITY AND LIABILITIES
Equity attributable to owners of the parent
Share capital
Retained earnings
Other components of equity
Minority interests
Total equity

Non-current liabilities
Long-term borrowings
Deferred tax
Long-term provisions
Total non-current liabilities

Current liabilities
Trades and other payables
Short-term borrowings
Current portion of long-term borrowings
Current tax payable
Short-term provisions
Total current liabilities
Total liabilities
Total equity and liabilities

12.4 Statement of Comprehensive Income

A company has the choice to present all its income and expenses in a single Statement of Comprehensive Income or in two statements. If it chooses to use two statements, one will be a separate Income Statement showing the components of profit or loss, and the second statement will start with the profit or loss for the period as shown on the Income Statement and then display the components of other comprehensive income.

In Chapter 3 we explained the Income Statement using the function of expenses approach. In this chapter we will continue with the two statements approach, but show the Income Statement using the classification of expense by nature.

To emphasise the relationship of the Income Statement and the other components of comprehensive income, we will use the layout illustrated in the standard but summarised to capture the main points. As with the balance sheet, a company is required to present not only the information for the present financial period but also for the previous period.

A Company
Income Statement for the year ended 31 December 2011

	2011	2010
Revenue		
Other income		
Changes in inventories of finished goods and work-in-progress		
Raw materials and consumables used		
Employee benefits expense		
Depreciation and amortisation expense		
Impairment of property, plant and equipment		
Finance costs	———	———
Profit before tax		
Income tax expense	———	———
Profit for the year from continuing operations		
Loss for the year from discontinued operations	———	———
PROFIT FOR THE YEAR	═══	═══
Profit attributable to:		
Owners of the parent		
Minority interests	———	———
	═══	═══
Earnings per share Basic and Diluted		

Before we continue with the Statement of Comprehensive Income, we need to make a few comments. Most of the terms above you should know and we have discussed the relevant standards and their requirements in earlier chapters. Towards the end of the Income Statement is the phrase PROFIT FOR THE YEAR. A calculation beneath this shows how the profit is divided between the owners of the parent company and the minority interests. It is the profit for the year which is the amount first shown on the Statement of Comprehensive Income.

A Company
Statement of Comprehensive Income for the year ended 31 December 2011

	2011	2010
Profit for the year		
Other comprehensive income		
Exchange differences on translating foreign operations		
Available-for-sale financial assets		
Cash flow hedges		
Gains on property revaluation		

Actuarial gains (losses) on defined benefit pension plans
Income tax relating to components of other
   comprehensive income
Other comprehensive income for the year net of tax
TOTAL COMPREHENSIVE INCOME
   FOR THE YEAR

Total comprehensive income attributable to:
   Owners of the parent
   Minority interests

12.5 Statement of Changes in Equity

The standard requires a company to present a Statement of Changes in Equity. This takes the equity section of the Statement of Financial Position and shows the movements during the year.

The contents required by the standard are:

(a) total comprehensive income for the period, showing separately the total amounts attributable to owners of the parent and to minority interests;
(b) for each component of equity, the effects of retrospective application or retrospective restatement recognised in accordance with IAS 8;
(c) the amounts of transactions with owners in their capacity as owners, showing separately contributions by and distributions to owners; and
(d) for each component of equity, a reconciliation between the carrying amount at the beginning and at the end of the period, separately disclosing each change.

In addition, an entity shall present, either in the Statement of Changes in Equity or in the Notes, the amount of dividends recognised as distributions to owners during the period, and the related amount per share.

Most companies find that the information is most clearly shown in the form of a table:

	Share capital	Share premium	Revaluation reserve	Retained earnings	Total
Balance at 1 January 2009					
Changes in accounting policy					
Changes in equity for 2009					
Total comprehensive income for the year					
Issue of share capital					
Balance at 31 December 2009					

Some of the above terms may be unfamiliar to you or you may have forgotten them, so we give brief descriptions below:

- **Share capital** — the finance an organisation receives from its owners (members or shareholders) in exchange for shares.
- **Share premium** — this is the difference when shares are issued between the market price and the par value of the share, assuming that the market price is higher.
- **Revaluation reserve** — an account showing the difference between the historical cost of an asset less depreciation and the fair value where the company decides to revalue non-current assets.
- **Retained earnings** — the net profit retained in the organisation after dividends and any other distributions have been made to investors.

12.6 A Look at Changes in the Future

Although the revisions to IAS 1 are recent, changes have already been taking place and we can expect to see other changes in the future. You will have noticed that the term "minority interests" is used above, whereas the term "non-controlling interests" is beginning to appear in financial statements. You can expect in the next few years to see a mixture of old and new terms and presentations as countries adjust to the requirements. There are, however, even more substantial changes likely to take place in respect to the presentation of financial statements.

There are proposals to change the format of the financial statements to achieve cohesiveness. At present, the financial statements all have their own individual formats and it is difficult to see the links between them. Under the new proposals, all statements will be divided into the same general categories: a business section; a financing section; income taxes; discontinued operations; and equity. This is very similar to the sections of our present Cash Flow Statement and the following table illustrates how it may work:

Proposed structure of financial statements

Statement of Financial Position	Statement of Comprehensive Income	Statement of Cash Flows
Business section	Business section	Business section
• Operating assets and liabilities	• Operating income	• Operating cash flows
• Investing assets and liabilities	• Investing income	• Investing cash flows

(Continued)

(Continued)

Statement of Financial Position	Statement of Comprehensive Income	Statement of Cash Flows

Financing section
• Financing assets
• Financing liabilities
Discontinued
   operations
	Financing section
	• Financing income
	• Financing expense
	Discontinued operations
	   (net of tax)
	Other comprehensive
	   income (net of tax)
		Financing section
		• Financing asset cash flows
		• Financing liabilities cash flows
		Discontinued operations

Equity		Equity

In addition to the above, the proposed Cash Flow Statement would be presented using the direct method. With the direct method, an entity presents separately cash receipts and payments. In Chapter 5 we claimed that most companies use the indirect method, which reconciles net income, pre-tax profit or net operating income to cash flow from operations. The indirect method is not so valuable to the users.

Companies would also be required to present a new reconciliation schedule reconciling the income to the cash flow statement. This would be shown as a footnote disclosure. This schedule would separate cash flows, fair value remeasurements and changes in accruals.

These proposals would bring about significant changes. The proposals for the change in format should bring about greater clarity and better understanding for the users. There is also the danger that it will produce confusion as users have become familiar with certain formats. Some users, for example banks and financial analysts, use financial models that capture certain totals in the current financial statements. This information may be lost or will require effort to retrieve.

12.7 IAS 33 Earnings per Share

Definitions

An ordinary share is an equity instrument that is subordinate to all other classes of equity instruments. Also known as a common share or common stock.

An equity instrument is any contract for the residual interest in a company after deducting all of its liabilities.

Options and warrants are financial instruments that give the holder the right to purchase an ordinary share.

An important item of information for users of financial statements is the Earnings Per Share (EPS). Simply explained, it is the portion of the total profit that is earned by each ordinary share. This ratio allows users to make performance comparisons between different enterprises in the same period and between different accounting periods for the same enterprise. IAS 33 sets out the principles for the determination and presentation of earnings per share (EPS) amounts.

The standard applies to companies whose securities are publicly traded or who are in the process of issuing securities to the public. If both parent and consolidated statements are presented in a single report, EPS is required only for the consolidated statements.

Companies must calculate and disclose the basic EPS on the face of their Income Statement. The basic EPS is calculated by dividing the profit or loss attributable to ordinary equity holders of the parent entity (the numerator) by the weighted average number of ordinary shares outstanding (the denominator) during the period. This is all ordinary shares in issue during the year. If a company has not issued further shares during the year, the calculation is shown in Example 1.

Example 1: Basic EPS calculation

Profit for year ended 31 December 2010: $3,500,000
Weighted average number of shares in issue: 25,000,000

$$\text{Basic EPS} = \frac{\$3,500,000}{25,000,000} = 14 \text{ cents.}$$

A company may issue shares during the course of the year to obtain cash, acquire an interest in another company or to redeem a debt. There is the assumption that the issue of shares for some form of consideration will result in the company having more resources. The increase in resources will lead to an increase in earnings and this will be reflected in the EPS.

If the shares are issued in exchange for cash, the date taken for the issue of shares is when the cash is received by the company. If they are issued to settle a liability, the date is the settlement date of that liability. If the shares are issued for the acquisition of an asset other than cash, the date of issue of the shares is when the acquisition is made.

The earnings numerator (profit or loss from continuing operations and net profit or loss) used for the calculation should be after deducting all expenses including taxes, minority interests, and dividends on other classes of shares such as preference shares. The denominator is calculated by adjusting the shares in issue at the beginning of the period by the number of shares bought back or issued during the period, multiplied by a time-weighting factor. This is known as the weighted average number of shares.

Example 2: Calculation of weighted average number of shares

A company has 20,000,000 ordinary shares in issue on 1 January 2009. During the year the following events take place:

   1 April 2009 — 4,000,000 shares issued to acquire a subsidiary
   1 October 2009 — 8,000,000 shares issued to raise cash to repay borrowings

Calculation:

1 January, number of shares in issue for 12 months =	20,000,000
1 April, number of shares in issue for 9 months = 4m × 9/12 =	3,000,000
1 October, number of shares in issue for 3 months = 8m × 3/12 =	2,000,000
Weighted average number	25,000,000

Having calculated the denominator, the EPS is calculated by applying the following formula:

$$EPS = \frac{\text{Net profit or loss attributable to ordinary shareholders}}{\text{Weighted average number of ordinary shares outstanding during the period}}.$$

There are times when companies will issue shares but will receive no consideration or only part consideration. The result is that the number of shares in issue has increased but there has not been the corresponding increase in resources. The standard identifies four such events and we will explain two of them.

The first is the bonus issue, also known as a stock dividend, where the shares are issued free to existing shareholders. The second is a rights issue where existing shareholders have the right to purchase shares at a price below the current market price. In both these cases, the weighted average number of shares should be adjusted by assuming that the "bonus" occurred at the beginning of the earliest period reported. The EPS calculation for the previous period should also be adjusted so that there is a fair comparison.

Example of a bonus issue

Bonus shares are issued when a company decides to issue more ordinary shares to its shareholders without expecting them to pay. It may do this because it considers that the current share price in the market is too high and more shares in circulation would lower the price. A bonus issue is sometimes referred to as stock dividends or a capitalisation issue.

The bonus shares are usually issued in proportion to the existing holdings of shareholders. For example, for every two shares you hold at a specific date, you will receive one bonus share. The EPS must be calculated for the earliest period presented.

A company has a year end at 31 December. At the beginning of 2009 it has 600,000 shares in issue. On 30 September that year it makes a bonus issue of one share for every three shares held. At 31 December 2009 its earnings were $160,000 and for the previous year the earnings were $150,000.

	2009	**2008**
Earnings	$160,000	$150,000
Shares in issue on 1 January	600,000	600,000
Bonus issue on 30 September 2009	200,000	200,000
Total shares	800,000	800,000
EPS	20 cents	18.75 cents

Example of a rights issue

A rights issue occurs when a company wishes to raise more money but also wishes to give some benefit to existing shareholders. If your existing shareholders are satisfied with the company's performance, it is preferable to go to them rather than to issue on the open market. The rights issue usually involves an exercise price that is less than the current value of the currently issued shares. For example, the current market price may be $4.75, but existing shareholders can purchase one share for $4.00 for every six shares they hold. This gives the shareholder the right to buy shares from the company at a price below the current market price.

Like a bonus issue, the shareholders have the right to a certain number of shares depending on the number they currently hold. However, unlike the bonus issue, the shareholders have to pay for the shares, but at a reduced price compared to the market.

A company has a financial year end at 31 December. The following events took place during the year:

	2009
Earnings	$2,800
Shares outstanding on 1 January 2009	1,000
Rights issue on 1 March 2009: 1 share for five	200
Market price of share on 1 March 2009	$11.00

The first stage is to calculate the theoretical rights value of each share. In other words, what is the value of the rights the existing shareholder is getting by being able to purchase a share under market price? The steps to do this calculation are:

1. Calculate the total value of the shares before the rights issue (number of shares multiplied by market price = 1,000 × $11.00). This is known as the cum rights price because the buyer of the shares at that time would have the right to purchase another share at $5.00 for every five shares held.
2. Calculate the total proceeds from the rights issue (number of shares multiplied by issue price = 200 × $5.00).
3. Add these two amounts together.
4. Divide by the total number of shares in issue (including rights shares).

Applying this formula to calculate the theoretical ex-rights price:

$$\frac{\$11,000 + \$1,000}{1,200} = \frac{\$12,000}{1,200} = \frac{\$10.00}{}.$$

The second stage is to calculate the weighted average number of shares. This is done by taking the 1,000 shares in issue for 2 months and adjusting for the bonus portion by the market price and adding to this the 1,200 shares in issue for 10 months:

$$1,000 \times \frac{2}{12} \times \frac{\$11}{\$10} + 1,200 \times \frac{10}{12} = 1183 \text{ (the weighted average number of shares)}.$$

The EPS for 2009 is: $\frac{\$2,800}{1183} = 2.37$ cents.

The EPS for 2008 is adjusted by the bonus element:

Original EPS = 2.5 cents per share

Adjusted for the bonus element = $2.5 \text{ cents} \times \frac{\$10}{\$11} = 2.27 \text{ cents}.$

The above situations and their different treatments are important, so we will summarise the main points in the following table:

Transaction	Basic calculation	Weighted average
Situation	No new shares issued during the year	New shares issued at full market price during the year
Impact	None	Earnings expected to rise because new shares in issue
Calculation	Divide net profit attributable to ordinary shareholders by weighted average number of shares	Use time-weighted average number of shares
Impact	None	On current year, but no retrospective effect
Transaction	**Bonus issue**	**Rights issue**
Situation	Shares issued free to shareholders during period, in proportion to current holdings	Shares issued at lower than market price, in proportion to current holdings

(*Continued*)

		(Continued)
Impact	Earnings will not change but number of shares will rise	Earnings increased by adding back finance charges and number of shares will increase
Calculation	Treat bonus shares as if in issue for full year	Use weighted average of shares adjusted by applying calculation (actual cum-rights price)/(theoretical ex-rights price)
Impact	Retrospective application reducing EPS for previous year	Earnings will increase and number of shares will increase

Diluted earnings per share

There may be a situation where some people have certain rights that will enable them to receive ordinary shares in the future. For example, they may have preference shares or convertible debt that they can convert into ordinary shares in the future. If they choose to do this, there will be more ordinary shares in issue, so the EPS will decline. Companies must disclose their diluted EPS in addition to their basic EPS. The diluted EPS is a warning to existing shareholders that there is the risk that more ordinary shares will be in issue in the future.

> **Definition — dilution**
>
> A reduction in earnings per share or an increase in loss per share resulting from the assumption that convertible instruments are converted, that options or warrants are exercised, or that ordinary shares are issued upon the satisfaction of specified conditions.

In referring to these potential ordinary shares, we are including all financial instruments or contracts that allow the holder to obtain ordinary shares of the company. Examples of potential ordinary shares are convertible debt, share warrants, convertible instruments, share rights and employee stock purchase plans.

The number of ordinary shares is the weighted average number of ordinary shares outstanding, as calculated for basic earnings per share, plus the weighted average number of ordinary shares that would be issued on the conversion of all potential dilutive ordinary shares into ordinary shares. The calculations are:

- Start with the basic EPS.
- Increase the net profit by the amount of financing costs the company will save by not having convertible instruments in issue.

- To the weighted average number of shares, add the number of shares that would be issued if the convertible instruments were converted. Assume that conversion takes place at the beginning of the period.

The following data is for 2009 (taxation is ignored):

	2009
Earnings (including finance charges for Convertible Loan Stock)	$150,000
12% Convertible loan stock	$100,000
Loan stock convertible at 4 ordinary shares for every $5 of stock	
Number of ordinary shares in issue	200,000

$$\text{Basic EPS} = \frac{\$150,000}{200,000} = 75 \text{ cents.}$$

In calculating the diluted earnings per share, we must add back the finance charges of $12,000 (12% × $100,000 loan) to the earnings to arrive at the amount of earnings before finance charges.

Calculation of diluted EPS:

Earnings add back finance charges = $162,000

$$\text{Number of shares} = 200,000 + \frac{\$100,000}{\$5} \times 4 = 280,000$$

$$\text{Diluted EPS} = \frac{\$162,000}{280,000} = 58.8 \text{ cents.}$$

The information that a company must provide in its financial statements is:

- details of basic and diluted EPS on the face of the Income Statement;
- the amounts used as the profit or loss for ordinary shareholders in calculating basic and diluted EPS;
- the weighted average number of ordinary shares used in calculating basic and diluted EPS;
- a description of those ordinary share transactions or potential ordinary share transactions that occur after the balance sheet date and would have had a significant effect on the EPS.

The following is taken from the Notes to the 2007 Annual Report for J Sainsbury:

Basic earnings per share is calculated by dividing the earnings attributable to ordinary shareholders by the weighted average number of ordinary shares in issue during the year, excluding those held by the Employee Share Ownership Plan trusts (note 25), which are treated as cancelled.

For diluted earnings per share, the weighted average number of ordinary shares in issue is adjusted to assume conversion of all potential dilutive ordinary shares. These represent share options granted to employees where the exercise price is less than the average market price of the Company's ordinary shares during the year.

12.8 IAS 34 Interim Financial Reporting

The purpose and basis of interims

Investors, creditors, and others relying on annual financial statements do not receive a sufficiently frequent flow of information for decision-making. By the time the annual financial statements are published, the economic environment may have changed dramatically since several of the reported events took place.

To reduce the problem of the lack of up-to-date information, most stock exchanges around the world require companies listed on the exchange to produce interim financial reports to produce timely and reliable information. The stock exchange may require companies to issue these at the six-month stage (half-yearly) as in the UK, or to issue them every three months (quarterlies) as in the USA.

It is normal that the Stock Exchange regulations for half-yearly interims will require them to be produced for the first six months of the financial year, but not for the second six months as the company will be producing annuals. For quarterlies, the Stock Exchange normally requires companies to produce interim financial statements for the first three quarters of the year but not for the fourth quarter as the annual financial statements will be produced.

One dilemma concerning the preparation of interim statements is whether they should be drawn up using the discrete, integral or the composite approach (a mixture of the two). With the discrete approach, each half-yearly or quarterly period is treated as a self-contained period. Costs and revenues are matched in each period and the same accounting policies and treatments are used for the interim period as for the annual accounts. With the integral approach, each shorter period is treated as part of the longer period. This approach recognises that business activity may be cyclical with profits being earned unevenly throughout the year. The integral approach attempts to match planned costs and profits on a basis relating to the year as a whole.

The problems of which approach to use include the following:

(a) Seasonal fluctuations of revenue;
(b) Substantial fixed costs in some periods;
(c) Costs/expenses incurred at infrequent intervals during the year which relate to a full year's activities;
(d) The limited time to obtain the information for the interim period which leads to numerous estimates being made. These have to be corrected in subsequent periods, leading to the distortion of those results;
(e) Infrequent or unusual events or transactions have a more substantial effect on the results of operations for an interim period.

An example of the difference between the two approaches is of a company that in December of each year carries out annual maintenance when the factory is closed. We will assume that the company is required to produce half-yearly interims. Should the company charge half of the maintenance cost to the first six months, although the cost has not been incurred (integral approach), or should the company put the full cost in the last six months (discrete approach)? Another example is a company that produces quarterly interim financial statements and has a large advertising campaign in January intended to generate sales for the entire year. Should the advertising expense be charged completely to the first quarter or spread over the entire year?

There are arguments in favour of and against both approaches. The criticisms of the discrete approach are:

• Interim statements prepared using the discrete approach give little guidance as to management expectations for the remainder of the year. The statements therefore have a lower predictive value, but that is exactly what users want to do with the information.
• Results can fluctuate dramatically from period to period and this can be misleading.
• If tax expense is calculated on a period-by-period basis, it becomes very distorted.
• The calculation of financial ratios will be distorted.

The criticisms of the integral approach are:

• The spreading of costs over the different periods is very subjective with the possibility of errors and manipulation. The figures can be unreliable for the quarter with major events being hidden.
• Over- or under-allocation of part of the costs to one period can lead to distorted or inaccurate results in the subsequent periods.
• Management has the opportunity to artificially smooth or disguise significant trading changes and conceal the actual level of activity in the period.

- Concepts of consistency are ignored as interim practices and policies may differ from those used in the preparation of the annual report and accounts.
- The results for interim periods should not be adjusted for one period to allow predictions of operations for subsequent periods.

Given these conceptual difficulties, it is not surprising that IAS 34 Interim Financial Reporting is not always as clear as one would wish. The standard setters confronted a wide range of approaches adopted by companies and what the IASB tried to achieve was to introduce consistency to those practices.

There is a certain amount of inconsistency in the requirements of IAS 34. At some stages in the standard it seems that companies should be using a discrete approach, and at other stages an integral approach is being put forward. As we will explain later, the standard has the requirement that the same accounting policies should be applied in the interim financial statements as are applied in annual financial statements. This represents a "discrete period" approach to interim reporting. On the other hand, the standard requires that measurements for interim reporting purposes should be made on a year-to-date basis so that the frequency of the entity's reporting does not affect the measurement of its annual results. This represents an "integral period" approach.

This ambiguity leads to conflicts with certain transactions and at the end of this section we will list the guidance of the standard for certain transactions.

Main requirements

It is important to emphasise that IAS 34 is not mandatory — it does not absolutely require companies to produce interim financial statements. The standard does not contain any rules as to which companies should publish interim financial reports, how frequently, or how soon after the end of an interim period. Governments, securities regulators, stock exchanges, and accountancy bodies often require companies with publicly-traded debt or equity to publish interim financial reports. Their regulations generally specify the frequency and timing of such reports.

IAS 34 *encourages* companies to provide interim financial statements at least at the end of the first six months of their trading year and to make these statements available no later than 60 days after the end of the interim period. IAS 34 applies to interim financial reports that are described by the issuing companies as complying with International Financial Reporting Standards (IFRSs).

This requirement on compliance means that each annual or interim financial statement is considered separately as far as compliance with IFRSs is concerned. Companies can, if they choose, prepare annual financial statements in accordance with IFRSs but prepare interim financial reports that do not comply with IFRSs. In such cases, the company cannot claim that the interim report does comply.

A company can decide to issue either a complete set of financial statements for interim reporting purposes or a condensed set of financial statements which we will describe later in this chapter. If it presents a complete set of financial statements for interim purposes, it must apply IAS 1 *Presentation of Financial Statements* in full.

If a company chooses to present a condensed set of financial statements for interim reporting purposes, it will not comply with all of the requirements of IAS 1 but will comply with the following requirements from IAS 1:

- fair presentation and compliance with IFRSs;
- going concern;
- accrual basis of accounting;
- materiality and aggregation; and
- offsetting.

IAS 34 defines the minimum content of an interim financial report as a condensed balance sheet, condensed income statement, condensed statement showing changes in equity, condensed cash flow statement and selected explanatory notes. The standard also prescribes the principles for recognition and measurement in financial statements presented for an interim period.

The periods and items to be covered by the interim financial statements are:

- balance sheet as of the end of the current interim period and a comparative balance sheet as of the end of the immediate, preceding financial year;
- income statements for the current interim period and cumulatively for the current financial year-to-date, with comparative income statements for the comparable interim periods (current and year-to-date) of the immediate, preceding financial year;
- statement showing changes in equity cumulatively for the current financial year-to-date, with a comparative statement for the comparable year-to-date period of the immediate, preceding financial year; and
- cash flow statement cumulatively for the current financial year-to-date, with a comparative statement for the comparable year-to-date period of the immediate, preceding financial year.

The interim financial reports should present each of the headings and the subtotals as illustrated in the most recent annual financial statements and the explanatory notes as required by IAS 34. Additional line items should be included if their omission would make the interim financial information misleading. If the annual financial statements were consolidated (group) statements, the interim statements should be group statements as well.

An enterprise should use the same accounting policy throughout the financial year, with the same policies for interim reporting and for annual financial statements. The exceptions are accounting policy changes made after the date of the most recent annual financial statements and which would be incorporated in the next annual financial statements. If a decision is made to change a policy mid-year, the change is implemented retrospectively, and previously reported interim data are restated.

The notes to the interim financial statements are essentially an update. They include disclosures about changes in accounting policies, seasonality or cyclically, changes in estimates, changes in outstanding debt or equity, dividends, segment revenue and result, events occurring after balance sheet date, acquisition or disposal of subsidiaries and long-term investments, restructurings, discontinuing operations, and changes in contingent liabilities or contingent assets.

The standard provides guidance for applying the basic recognition and measurement principles at interim and the main points are as follows:

- Revenues received seasonally, cyclically or occasionally within a financial year should not be anticipated or deferred at the interim date if this practice is not used at the financial year-end.
- Costs that are incurred unevenly during a financial year should be anticipated or deferred if this practice is appropriate at the end of the financial year.
- Income tax expenses should be recognised based on the best estimate of the weighted average annual income tax rate expected for the full financial year.

An example of the basis on which the interim reports are prepared is shown below. This is from China Food Group plc 2008 Interim Report:

Basis of preparation

These condensed consolidated interim financial statements are for the six months ended 30 June 2008 and have been prepared in accordance with IAS 34 "Interim Financial Reporting". They do not include all of the information required for full annual financial statements, and should be read in conjunction with the consolidated financial statements of the Group for the year ended 31 December 2007.

The condensed consolidated financial statements comprise the financial statements of all the entities within the Group. The financial statements of the subsidiaries are prepared for the same reporting date as the parent company. Consistent accounting policies are applied for like transactions and events in similar circumstances.

The condensed consolidated financial statements of the Group and the individual financial statements of the company have been prepared in accordance with IFRS as adopted by the EU and under the historical cost convention, except that they have been modified to include the revaluation of certain financial assets and liabilities.

Minimum contents

Where a company chooses to present a complete set of financial statements in its interim financial reports, the form and content of the financial statements must conform to the requirements of IAS 1 *Presentation of Financial Statements*. Therefore, the measurement and disclosure requirements of all relevant Standards apply. These include all measurement and disclosure requirements of IAS 34 and, in particular, the selected explanatory note disclosures listed in that standard.

Companies complying with IAS 34 but issuing a condensed interim report must, at a minimum, include the following information:

- condensed statement of financial position;
- condensed statement of comprehensive income, presented as either:
  - condensed single statement; or
  - condensed separate income statement and a condensed statement of comprehensive income if it does this in its annual financial statements;
- condensed statement of changes in equity;
- condensed statement of cash flows; and
- selected explanatory notes.

With the condensed financial statements, each of the headings and subtotals that were included in the company's most recent annual financial statements should be disclosed. Additional line items are required if their omission would make the condensed interim financial statements misleading. The result of this requirement is that at least some statements will include all of the line items, headings and subtotals that were presented in the most recent annual financial statements. However, under IAS 34, the notes supplementing the interim financial statements are limited, which means that the interim report will be condensed compared to what would be reported in a complete set of financial statements under IAS 1 and other Standards.

All of the supplementary notes in the annual financial statements are not required for interim reporting purposes, since this would result in repetition, or the reporting of relatively insignificant changes. The explanatory notes included with the interim financial information are intended to provide an explanation of events and transactions that are significant to an understanding of the changes in financial position and performance of the entity since the last annual reporting date.

As with the annual financial statements, interims should include comparative information: the amounts for the comparable financial period. The main requirements are:

- Balance sheet as of the end of the current interim period and a comparative balance sheet as of the end of the immediately preceding financial year.
- Income statements for the current interim period and cumulatively for the current financial year-to-date, with comparative income statements for the

comparable interim periods (current and year-to-date) of the immediately preceding financial year.

- Cash flow statement cumulatively for the current financial year-to-date, with a comparative statement for the comparable year-to-date period of the immediately preceding financial year.

- If the company's business is highly seasonal, IAS 34 encourages disclosure of financial information for the latest 12 months, and comparative information for the prior 12-month period, in addition to the interim period financial statements.

Relationship with annual financial statements

In most countries, companies do not prepare a separate report for the final interim period in a financial year whether this is the second half-year or the fourth quarter. In such circumstances, IAS 34 requires disclosure in the notes to the *annual* financial statements where an estimate of an amount reported in an earlier interim period is changed significantly during the final interim period. In other words, if a company in the first half-year or in the first three-quarters estimates incorrectly the amount for the entire year, that fact must be stated in the annual financial statements.

The accounting policies applied in the interim financial statements should be consistent with those applied in the most recent annual financial statements. We discussed the importance and nature of accounting policies in Chapter 7. Companies must state in the interim report that they have met this requirement. This is to ensure that companies do not change their accounting policies at the interim stage to make their results look more favourable.

However, changes in the accounting policies for the next annual financial statements may be intended to be applied and this is known at the interim stage. These changes may be because of a new IFRS being introduced or changes are being made on the basis that the new accounting policies will result in the financial statements providing more reliable and relevant information. Preparers of interim financial reports in compliance with IAS 34 are required to consider any changes in accounting policies that will be applied for the next annual financial statements, and to implement the changes for interim reporting purposes.

Where there is a change in accounting policy, the financial statements of prior interim periods of the current financial year should be restated and the comparable interim periods of prior financial years that will be restated in annual financial statements in accordance with IAS 8. As we discussed in Chapter 7, the concept of impracticability applies where a company cannot make the changes after every reasonable effort to do so.

Guidance on specific transactions

Revenues

Revenues that are received seasonally, cyclically or occasionally within a financial year should not be anticipated or deferred as of an interim date, if anticipation or deferral would not be appropriate at the end of the financial year. This would be the same policy that companies would adopt for their annual financial statements. For example, a retailer does not divide forecasted revenue for the entire year by two to arrive at its half-year revenue figures. It must report its actual revenue for the first six months.

To assist the user in appreciating the cyclical nature of its business, the retailer could include additional information on the actual revenue for the 12 months up to the end of the interim reporting period and comparative information for the corresponding previous 12-month period.

Uneven costs

Costs that are incurred unevenly during an entity's financial year should not be anticipated or deferred for interim reporting purposes. In other words, a company cannot spread its costs evenly over the entire year. At the beginning of this section we gave the example of the company that incurred large advertising costs in the first part of the year. These must be recognised in full in the period in which they are incurred. There is an exception to this. If the company's policy is to anticipate or defer that type of cost at the end of the financial year, it can apply this policy at the interim stage.

Employer payroll taxes and insurance contributions

If employer payroll taxes or contributions to government-sponsored insurance funds are assessed on an annual basis, the employer's related expense is recognised in interim periods using an estimated average annual effective payroll tax or contribution rate.

Major planned periodic maintenance or overhaul

The cost of a planned major periodic maintenance or overhaul or other seasonal expenditure that is expected to occur late in the year is not anticipated for interim reporting purposes. We gave an explanation of this instance earlier in this section. There is an exception to this requirement and that is where an event has caused the entity to have a legal or constructive obligation. The mere intention or necessity to incur expenditure related to the future is not sufficient to give rise to an obligation.

Provisions

You may recall from Chapter 7 that the making of provisions by companies is a very controversial area and the IASB has been trying to make the requirements less open to abuse. This is reflected in IAS 34 which states that a provision is recognised when a company has no realistic alternative but to make a transfer of economic benefits as a result of an event that has created a legal or constructive obligation. IAS 34 requires that a company apply the same criteria for recognising and measuring a provision at an interim date as it would at the end of its financial year. The existence or non-existence of an obligation to transfer benefits is not a function of the length of the reporting period; it is a question of fact.

Year-end bonuses

In some organisations, employees may receive a bonus at the year end based on the profitable performance of the company or other measures of performance. Some are earned simply by continued employment during a time period. They may be purely discretionary, contractual, or based on years of historical precedent. A year-end bonus can be anticipated at the interim stage if, and only if:

- the bonus is a legal obligation, or past practice would make the bonus a constructive obligation and the entity has no realistic alternative but to make the payments; and
- a reliable estimate of the obligation can be made.

Pensions

The pension cost for an interim period is calculated on a year-to-date basis by using the actuarially-determined pension cost rate at the end of the prior financial year, adjusted for significant market fluctuations since that time and for significant curtailments, settlements or other significant one-time events.

Contingent lease payments

Contingent lease payments can be an example of a legal or constructive obligation that is recognised as a liability. If a lease provides for contingent payments based on the lessee achieving a certain level of annual sales, an obligation can arise in the interim period of the financial year before the required annual level of sales has been achieved, if that required level of sales is expected to be achieved and the entity, therefore, has no realistic alternative but to make the future lease payment.

Intangible assets

Companies cannot defer expenses at the interim stage in the belief or hope that these expenses will meet at a later date the criteria to be capitalised as an intangible asset. IAS 38, which we explained in Chapter 6, requires that asset recognition (cost capitalisation) should begin at the point in time at which the recognition criteria are met, not at the start of the financial reporting period in which those criteria are met.

Vacations, holidays, and other short-term compensated absences

We explained in Chapter 8 that IAS 19 Employee Benefits requires a company to measure the expected cost of and obligation for accumulating compensated absences at the amount the entity expects to pay as a result of the unused entitlement that has accumulated at the end of the reporting period. That principle is also applied at the end of interim financial reporting periods.

Irregularly occurring and discretionary costs

A company may budget for such costs as charitable donations and training of employees to be incurred at some time during the financial year. Although the company may plan and intend to incur these costs, they are usually discretionary and can be avoided if the company wishes not to make the payments. A company cannot recognise at the end of the interim period that it intends to make these payments later in the year.

Volume rebates

In some industries it is practice for suppliers to give a rebate on the purchases made by a customer based on the volume. This rebate is frequently made at the year end and is anticipated by both the buyer and the seller. If these rebates are contractual in nature and it is probable that they have been earned or will take effect, they can be anticipated in the interim financial statements. This is contrary to what you may have thought would be the position, but one suspects that these practices were established long before the standard was issued. The IASB may well have decided that there was no benefit to be gained from trying to change what had already been established as normal business practice.

Inventories

Inventories are measured for interim financial reporting using the same principles as at financial year end. In Chapter 3 we described the recognition and measurement criteria of IAS 2 Inventories. The valuation of inventories is a large task and to save cost and time, companies often use estimates to measure inventories at interim dates.

Earnings per share

Although IAS 34 does not make any specific reference to earnings per share but to enable users to compare trends, the same EPS figures should be presented in the interim financial report as in the annual financial statements.

The following example from the Notes for the first quarter of 2009 for Intercontinental Hotels shows the position of its capital commitments and contingent liabilities:

At 31 March 2009, the amount contracted for but not provided for in the financial statements for expenditure on property, plant and equipment was $33m (2008 31 December $40m; 31 March $18m).

At 31 March 2009, the Group had contingent liabilities of $10m (2008 31 December $12m; 31 March $20m), mainly comprising guarantees given in the ordinary course of business.

12.9 Chapter Summary

IAS 1 Presentation of Financial Statements

☞ Balance Sheet is now called Statement of Financial Position.
☞ Cash Flow Statement is now called Statement of Cash Flows.
☞ There is now a Statement of Comprehensive Income showing all items of income and expense.
☞ Two formats are offered for the Income Statement: by function or by nature.
☞ Formats for the financial statements are given but flexibility is allowed.
☞ Current and non-current assets are distinguished.
☞ A Statement of Changes in Equity is required, showing all movements in the equity section of the Statement of Financial Position.

IAS 33 Earnings per Share

☞ Companies are required by IAS 33 to disclose their Basic Earnings per Share and their Diluted Earnings per Share.
☞ Basic earnings per share is the profit attributable to ordinary shareholders divided by the weighted average number of shares.
☞ If shares are issued for cash during the year, then the number of shares are weighted proportionately.
☞ If bonus shares are issued, it is assumed that they were issued at the beginning of the period.

☞ Diluted earnings per share demonstrates the risk to existing shareholders of there being people who have the right to ordinary shares in the future.

☞ To calculate diluted EPS, the net profit is increased by the financing costs no longer payable on these convertible instruments.

☞ The weighted average number of shares used in the basic EPS calculation is increased by the number of shares that would be issued if the convertible instruments were converted. Assume conversion takes place at the beginning of the year.

IAS 34 Interim Financial Reporting

☞ An interim period is a financial period less than a year.
☞ The standard does not make interim reports mandatory.
☞ The standard applies to those companies stating that they comply with IFRSs.
☞ Companies can present either full or condensed financial statements.
☞ The dilemma of the discrete or integral approach has not been resolved.
☞ The standard offers guidance on the treatment of certain transactions.
☞ The standard sets out minimum contents and reporting periods.

Progress Test

1. Under IAS 33 Earnings per Share (EPS), which ONE of the following must a company disclose?

   a) A ten-year trend of EPS
   b) A prediction of the EPS for the following year
   c) A comparison of the EPS against the market price
   d) The weighted average number of ordinary shares used to calculate EPS

2. At the year ended 31 March 2008, a company has 6 million ordinary shares of $1 each and 500,000 $1 irredeemable preference shares at 10%. The profit before tax was $500,000. Ignore any tax. What is the EPS?

   a) 0.60
   b) 0.75
   c) 0.83
   d) 0.90

3. Which TWO of the following must be included in a complete set of financial statements?

   a) A Statement of Changes in Equity
   b) A five-year financial summary of the entity
   c) A Statement of Cash Flows
   d) A Chairman's Statement

4. Which one of the following statements is true in regard to bonus shares when calculating the weighted average number of ordinary shares?

   a) They are time-apportioned from the date of their issue
   b) They are treated as if they were issued at the beginning of the year
   c) They are treated as if they are issued at the end of the year
   d) They are not included in the calculations

5. Which one of the following statements is true in regard to shares issued for cash when calculating the weighted average number of ordinary shares?

   a) They are time-apportioned from the date of their issue
   b) They are treated as if they were issued at the beginning of the year
   c) They are treated as if they are issued at the end of the year
   d) They are not included in the calculations

6. Which two of the following statements in relation to an interim financial report are true according to IAS 34?

   a) It must contain a summary of financial performance
   b) It may contain a complete set of financial statements
   c) It may contain a condensed set of financial statements
   d) It must contain both a condensed and a complete set of financial statements

7. A company which believes that compliance with the regulations of a particular standard would make its financial statements misleading should:

   a) still comply with the standard
   b) ignore the standard completely
   c) depart from the standard but disclose certain information
   d) comply with the standard but disclose certain information

8. In an interim financial report, IAS 34 proposes that a company should:

   a) include all the same Notes to the Accounts as in the annual reports
   b) include a limited number of Notes to the Accounts
   c) omit the Notes to the Accounts

9. A retailer has cyclical revenue throughout the year. At the half-year the revenue is $30m and the retailer predicts that for the entire year it will be $90m. What is the amount of revenue to be shown in the Interim Report?

   a) $45m
   b) $30m
   c) $60m
   d) None of these

10. A company always receives a volume rebate from one of its suppliers. It is calculated at 5% on the value of the business conducted. The company anticipates that
the total value of business for the year 2009 will be $80,000. What amount for
the rebate should be shown in the half-year interim report for 2009?

a) Zero
b) $4,000
c) $2,000
d) $1,000

13

Foreign Operations and Segmental Reporting

Learning Objectives

At the end of this chapter you should be able to:

☞ Explain the issues regarding changes in exchange rates
☞ Differentiate between functional and presentational currencies
☞ Explain and carry out the calculations for transactions in foreign currencies
☞ Adjust for exchange differences where there are foreign operations
☞ Identify a hyperinflationary economy
☞ Explain the accounting treatments in a hyperinflationary economy
☞ Explain the importance of identifying and reporting operating segments.

13.1 Introduction

This chapter discusses three different standards. The first two are very much related to business being carried out in a global environment. IAS 21 discusses the effects of changes in foreign exchange rates for those companies with international transactions or operations in other countries. IAS 29 is concerned with financial reporting in hyperinflationary economies.

The development of global business has resulted in many entities being involved in various forms of relationships with other entities in different countries. These may include transactions conducted with foreign buyers or sellers or participation in foreign operations and, in these circumstances, foreign currencies are involved. Guidance is required to ensure that these currencies are translated in a consistent manner.

The main requirements are that the transactions in foreign currencies must be expressed in the entity's reporting currency and the financial statements of foreign operations must be translated into the entity's reporting currency. The standard sets out guidance for the selection of the exchange rate to be used and the recognition of the financial effects of changes in exchange rates.

IAS 29 is concerned with a less common but important situation. Unfortunately, inflation is a fact of life and its effects can distort the financial reports of companies. We discussed the weaknesses of using money measurement in Chapter 1. For many countries, the inflation rate is not sufficiently significant to cause problems for accounting in the short-term. In some countries, however, the inflation rate is so high that the financial reports are meaningless unless adjustments are made. IAS 29 explains those adjustments.

The third standard, IFRS 8 Operating Segments, mainly affects the larger companies. Where you have large companies offering a wide range of products and services, often in several different countries, more detail on the different areas of activity is valuable to the user. The standard sets the criteria for identifying different operating segments and the disclosure requirements.

13.2 IAS 21 The Effects of Changes in Foreign Exchange Rates

There are several reasons why a standard was required to provide guidance on the accounting treatments companies should take in respect of changes in foreign exchange rates. Companies conduct transactions internationally and may operate in several foreign currencies. Where there are consolidated accounts to be prepared, there may be foreign operations maintaining their records in a foreign currency. Also, companies sometimes wish to provide their financial statements to users in other countries in the currency of that country.

Unfortunately, the relative values of foreign currencies are rarely fixed. Variable exchange rates over time make comparisons between companies or even within the same company difficult. A standard was therefore required to bring order to what could have been a very confusing area of business. The standard is not about conversion, which is the physical exchange of one currency for another. The standard is concerned with translation, which is changing the foreign currency balances into the domestic currency equivalents by the application of the foreign exchange rate at a particular time.

Main requirements

In considering foreign exchange rates, we can divide the issues into two different situations. First are those companies that are carrying out transactions in foreign currencies, e.g., exporting goods to foreign customers; purchasing supplies, machinery and equipment from foreign sources. Second are those companies which have business operations in another country, i.e., a subsidiary or branch located overseas.

Definition — functional currency

The currency of the primary economic environment in which the company operates.

The general principle for the first situation is that a company should translate foreign currency items and transactions into its functional currency. To do this translation, the spot exchange rate between the functional currency and the foreign currency at the date of the transaction is used. Average rates can be used, but care must be exercised. If exchange rates fluctuate significantly over time or if there are a small number of irregular transactions, the average can be distorted.

At each balance sheet date, the following actions are taken:

- use the closing rate to report foreign currency monetary items (e.g., cash held, and assets to be received and liabilities to be paid in either fixed amounts or amounts that can be determined);
- use the exchange rate at the date of transaction to report non-monetary items carried at historical cost;
- use the exchange rate at the time when fair values were determined for non-monetary items carried at fair value.

Exchange differences will often arise because you are using the same monetary items at different exchange rates. These differences normally occur due to the settlement amounts payable or receivable in a foreign currency and the re-translation during the preparation of financial statements at the period-end.

Definition — presentation currency

The currency in which the financial statements are presented.

The general principle for the second situation is that the results and financial position of a foreign operation are translated in the reporting entity's financial statements (the presentation currency) as follows:

- assets and liabilities for each Balance Sheet presented (including comparatives) are translated at the closing rate at the date of that Balance Sheet;

- income and expenses for each Income Statement (including comparatives) are translated at exchange rates at the dates of the transactions;
- all resulting exchange differences are recognised as a separate component of equity.

13.3 Functional Currency

Definition — foreign currency

A currency other than the functional currency.

Every individual company complying with IAS 21 must measure its results and financial position in its functional currency, i.e., the currency of the primary economic environment in which the company operates. If we are considering consolidated financial statements, each individual company in the group, wherever it is situated in the world, must prepare its financial statements in its functional currency. There is no such thing as a group functional currency and we will discuss this later.

It is critical to understand the importance of identifying a company's functional currency, as this serves the basis for determining whether the company has any foreign exchange transactions. By identifying its functional currency, a company will also be identifying the treatment of exchange gains and losses arising from the translation process and its reported results. The functional currency must be determined at the lowest foreign operational level, i.e., a subsidiary, associate, branch or joint venture whose activities are based or conducted in a country or currency other than that of the reporting entity.

The identification of the correct functional currency is essential but can be difficult in some countries and for some companies. A company does not have a free choice for determining its functional currency. For example, if it is operating in a country with hyperinflation, it cannot choose a more stable currency but must use the local currency if that is the one of its primary economic environment.

Because of the potential difficulties in identifying the functional currency, the standard offers the following guidance. One important characteristic is the currency in which transactions are normally conducted.

Primary indicators of the functional currency:

- The currency that *mainly influences* sales prices for goods and services. This is normally the currency in which sales prices for goods and services are denominated and settled. For example, the company may operate in an active local sales market where its products are priced in the local currency and payments are made primarily in that local currency.

- The currency of the country whose competitive forces and regulations *mainly determine* the sales prices of goods and services. For example, a company may be pricing its manufactured products in Euros, but the legal and regulatory environment of the country in which it is located may prohibit the company from trading in hard currency and the local currency will be the functional currency.
- The currency that mainly influences the costs of labour, materials, goods and services. If such costs are incurred and settled in the local currency, this will be the functional currency.

Secondary indicators of the functional currency:

- The currency in which finance is generated as, if this is done locally, it may indicate that is the functional currency.
- The currency in which the receipts from operating activities are normally retained.

Where the company is a foreign operation, e.g., subsidiary, branch, associate or joint venture, there are four further factors to be considered in addition to those above:

1. A foreign operation that operates with significant autonomy and not as an extension of the reporting entity would normally use the local currency as the functional currency. A foreign operation that only sells the goods and sends the proceeds to the reporting company in another country would not normally use the local currency as the functional currency to prepare its financial statements.
2. A foreign operation that has few transactions with the reporting entity would normally use the local currency as the functional currency.
3. If the cash flows of the foreign operation do not affect the cash flows of the reporting company and are mainly in the local currency, that will be the functional currency.
4. If the foreign operation can maintain its activities from its own cash flows in the local currency, that will be the functional currency.

In some instances it will be difficult to determine the functional currency and each situation must be determined by its own characteristics. Management may have to determine the relative importance of each of the indicators in the particular circumstances. The operation may be diverse, with cash flows, financing and transactions occurring in more than a single currency. The standard states that, in making its judgement, management must give priority to the primary indicators before considering the secondary indicators. If a decision can be made on the basis of the primary indicators, there is no need to consider the secondary indicators.

In most cases, the functional currency will be the currency of the country whose economy drives the business and reflects the economic effects of the underlying transactions, events and conditions. There are variations and one example is where a company may have several foreign operations in one country. It is possible that these have different functional currencies. One may be operating in the local currency, whereas another may meet the characteristics of the primary indicators.

13.4 Foreign Currency Transactions

Foreign currency transactions are transactions denominated in a currency other than the company's functional currency. These transactions may result in accounts payable or accounts receivable that are fixed in terms of the foreign currency. For example, a Chinese company may purchase goods from a Canadian company where the price is set in Canadian dollars. When the Chinese company has to pay, the cost in Chinese Renminbi (CNY) will depend on the exchange rate at that date.

There are two stages in translating foreign currency transactions. The first is the initial recognition and the second is at the subsequent balance sheet date. To apply the guidelines, you need to understand some of the terms used with currency exchanges:

- *Spot rate* — the exchange rate for immediate delivery.
- *Closing rate* — the spot exchange rate at the balance sheet date.
- *Exchange differences* — the difference resulting from translating a given number of units at one currency into another currency at different exchange rates.

Initial measurement

A foreign currency transaction should be recorded initially on recognition in the functional currency by applying to the foreign currency amount, the spot exchange rate between the functional currency and the foreign currency at the date of the transaction. For revenues, expenses, gains and losses, the spot exchange rate at the dates on which those elements are recognised should be applied.

For a company that has few transactions or large, one-off transactions, the actual spot exchange rate can be used. For a company of any size, it is usually impracticable to apply the spot rate on the dates that all the transactions are taking place. It is usual in these cases to use a rate that approximates the actual rate, such as an average rate for the period. The standard allows this as long as there are no significant changes in rates during the period.

Depending on the circumstances, a company may use an actual average rate or an estimated average rate. An actual average rate is usually used where there is some delay between the date when the transaction occurred and the recorded date. The estimated average rate may be used where the company is unable to wait for the period end to obtain the actual average rate.

Example of initial measurement

Into Inc. has a functional currency in Canadian dollars. It buys machinery from Sweden for 4 million Swedish krona. At that date, the spot exchange rate is CA$1 = SEK4. The transaction will be recorded at CA$1,000,000.

There are difficulties in determining the average spot rate and these can be made even more complex by any regulations that prevail in the country at that time. The following example is from the Annual Report of Sinopec:

> **Currency risk**
>
> Substantially all of the revenue-generating operations of the Group are transacted in Renminbi, which is not fully convertible into foreign currencies. Approval of foreign currency payments by the PBOC or other institutions requires submitting a payment application form together with suppliers' invoices, shipping documents and signed contracts. With the authorisation from the PRC government, the PBOC announced that the PRC government reformed the exchange rate regime by moving into a managed floating exchange rate regime based on market supply and demand with reference to a basket of currencies on 21 July 2005.

Subsequent measurement

In considering subsequent measurement, we are normally concerned with the balance sheet. At the end of the financial period when the balance sheet is being prepared, items fall into three classifications:

1. Monetary items
2. Non-monetary items measured at historic cost
3. Non-monetary items measured at fair value.

For an item to qualify as a monetary item, it is not necessary for it to be recovered or settled in cash. Monetary items are units of currency held and assets and liabilities to be received or paid in a fixed or determinable number of units of currency, such as cash, bank balances and receivables and financial liabilities such as debt, provisions that are settled in cash, pensions and other employee benefits to be paid in cash, deferred taxes and cash dividends that are recognised as a liability.

IAS 21 requires that an entity should translate its foreign currency monetary items outstanding at the end of each reporting period using the closing rate. If you refer back to our definitions, you will see that this is the spot exchange rate at the end of the reporting period.

Non-monetary items are items other than monetary items such as intangible assets, plant and equipment, and inventories. Translation of non-monetary items depends on whether they are measured at historical cost or at fair value. For example, under IAS 16 Property, Plant and Equipment, companies can choose to either use historical cost or carry out a revaluation of property, plant and equipment and measure at fair value.

Non-monetary items that are measured in terms of historical cost in a foreign currency should be translated using the exchange rate at the date of the transaction. Non-monetary assets that are measured at fair value in a foreign currency should be translated using the exchange rate at the date when the fair value was determined.

We have summarised the above regulations in the following table:

Item	Exchange Rate
Monetary items	Closing rate (spot exchange rate at balance sheet date)
Non-monetary items measured at historic cost	Rate of exchange at the date of the original transaction
Non-monetary items measured at fair value	Exchange rate at the date when fair value was determined

You will have realised that if we are translating a transaction at the spot rate when it took place and at the balance sheet using the closing rate, there is likely to be a difference.

Definition — exchange differences

The difference due to translating the same amounts at different exchange rates is referred to as an exchange difference. These differences usually arise from the payment or receipt of monetary amounts in a foreign currency and the retranslation at the period end when the financial statements are prepared.

Monetary items may be settled within the financial period or may be still outstanding at the balance sheet date. Exchange differences arising on the settlement of monetary items or on translating monetary items at rates different from those at which they were translated on initial recognition during the period or in previous financial statements, should be recognised in profit or loss in the period in which they are settled.

Monetary items arising from a foreign currency transaction that remain outstanding at the balance sheet date should also be reported as part of the profit or loss for the year.

Non-monetary items that are measured at historical cost are translated at the date of the transaction.

With non-monetary items remeasured at fair value, for example, where property is revalued, any gain or loss should be recognised in comprehensive income.

Example

Intco Inc. uses the Canadian dollar as its functional currency; in other words, it uses that currency for its financial statements. On 1 October it buys goods from an overseas supplier in Sweden. The cost is 300,000 Swedish krona (SEK). The following information is available on exchange rates:

$$1 \text{ October CA\$1} = \text{SEK5}$$
$$1 \text{ November CA\$1} = \text{SEK4.50}$$
$$31 \text{ December CA\$1} = \text{SEK4}$$

The transaction occurs on 1 October so Intco is going to use the exchange rate at that date to incorporate the transaction into its financial statements:

$$\text{CA\$1} = \text{SEK5}$$
$$\text{SEK300,000}/5 = \text{CA\$60,000}$$

Asset of inventory will appear in accounting records as CA$60,000. Liability (supplier) will appear in records as CA$60,000.

Let us assume that Intco pays the Swedish company on 1 November but still has the inventory at that date:

$$\text{CA\$1} = \text{SEK4.5}$$
$$\text{Cost of settled liability is (SEK300,000}/4.5) = \text{CA\$66,600}$$

The exchange difference between settlement of CA$66,600 and original figure of CA$60,000 will be shown as loss in Income Statement. Inventory (non-monetary item) stays at CA$60,000 in the accounting records.

Let us now assume that Intco does not pay the liability but at 31 December still owes the money to the Swedish company and still has the inventory:

$$\text{SEK300,000}/4 = \text{CA\$75,000}$$

The liability will appear in the balance sheet at CA$75,000. The inventory (non-monetary item) will appear in balance sheet as asset at CA$60,000. Exchange difference of CA$15,000 is reported in the Income Statement as a loss.

13.5 Foreign Exchange and Consolidated Financial Statements

Where we have a group of companies with foreign operations, there are some particular issues. Where the foreign operation has the same functional currency as the reporting company, any movements in exchange rates will have an immediate impact on the reporting company's cash flows. Where the foreign operation's functional currency is different, we need to adopt a two-stage approach:

1. At the individual level, the foreign exchange transactions are conducted in the foreign currency and the financial statements prepared in that currency.
2. When consolidation is taking place, the financial statements of the individual foreign operations must be translated into the presentation currency of the reporting company.

The main rules for translating from the functional currency into the presentation currency are:

- Statement of Financial Position: The assets and liabilities of the foreign operation are translated at the closing rate at the year end.
- Statement of Comprehensive Income: The amounts should be translated at the date of transaction (an average rate may be used).
- Exchanges in the parent's investment shown on the Statement of Financial Position of the foreign operation should be taken to equity.

Other considerations:

Different reporting dates

IAS 27 permits the use of a different reporting date that is within three months either side of the reporting company's statement of financial position date. Where a foreign subsidiary's financial statements are drawn up to a date that is different from that of the parent, the foreign operation can prepare additional financial statements with adjustments for any significant changes in exchange rates.

Non-controlling interest

Where the foreign operation is not wholly-owned, the exchange differences that are attributable to non-controlling interest should be allocated to and reported as part of the non-controlling interest in the Consolidated Statement of Financial Position.

Goodwill and fair value adjustments

Goodwill arising in a business acquisition is the excess of the cost over the acquirer's interest in the net fair value of the acquiree's identifiable assets, liabilities and contingent liabilities. Any goodwill arising because of the acquisition of a foreign operation and any fair value adjustments to the carrying amounts of assets and liabilities arising on a foreign operation's acquisition should be treated as the foreign operation's assets and liabilities. They should be translated at the closing rate.

Change in functional currency

Once the functional currency of a foreign operation is determined, it should be used consistently, unless significant changes in economic facts, events and conditions indicate clearly that the functional currency has changed. Where there is a change in the functional currency, the company translates all items into the new functional currency from the date of the change using the exchange rate at that date. The change in functional currency is treated prospectively and it is not a change in accounting policy under IAS 8.

Consolidation procedures

The approach is very similar to the normal consolidation procedures. The one difference is where exchange differences arise on long-term or short-term intra-group monetary items, they cannot be offset against intra-group balances. The reason is that such balances are commitments to exchange one currency into another, leading to a gain or loss through currency fluctuations.

13.6 IAS 29 Financial Reporting in Hyperinflationary Economies

The financial statements prepared in a hyperinflationary economy are misleading as the loss in purchasing power of money makes comparisons of transactions and events at different periods unreliable. Where there is hyperinflation, the standard specifies the accounting treatment and disclosures required. The requirements apply to the primary financial statements of the entity, including group accounts where the functional currency is that of the hyperinflationary economy.

The only quantitative guidance to hyperinflation given in the standard is a cumulative inflation rate of approximately 100% or more over a three-year period. The standard also gives examples that indicate there is hyperinflation. These include:

* the holding of wealth in non-monetary assets such as land and works of art or in a stable currency;
* monetary amounts being expressed in a stable currency rather than the local currency, with prices sometimes being quoted in the stable currency;
* sales and purchases on credit are transacted at prices that adjust for the expected loss of purchasing power during the credit period;
* interest rates, wages and prices are linked to a price index.

To some extent, IAS 29 relaxes the concept of reliability, as discussed in Chapter 1, in an attempt to introduce consistency in accounting treatment and provide information that reflects the impact of the hyperinflationary economy on the entity.

To achieve these aims, the standard requires that financial statements of an entity that reports in the currency of a hyperinflationary economy should be restated in terms of the measuring unit current at the balance sheet date. There has been some confusion as to what the intention of this requirement is and IFRIC Interpretation 7 *Applying the restatement approach under IAS 29* was issued to clarify the matter.

In that interpretation, the guidance is that it must be assumed that the economy has always been hyperinflationary. This means that for non-monetary items measured at historical cost, the opening balance sheet at the beginning of the earliest period presented in the financial statements must be restated to show the effect of inflation since the assets were acquired and the liabilities incurred until the closing date of the reporting period.

Restatement of the Balance Sheet

Assuming that the historical model has been used to draw up the original financial statements, the procedures an entity should follow to carry out the restatement are:

- If any items are not already valued in terms of measuring units current at the year end, a general price index should be used to restate them.
- Monetary assets and liabilities are not restated because they should already be valued in terms of measurement units current at the year end.
- If assets are already stated at market value or net realisable value, they are consequently already valued in measurement units current at the year end and need not be restated.
- If the entity has any assets or liabilities linked by agreement to changes in the general level of prices, these should be adjusted according to the agreement. These would include such items as index-linked bonds.
- All other non-monetary assets such as plants, machinery, intangible assets and inventories should be restated, by using the general price index, at measurement units current at the year end.

Restatement of the Comprehensive Income Statement

Assuming that historical cost is used, all amounts of income and expense should be restated in terms of measuring units current at the year end. This entails using a factor that adjusts for the change in the price index since the item of income or expense was first recorded.

Once the assets, liabilities, equity and Statement of Comprehensive Income have been restated, there will be a net gain or loss on monetary assets and liabilities.

This is known as the net monetary position and must be recognised separately in the profit or loss for the period.

Example

To put these procedures into practice, we will take a simple example. This will use the Statement of Financial Position at the beginning of the year which has been restated at the general price index at that time, and restate it at the general price index at the end of the year. We will assume that the general price index was 100 at the beginning of the year and 200 at the end of the year.

Statement of Financial Position at the beginning of the year

	$000
Non-monetary assets	3,000
Monetary assets	3,000
Total assets	6,000
Equity	4,000
Monetary liabilities	2,000
Total equity and liabilities	6,000

If you return to the list of procedures above, you will see that monetary assets and liabilities do not change as they are already valued at monetary units current at the year end. The non-monetary assets must be restated, so the Statement of Financial Position at the end of the year is:

Statement of Financial Position at the end of the year

	$000
Non-monetary assets	6,000
Monetary assets	3,000
Total assets	9,000
Equity	8,000
Monetary liabilities	2,000
Total equity and liabilities	10,000

The difference of $1,000,000 is the loss made by the entity because it held net monetary assets throughout the year of $1,000,000. This loss of $1,000,000 must be shown on the Comprehensive Income Statement.

As we stated earlier, IFRIC 7 has been issued to clarify some of the problems that have arisen and gives guidance on several issues that are outside of the explanations we provide in this book.

13.7 IFRS 8 Operating Segments

Because of the size and diversity of some companies, it is difficult for the user to analyse the overall results. The risks and returns of a diversified, multinational company can only be understood by examining and analysing the different groups of products or services or the geographic areas in which the company has interests. IFRS 8 is intended to assist the user in understanding past performance and risks and returns by providing this type of information.

Operating segments are determined based on the structure of the organisation and how information is reported to management. When we have looked at other standards, they have usually prescribed the measurement methods to be used. IFRS 8 uses what is known as the management approach. The disclosures required are mainly based on the information presented to management.

The IASB adopted the management approach because they considered it helpful to users to receive the type of information that internal management use to structure the organisation in line with the risks and opportunities that management consider important and to relate this information to other disclosures in the annual report. There is also the cost argument. As the information is already being collected and used internally by management, it is readily available to present to external users.

The disclosure of segmental information is required by those companies whose equity or debt securities are publicly traded, in other words on a stock exchange. With group accounts, only consolidated information needs to be shown.

It is important to note that there is no exemption from the disclosures on the grounds that management may consider the segment information sensitive or that its disclosure may cause "competitive harm". This has been an excuse in the past used by entities to restrict the information they present to users.

Some entities outside the scope of IFRS 8 may decide to disclose segmental information. If the information the entity discloses does not comply fully with IFRS 8, it should not be referred to as segment information and an alternative heading should be given. Entities should also use the guidance in IFRS 8 to identify operating segments when determining cash-generating units (CGUs) or groups of CGUs to which goodwill or mineral resource exploration and evaluation assets are allocated.

Determining what parts of the business are operating segments can be difficult. IFRS 8 defines an operating segment as a component of an entity:

(a) that engages in business activities from which it may earn revenues and incur expenses (including revenues and expenses relating to transactions with other components of the same entity);

(b) whose operating results are regularly reviewed by the entity's chief operating decision maker to make decisions about resources to be allocated to the segment and to assess its performance; and

(c) for which discrete financial information is available.

The standard makes clear that an operating segment may engage in business activities for which it has yet to earn revenues. This could be an operation started by the entity which is incurring costs but has not yet started to generate revenue.

In defining a segment, the standard uses the criteria that "results are regularly reviewed by the entity's chief operating decision maker". This is an important phrase and IFRS 8 explains that the term "chief operating decision maker" (CODM) is intended to mean a function rather than an executive with a specific title. The function is that of allocating resources to operating segments and assessing their performance, and the CODM is frequently the Chief Executive of the entity. However, the function could be carried out by others, such as a senior management team or the board of directors.

The standard does not clarify what it means by "regularly reviewed" and we can conclude that monthly or even quarterly would suffice. It is not the frequency of the review that is important but the fact that it is a part of the normal procedures for decision making in the entity.

Reportable segments

Once the entity's operating segments have been identified, the entity must then determine which operating segments are reportable. Reportable segments are those operating segments, or groups of operating segments, that meet the quantitative thresholds for separate disclosure. IFRS 8 has established quantitative thresholds so as not to place too large a disclosure burden on entities:

(a) Its reported revenue, including both sales to external customers and inter-segment sales or transfers, is 10% or more of the combined revenue, internal and external, of all operating segments.

(b) The absolute amount of its reported profit or loss is 10% or more of the greater, in absolute amount, of:

  (i) the combined reported profit of all operating segments that did not report a loss; and

  (ii) the combined reported loss of all operating segments that reported a loss.

(c) Its assets are 10% or more of the combined assets of all operating segments.

There is some relief from being compelled to report all operating segments. An entity can aggregate two or more segments into one single operating segment. To do this, the segments must be similar in each of the following respects:

(a) the nature of the products and services;
(b) the nature of the production processes;
(c) the type or class of customer for their products and services;
(d) the methods used to distribute their products or provide their services; and
(e) if applicable, the nature of the regulatory environment.

If one or more of the aggregated segments has reported a profit but another has reported a loss, the net profit or loss is considered for the purpose of determining the reportable threshold for segment results. In some cases, this can change the number of reportable segments identified. However, the fact that one segment did not meet the quantitative thresholds prior to the aggregation with other segments does not preclude it from being considered a reportable segment subsequent to that aggregation.

Once an entity has identified and, where appropriate, aggregated its reportable segments, it must apply the 75% test. The external revenue of reportable segments must constitute at least 75% of total consolidated revenue. If the external revenue of the reportable segments is above 75%, the entity is not required to report additional segments. If the 75% threshold is not met, additional operating segments or aggregated operating segments must be identified as reportable segments until at least 75% of the entity's revenue is included in reportable segments.

13.8 Chapter Summary

IAS 21 The Effects of Changes in Foreign Exchange Rates

☞ Transactions conducted in foreign currencies lead to exchange differences.
☞ The standard sets out how you translate the foreign currencies into the functional currency.
☞ For initial recognition, you use the spot exchange rate.
☞ For subsequent recognition, the rules are different for monetary and non-monetary items.
☞ Exchange differences normally go to the Income Statement.

IAS 29 Financial Reporting in Hyperinflationary Economies

☞ Non-monetary assets and liabilities must be restated using the general price index.
☞ Income and expenses must be restated.

☞ Monetary assets and liabilities need not be restated.

☞ The gain or loss on net monetary items (monetary assets – monetary liabilities) must be reported in the profit or loss for the year.

Progress Test

1. At the balance sheet date, what is the rate that should be used for monetary items?

   a) The spot exchange rate at the balance sheet date
   b) The rate of exchange at the date of the original transaction
   c) The exchange rate at the date the fair value was determined
   d) Any of these rates

2. What is the correct term for the currency of the primary economic environment in IAS 21?

   a) Foreign currency
   b) Presentation currency
   c) Functional currency
   d) Reporting currency

3. At the balance sheet date, what is the rate that should be used for non-monetary items measured at historic cost?

   a) The spot exchange rate at the balance sheet date
   b) The rate of exchange at the date of the original transaction
   c) The exchange rate at the date the fair value was determined
   d) Any of these rates

4. Which of the following facts would not apply in determining a company's functional currency?

   a) The currency that influences the costs of the company
   b) The currency that is internationally accepted for trading
   c) The currency in which finance is generated
   d) The currency in which receipts from operating activities are retained

5. Where a company has a foreign operation that functions independently from the parent, the functional currency would be:

   a) the same as the parent
   b) the same as the presentation currency
   c) the currency most used internationally
   d) none of these

6. IAS 29 gives indications of a hyperinflationary economy. Which one of the following is not an indication?

   a) The holding of wealth in non-monetary assets
   b) Monetary amounts being expressed in a stable currency rather than the local currency
   c) Inflation is over 50% for at least three months
   d) Sales and purchases on credit are transacted at prices that adjust for the expected loss of purchasing power during the credit period

7. Which one of the following is not part of IFRS 8's definition of an operating segment?

   a) It engages in business activities from which it may earn revenues and incur expenses
   b) The operating results are regularly reviewed by the entity's chief operating decision maker to make decisions about resources to be allocated to the segment and to assess its performance
   c) It operates independently of the main company in conducting its operations
   d) Discrete financial information is available

8. Which of the following statements is incorrect under IFRS 8?

   a) If an entity changes the way it is structured internally so that its reportable segments change, the comparative information for earlier periods must be restated
   b) Disclosure is always required of the total assets of each reportable segment
   c) The measurement of the profit or loss to be disclosed for each reportable segment is defined in IFRS 8
   d) The identities of major customers need not be disclosed

9. Under IAS 29, which one of the following does not have to be restated on a measuring unit current at the year end?

   a) Non-monetary assets and liabilities
   b) Monetary assets and liabilities
   c) Items of income and expense

10. Which one of the following statements best describes currency conversion?

   a) The restatement of the value of one currency in another currency
   b) The spot exchange rate at the year end
   c) The identification of exchange differences
   d) The process of exchanging one currency for another

14

Evaluating IFRS Financial Statements

Learning Objectives

At the end of this chapter you should be able to:

☞ Describe the purpose of ratio analysis
☞ Explain the sources and types of data available for ratio analysis
☞ Calculate and interpret the main accounting ratios from a set of financial statements
☞ Calculate and interpret investment ratios
☞ Explain and calculate the main cash flow ratios.

14.1 Introduction

A ratio describes a quantitative relationship between 2 values (usually expressed as x:1 or x%). Ratio analysis is not only about calculating the ratios but mainly their analysis and their interpretations. A simple spreadsheet model will calculate as many ratios as you want, but it is only you who can conduct the analysis and interpretation. Experience will help you produce a more sophisticated analysis, but this chapter will provide you with all the tools and advice on how to calculate ratios and to analyse and interpret your findings.

In this chapter we discuss accounting ratios, investment ratios and cash flow ratios. There is some overlap between these three categories, but for the purposes of

323

this chapter, we regard accounting ratios as those that are constructed from the data contained in the Statement of Comprehensive Income, the Statement of Financial Position and the Notes to the Accounts. By investment ratios we mean those that are focused on the performance of shares and of the stock market. We have separated cash flow ratios into a separate category. It is really a part of accounting ratios but has some particular techniques and approaches of its own. An overview of ratio analysis is given in the following diagram:

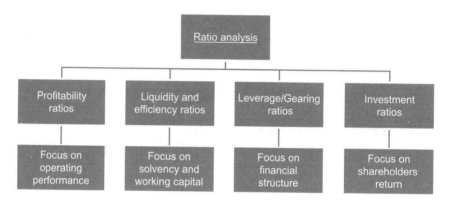

In conducting an analysis, it is essential that you refer to the earlier chapters and the effect of international accounting standards on the financial statements of companies. When discussing topics such as goodwill, intangible assets, impairment and leasing, we explained the impact the application of these standards could have on the individual entity's financial statements. The extent to which a company complies with the standards or adopts a particular method will influence your interpretation of the ratios you calculate.

Definition — ratio analysis

This is a technique for evaluating the financial performance and stability of an entity, with a view to making comparisons with previous periods, other entities and industry averages over a period of time.

Ratios are widely used by various groups and individuals — present and potential investors, managers, lenders, trade unions, suppliers and other trade creditors — but also by credit rating agencies, investment analysts and financial journalists. Whatever your future career, you will need the knowledge of ratio analysis that is explained in this chapter.

A few words of caution before we begin to explain the details. There are no set definitions of the various terms used in ratio analysis and there are different approaches to calculating them. There are also many different ratios that can be calculated. In this chapter we explain the main ratios and use the most common definitions of terms and methods of calculation. Where there are frequently used alternatives, we make reference to them in the text.

14.2 Establishing the Context

It is important that you do not rush into calculating and analysing ratios without an exploration of the context in which your study is taking place. Whether you are looking at the financial statements of one company or the share prices of several companies or the market index, you need to take a broader view. The main sources for your information will be:

- Daily newspapers, e.g., *Wall Street Journal, Financial Times,* for an overview and immediate information
- "Investment" magazines specifically related to the activities of the share markets
- General business magazines, e.g., *Forbes, Business Week*
- Newsletters issued by several government and industry bodies and departments
- Internet and various websites
- Companies, as they provide a substantial amount of information both in hard copy and on their websites.

From these sources you will be aiming to extract indicators of past performance, current events and predictions of future trends. The types of indicators you will find useful are:

Economic indicators

- Inflation
- Economic growth or decline
- Consumer confidence
- Commodity prices

Inflation indicators

- Retail price index or similar
- Bank or government inflation/economic reports
- Reports from industry
- Reports from private sector

Consumer confidence indicators

- Housing starts
- Mortgage applications

- Retail sales
- Industry reports
- Corporate reports

In addition to the above indicators, there is also data and information that influences change as much as it indicates change. The information not only captures what has happened but also sets off a series of other changes. As far as share prices and stock markets are concerned, the main influencers are:

- Company results
- Results of competitors
- Revisions in broker forecasts
- Opinion on market and industry
- Exchange rates
- Political upheavals
- Rumours
- Greed.

As well as indicators and influencers, there is also informed opinion, speculation and rumour. It is sometimes difficult to differentiate between good and poor information. Ratios are used by individuals and groups who are either hoping to make money or to ensure that they do not lose the money they have. They need information to make their decisions and sometimes speculation can be more exciting than good, sound evidence.

14.3 Accounting Ratios

Sometimes known as accounting ratios or fundamental analysis, there are three key points in the definition:

- The analysis is usually conducted on the financial statements of an organisation. These may be the annual or interim report, but can also be internal financial statements if they are available. Usually the internal documents will provide much more detail and therefore are much more useful.
- The analysis is conducted for a single entity or a number of entities.
- There must be comparative figures, otherwise the analysis will not be revealing. Ratio analysis helps in the comparison between different size organisations, specific organisations and the relevant industry ratios, and over different time periods.

Taking this last point, we will demonstrate with a simple example the conduct of an analysis.

Example

There are two companies and their revenue and gross profits for 2009 are:

	Company X	Company Y
	$000	$000
Sales	80	160
Gross profit	20	30

It is easy from this example to see which company makes the most gross profit. As Company Y is twice the size (as measured in sales) than X, we would expect it to earn more profit. But which company is the most profitable? To find this we can calculate the gross profit margin by expressing the gross profit as a percentage of sales:

$$\text{Gross profit margin} \qquad \underset{\text{Company X}}{\frac{20}{80} = 25\%} \qquad \underset{\text{Company Y}}{\frac{30}{160} = 18.75\%}$$

Company X is therefore more profitable, although Company Y is the larger. The question is the reason for Company X being more profitable, and we will explain the possible reasons in this chapter when we look at examples with more information.

Of course, we could extend our analysis by comparing the performance of these two companies against the average for the industry in which they are operating. We could also calculate the ratios for a number of previous years and ascertain whether the ratios for 2009 are part of a trend or are unusual in some way.

When you are interpreting ratios, you will find that they are related and the analysis of one ratio will help to explain another. We are now going to look in depth at the four sets of ratios:

- **Profitability ratios** — reveal a company's ability to generate profits.
- **Turnover ratios** — reveal the company's efficiency with regard to the use of its assets.
- **Liquidity and efficiency ratios** — reveal a company's ability to repay its obligations.
- **Gearing (leverage) ratios** — reveal how a company's financial structure influences its financial performance.

We will now complete an analysis on the first three categories of ratios and we will discuss gearing ratios at the end of this section. We are using the financial statements of two small companies that are not listed on a stock exchange and do not necessarily comply with international standards. We will assume that they both supply animal feedstuff and they have been in business for some years.

Taking this simple form of a company allows us to conduct an in-depth analysis. You would use exactly the same procedures for a large, listed company, but the volume of data and the variety of the transactions would be much greater.

M. Arnold
Income Statement to 31 December 2009

	$	$
Revenue		108,665
Cost of sales:		
Opening inventory	41,650	
Purchases	78,435	
	120,085	
less closing inventory	57,420	62,665
Gross profit		46,000
Operating expenses:		
Delivery costs	1,214	
Interest on loan	2,000	
Wages	16,400	
Office costs	3,962	
Bad debts	400	
Depreciation	1,000	24,976
Net profit		21,024

Balance Sheet as at 31 December 2009

	$	$	$
Current assets:			
Cash	654		
Accounts receivable	15,850		
Inventory	57,420		73,924
Non-current assets:			
Premises at cost		40,000	
Weighing machinery cost	10,000		
less depreciation	4,000	6,000	46,000
Total assets			119,924
Current liabilities			11,500
Long-term liabilities			40,000
Total liabilities			51,500
Owner's equity:			
Capital	47,400		
Profit for the year	21,024		68,424
Total liabilities and owner's equity			119,924

L. Porter
Income Statement to 31 December 2009

	$	$
Revenue		14,800
Cost of sales:		
Opening inventory	1,750	
Purchases	10,000	
	11,750	
less closing inventory	2,050	9,700
Gross profit		5,100
Less expenses:		
Rent of weighing machinery	300	
Miscellaneous operating costs	600	900
Net profit		4,200

Balance Sheet as at 31 December 2009

	$	$
Current assets:		
Bank	3,100	
Inventory	2,050	5,150
Non-current assets:		
Premises at cost		18,000
Total assets		23,150
Current liabilities		950
Owner's equity:		
Share capital	18,000	
Profit for the year	4,200	22,200
Total liabilities and owner's equity		23,150

Using the above data, we will calculate the following ratios.

Profitability ratios are used to assess the operating performance of a business. The main ratios are:

- Return on net assets or RONA (also known as return on capital employed)
- Net asset turnover (also known as capital turnover)
- Net profit margin (also known as return on sales or ROS)
- Gross profit margin.

As there are no standard definitions, we will use the following explanations of the terms. *Return* is profit before interest and tax (PBIT), which is shown as operating profit in some financial statements. It is also known as EBIT — earnings before interest and tax. *Net assets* is total assets – current liabilities.

Return on net assets measures the percentage return on the investment of funds in the business. It provides information on how effective the business is in generating revenue from resources and management's ability to control costs.

Net asset turnover measures the number of times the net assets have been used during the year to achieve the sales revenue.

Net profit margin is the profit before interest and tax expressed as a percentage of the sales figure. It shows the percentage profit a company makes on sales after deducting all expenses.

Gross profit margin, which we calculated in the simple example at the beginning, measures gross profit as a percentage of sales and is a good indicator of how successful a company is in its basic trading operations.

Liquidity and efficiency ratios are used to evaluate the solvency and financial stability of a business and assess how effectively it has managed its working capital (i.e., current assets – current liabilities).

> ### Definition — working capital
>
> The amount of funding required for the organisation's day-to-day operations. It is the total of the current assets (e.g., inventories, accounts receivable and cash) less current liabilities (e.g., accounts payable, bank overdrafts).

The main ratios are:

- Current test
- Acid test
- Inventory turnover
- Accounts receivable period
- Accounts payable period.

The current test shows the solvency of the company in the short-term by comparing current assets and current liabilities: usually expressed as x:1.

The *acid test* is a liquidity ratio that shows the relationship between liquid assets and current liabilities, and is usually expressed as x:1. It is regarded as a more stringent test than the Current Test in assessing the solvency of a business. Liquid assets are all current assets except stock (inventories), which take longer to convert into cash.

The *accounts receivable period* is an efficiency ratio that measures the average time trade debtors, usually customers, have taken to pay the business for goods and services over the year.

The *accounts payable period* shows how long the entity is taking to pay its own debts.

Let us start by calculating the ratios for both companies before we do the analysis and interpretation. Usually in ratio analysis a great degree of accuracy is not required and calculations to one decimal point will suffice. It is always helpful when preparing an analysis to do it in tabular form:

PROFITABILTY RATIOS		Arnold	Porter
Return on net assets (%)	$\dfrac{\text{EBIT}}{\text{Net assets}}$	$\dfrac{23024}{108424} = 21.2\%$	$\dfrac{4200}{22200} = 18.9\%$
Gross margin (%)	$\dfrac{\text{Gross profit}}{\text{Sales}}$	$\dfrac{46000}{108665} = 42.3\%$	$\dfrac{5100}{14800} = 34.5\%$
Return on sales (%)	$\dfrac{\text{EBIT}}{\text{Sales}}$	$\dfrac{23024}{108665} = 21.1\%$	$\dfrac{4200}{14800} = 28.4\%$
Net asset turnover	$\dfrac{\text{Sales}}{\text{Net assets}}$	$\dfrac{108665}{108424} = 1.0$ time	$\dfrac{14800}{22200} = 0.66$ time

LIQUIDITY RATIOS		Arnold	Porter
Current test	$\dfrac{\text{Current assets}}{\text{Current liabilities}}$	$\dfrac{73924}{11500} = 6.43{:}1$	$\dfrac{5150}{950} = 5.42{:}1$
Acid test (Quick ratio)	$\dfrac{\text{(Current assets } - \text{ inventories)}}{\text{Current liabilities}}$	$\dfrac{16504}{11500} = 1.44{:}1$	$\dfrac{3100}{950} = 3.26{:}1$

WORKING CAPITAL MANAGEMENT		Arnold	Porter
Collection period	$\dfrac{\text{Receivables} \times 365}{\text{Sales}}$	$\dfrac{15850}{108665} = 54$ days	
Payment period	$\dfrac{\text{Payables} \times 365}{\text{Purchases}}$	$\dfrac{11500}{78435} = 54$ days	$\dfrac{950}{10000} = 35$ days
Inventory turnover	$\dfrac{\text{Cost of sales}}{\text{Inventory}}$	$\dfrac{62665}{57420} = 1.09$	$\dfrac{9700}{2050} = 4.73$

Notes:

1. In calculating the operating profit for Arnold, we added back the interest as we wish to know the profit that has been earned on the capital invested by the owner and the long-term liabilities.

2. We have expressed the payment period and the collection period in number of days, although some prefer to express it as a percentage or a ratio.
3. For this exercise, we have taken only the closing inventory amounts to calculate inventory turnover. Some claim that by calculating the average inventory (opening inventory + closing inventory divided by 2), you obtain a more accurate reflection of performance.

If we were only interested in the return the owner is getting on the capital invested, we would have used the profit after interest.

Analysis and interpretation

It is evident from the financial statements that Arnold is the larger company, but that does not necessarily make it the best. We are interested in its financial performance and stability as reflected in comparing the two sets of ratios.

The first part of our analysis focuses on what some people refer to as "the big three". These are the profitability ratios and are shown in the following diagram:

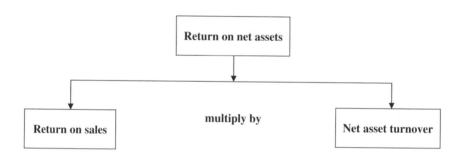

Return on net assets, sometimes referred to as return on capital employed, is also known as the "prime" ratio. It is the ratio that gives you the overview of the profitability performance. If we take Arnold's figure, we get a return of 21.2%. In other words, the money invested long-term in the business to acquire the net assets receives a return of 21.2%. Is that good or bad? One thing we can do is speculate what return Arnold could achieve if the same amount was invested in a bank — much lower than 21.2%, but such an investment would be safe, whereas the investment in Arnold's business has a degree of risk. The higher the level of risk, then the greater the return you would expect.

Porter is not doing quite so well as Arnold with a return on net assets of 18.9%. Porter wishes to improve this, so the company must look at the other two ratios. The return on sales is 28.4% and the net asset turnover is 0.66. Looking at the above diagram, you can see that if we multiply these two amounts together, the result is the prime ratio. So if Porter wishes to improve the prime ratio, the answer is in improving one of the other ratios.

Porter's return on sales is higher than Arnold's, so we need to suggest possible reasons for this. By comparing the financial statements you can see that Porter has fewer operating expenses, presumably because it is a smaller and less sophisticated business. For example, Arnold has deliveries, wages and office costs. Porter seems to operate its business with the minimum of costs. Also, Porter has no bad debts and as there is no accounts receivable on the balance sheet, we assume it is a cash-only business.

The return on net assets for Porter is much lower. Arnold "turned over" or used the net assets once in achieving its level of sales, but Porter only managed a miserable 0.66 times. To explain this, we need to look at the components of their net assets. The balance sheets reveal that the largest component is premises with Porter's being $18,000 against Arnold's $40,000.

If we look at the sales amounts on the income statements, Arnold has over seven times the sales of Porter, but the value of premises is only just over twice as much. Either Porter has premises that are too large for its needs or we need to look at the valuations. If both businesses are close, a quick visit would show whether Porter's premises is much larger and that would lead us to try to find a reason.

As far as the valuation of premises are concerned, we may be dealing with the deficiencies of historic cost or the revaluation method allowed in IAS 16 (see Chapter 4). If Arnold's premises were purchased many years ago, they will be shown at that figure. If Arnold purchased its premises recently, it would have paid current prices and the premises could be very similar. Of course, Porter may have revalued the premises using the alternative method allowed under IAS 16, although this is doubtful. Interestingly, neither company appears to depreciate its premises and this should be investigated.

From this initial analysis, it appears that Porter may have premises that are too large for its present needs or the valuations are not comparable. If it is a case of larger premises, Porter needs to increase its sales to improve the net asset turnover ratio. If the company could achieve the same ratio as Arnold, its return on net assets would be 28.4%, i.e., the return on sales multiplied by the net asset turnover ratio.

Our final analysis of profitability is the gross margin ratio. Arnold's ratio is much higher than Porter's, but the net profit ratio for Arnold is lower than Porter's. We need to find explanations for this. We have already offered the explanation because the expenses of Arnold are higher. If Arnold is going to offer delivery and credit to customers, it must be paid for in some way. Porter may therefore be competing more on price rather than services to customers. The other reasons may revolve around the selling price itself.

Arnold may be charging more for its goods. A quick telephone call to the two companies and a request for copies of their price lists would confirm if this is the case. It could also be that Arnold offers a wider range of products, some of high quality, and a higher price can be charged. Of course, the gross profit margin depends not just on the selling price but also the amount paid for the products. As a larger company, Arnold may be able to obtain a discount from its suppliers.

Finally, we will look at the management of the working capital. This is the difference between the total of current assets minus the current liabilities. It reflects how much investment a company has in its trading cycle.

It is always dangerous to say there is a ratio that is acceptable, but for the current test, usually a ratio between 1.6:1 to 2:1 is considered healthy. The reason for this is that at 1.6:1 it means that for every $1 of current liability, the company has $1.60 of current assets. In other words, if all the people that the company owes money to wanted to be paid tomorrow, the company should be able to manage to do so.

If we look at Porter and Arnold, they both have very high ratios with Arnold's being 6.43:1. Your reaction may be that this must be excellent because Arnold has such a large amount of current assets to cover the current liabilities. Unfortunately, a large ratio is not healthy but is a sign of financial mismanagement.

Arnold has $5.43 more in current assets than current liabilities. That excess amount has come from somewhere. Either the owners of the company have contributed as capital and they will expect to receive dividends. Alternatively, that difference is being funded by the loan that Arnold has of $40,000. If some of the loan was repaid, this would lessen the interest charges, thus improving the net profit. A high current ratio is a sign of financial mismanagement unless there are temporary conditions that would explain it.

The acid test has a similar objective as the current test, but inventories have been removed from the calculations. The reason for this is that if the company had to pay debts quickly, it needs cash and would not have time to sell its inventories to raise the cash.

Inventory turnover appears to be a problem for Arnold. In a year, it managed to sell its level of inventory just over once, whereas Porter sells its level of inventory 4.73 times. Imagine that you were selling cans of baked beans and on every can you make only 2 cents, and you sell five cans each day. One way to improve your daily profit would be to try to sell more cans, i.e., improve your inventory turnover.

A recommendation to Arnold would be to investigate the reason for this low turnover. One reason could be, as we said earlier, that Arnold carries a much wider range of products to provide service to the customers, but some of these products are slow-selling. The danger is that the products will decay or lose their value whilst in store.

The accounts receivable and payable are fairly self-explanatory. As Porter does not give credit, there is no accounts receivable ratio. As a rule of thumb, if a company normally gives one month's credit, then the usual accounts receivable ratio is 45 days. This is because customers pay in the month following the month they purchased the goods. Customers will have purchased throughout the month from day 1 to the last day, which gives the average of 15 days plus one month's credit period.

Arnold's accounts receivable ratio may be acceptable in that particular industry, and as the accounts payable ratio is also 54 days, this provides some reassurance.

Porter pays its suppliers much quicker, 35 days, and this may be evidence that Porter has not established itself as a financially stable and progressive business.

The above is only a brief analysis, and there are many other ratios that can be calculated and also questions asked just on the basis of the financial statements. The analysis and interpretation of the financial statements of a large company would be similar to our example but would take much longer. It would involve a close examination of the accounting policies of the company and a knowledge of accounting standards.

All international accounting standards are important, and in some industries and for certain transactions and events are critical for providing financial statements that can be analysed. Some examples of the types of topics you should investigate are:

1. IAS 16 and the use of the revaluation model and the depreciation methods used
2. IAS 17 and whether the company is identifying operating or financing leases
3. IAS 21 for those companies conducting transactions in foreign currencies or with foreign operations
4. IAS 36 and if there has been any impairment of assets
5. IAS 37 and whether provisions have been made and if there are disclosures on contingent liabilities
6. IAS 38 and the measurement and recognition of intangible assets
7. IFRS 3 and the treatment of goodwill in a business combination.

Financial instruments and the relevant standards are an analysis exercise by themselves. Do not, however, become confused by the complexity of the various standards; concentrate only on the calculation of the ratios. It is far better to understand the main accounting ratios well and to be able to analyse and interpret them.

14.4 The Process and Limitations of Ratio Analysis

In the course of your career, it is quite likely that you may be asked to conduct a ratio analysis. This could be for a department, the company itself, a competitor that you may try to acquire or even a complete industry. In this section we will provide a guide as to the steps you should take and also offer caution on the limitations of ratios.

We outline below a process for conducting an analysis that can be applied to most situations.

Accounting ratio analysis and interpretation

1. Acquire financial statements for several years, at least a minimum of three years although five years would be preferable. This should include annual and interim financial statements. If you are able to obtain any internal financial documents, it would be helpful.
2. Take a quick scan of all the documents to see if there have been any significant changes over a period of time. Putting the key figures for the main figures such as

revenue and earnings on a spreadsheet helps the comparison. It is also useful to include aggregations such as total assets, net current assets and working capital.

3. If you have the published documents, you must review the notes. You are looking for any note that calls your attention to unusual events, e.g., after the financial period, provisions, contingent liabilities, impairments.

4. Examine the Balance Sheet, Income Statement and Cash Flow Statement without calculating ratios. Your objective is to detect any items that look particularly large or unusual.

5. Identify and calculate the ratios that you consider to be the most important for your task and relevant to the company you are investigating.

6. If possible, obtain the ratios for a competitor and the industry averages. These are usually available in most libraries or on the Internet. Ensure that the definition of terms and method of calculation is comparable to your own.

7. Analyse and interpret the ratios using all the information you have collected. The process of interpretation may reveal additional information you require to complete your task.

8. If the management of the company has discussed their financial results and in an annual report they will have done so, compare it to your own interpretation. If there are differences, investigate them.

Put in wider context

9. Review the company's products and services and their long-term prospects.
10. Assess the strengths and weaknesses of senior managers of the company.
11. Evaluate the company's markets by product and region.
12. Assess the economies and political stability of the regions where the company operates.
13. Compare your findings with competitors.
14. Revisit your ratio analysis and interpretation and reevaluate your findings within the wider context.
15. Write your report, remembering to define the terms you have used and to present the calculations in a tabular format.

Despite the great value of ratio analysis properly conducted, there are deficiencies. Some of these we have already commented on, but we repeat them here for the benefit of completeness:

-   There are no agreed definitions of terms, so ratios based on different definitions cannot be compared. You must ensure that your comparisons with data obtained from other sources are valid.
-   Ratio analysis is only useful if comparisons are made and the choice of analysis depends on the user and the availability of data.
    -   If data is not disclosed, less precise alternatives will have to be used (but look first in the Notes to the Accounts).

— Comparative data may not be available for trend analysis (e.g., a new business has no track record) or for inter-company comparison (e.g., if company operates in a niche market or if there are no industry benchmarks).

• Figures in financial statements can be misleading.

— If there is high inflation or window dressing, unscrupulous manipulation or an unusual accounting treatment has been used. Window dressing is where companies present results in such a way that is favourable to the company but could mislead the unwary user.

• Financial statements do not take account of non-financial factors, such as:

— Are there sound plans for the future? Does the company have a good reputation, strong customer base, reliable suppliers, loyal employees? Does it have obsolete assets, strong competitors, poor industrial relations or operate in a high-risk industrial sector?

14.5 Types of Analysis

So far we have considered accounting ratios and emphasised the comparison with other companies and industry averages. There are other methods for analysing and presenting ratios and we will consider them in this chapter. The main ones used are:

• Trend analysis
• Common size statement analysis
• Vertical analysis
• Horizontal analysis.

Year-to-year change and trend analysis

With this technique, we are looking at data either with a simple comparison with the previous period or over an extended period of time. This could be years, months, weeks or even hours and minutes. The change could be for one item only or it could be for several items. In the table below, we are looking at the sales figure for one company. The comparison is from the previous year to the current year with the change being shown in dollars and percentages:

Year-to-year change

	Current year	Previous year	$ Change	% Change
Revenue	$70,150	$59,287	+$10,863	+18.3%

In a trend analysis, it is often more informative to take two or three key items and compare them over several years to reveal the changes in their relationship. For example, one could take the revenue each year and compare it to the profit before interest and tax as in the following example:

Comparison PBIT to revenue for 8 years ($000s)

	2002	2003	2004	2005	2006	2007	2008	2009
Revenue	96	102	112	105	108	110	115	118
Gross profit	56	60	72	65	70	65	62	55

The above figures demonstrate the trend, but it is often far more helpful for the user to show the data in the form of a chart. Below, we have used a two-line graph. At this stage it is not titled and there is no legend, but the message is very clear. Although the gross profit was complementary to the revenue for the first few years, in recent years the gross profit has been declining although the revenue has been increasing.

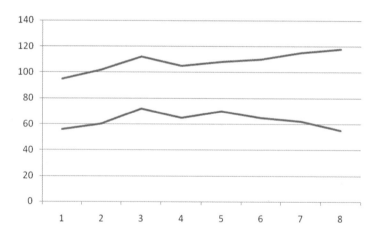

Same size and vertical analysis

The following example is sometimes referred to as a same size analysis or a vertical analysis. Revenue is considered as 100% and all the costs and the profit are expressed as a percentage of that amount. We could express all the separate assets on the Statement of Financial Position as a percentage of the total assets or the separate liability accounts as a percentage of total liabilities. These presentations and analyses of data are much more helpful if comparative figures are given for the previous financial period, if they are available.

	Income Statement for 2009	
	$	%
Revenue	500	100
Cost of sales	375	75
Salaries	30	6
Rent	10	2
Admin.	9	1.8
Depreciation	20	4
Interest	5	1
PBT	51	10.2

This has been a brief introduction to the different forms of analysis and presentation you can make. These approaches are often best presented as a chart to assist the user in understanding the relationship of the data.

14.6 Leverage or Gearing Ratios

The ratio that looks at the financial structure of the business is known as the leverage ratio in some countries and as the gearing ratio in others: they are exactly the same ratio. As with other ratios, however, there can be some differences in the calculation of the ratio.

Businesses fund their activities with the capital invested by the owners plus any retained earnings, which is known as equity in incorporated entities. They may also have to borrow funds from banks and other financial institutions and these will form the long-term liabilities, frequently referred to as debt. As with all ratios, definitions of these terms vary, but equity is normally the risk capital and debt is the total of all liabilities over 12 months old. If you consider all the elements on the Statement of Financial Position, then you will see that equity + debt is equal to the net current assets also known as capital employed.

Leverage or gearing refers to the relative proportions of equity and debt that a company has in its financial structure. A highly leveraged company is one that has a high proportion of debt in relation to equity. A company that has a low proportion of debt in relation to equity is a low leveraged company. The importance of leverage is the potential risks or rewards shareholders may enjoy in different economic conditions.

The different impact of high and low leveraged conditions is best explained by an example. To do this we will use two ratios: one is return on net assets and the other is return on equity. Return on net assets, or capital employed, we have already discussed in this chapter. This is the amount of earnings before interest and tax expressed as a percentage of the net assets. With the return on equity ratio, we are going to define return as the earnings after interest but before tax. In other words, we are calculating what the shareholders receive on their investment, excluding long-term liabilities from our consideration. The formula is:

$$\frac{\text{Earnings after interest but before tax}}{\text{Equity}} \times 100.$$

Example

Soprano Inc. is a low leveraged company and Alto Inc. is a highly leveraged company. For 2009 they both have the same amount of earnings before interest and tax. The details for the two companies are as follows:

	Soprano Inc.	*Alto Inc.*
Equity	$400,000	$200,000
Debt	$200,000	$400,000
Earnings before interest and tax	$80,000	$80,000
Interest charge on debt at 10%	$20,000	$40,000
Earnings after interest but before tax	$60,000	$40,000

We can now analyse these two sets of figures by calculating the Return (Earnings before interest and tax) on Net Assets (Debt + Equity) and the Return (Earnings after interest but before tax) on Equity:

	Soprano Inc.	*Alto Inc.*
Return on net assets	13.3%	13.3%
Return on equity	15.0%	20.0%

Although the two companies have the same profit before interest and tax, the return that the shareholders receive is very different because of the amount of debt that Alto has. This means that the profit after interest is $60,000 for Soprano but only $40,000 for Alto. However, Soprano has double the amount of equity than Alto.

From this example you can see that when companies are making healthy profits, the shareholders in the highly leveraged company will get a better return. This is because once the interest is paid, the profit after interest relates to the much smaller amount of equity.

If the economy were to change and the amount of earnings before interest and tax was only $40,000, we would get very different results:

	Soprano Inc.	*Alto Inc.*
Equity	$400,000	$200,000
Debt	$200,000	$400,000
Earnings before interest and tax	$40,000	$40,000
Interest charge on debt at 10%	$20,000	$40,000
Earnings after interest but before tax	$20,000	$0
Return on net assets	6.7%	6.7%
Return on equity	5%	0%

The shareholders in Soprano, the low leveraged company, may be disappointed that the return has dropped from 15% to 5%. The shareholders in the highly leveraged company, Alto, will be even more disappointed as there is no profit for them. The high interest charge has completely obliterated the profit, so there is zero return.

In the next section on investment ratios, you will see that this impact of the structure of the business is reflected in the ratio "interest cover".

14.7 Investment Ratios

Shareholders may conduct a fundamental analysis of the financial statements of a company, but they are likely to be aware of their deficiencies. They will realise that the financial statements do not reveal the value of a company. The use of historic cost does not result in a balance sheet that shows investors what a company is worth.

One way for investors to find out what the market seems to consider a company is worth is to calculate the market capitalisation. The formula is:

Current share price × Number of ordinary shares in issue.

You will realise that as share prices fluctuate, even on a daily basis, the "value" of the company is always changing. Remember that as we discuss the ratios used by investors, share prices go down as well as up.

Interest cover

One of the problems of leverage ratios is that they can be defined in several ways. An alternative ratio, interest cover, reveals the effect of leverage but avoids the definitional problems. The ratio is calculated by using the following formula:

$$\frac{\text{Earnings before interest and tax}}{\text{Interest charge}}.$$

What this ratio reveals is the number of times the interest charge could be paid out of the current earnings and we usually refer to the ratio as the number of times. If the interest charge can be paid, i.e., is covered, several times from the earnings, shareholders can have some confidence that they will receive some return even when the economy is bad. The low leveraged company has less risk in an economic downturn.

With a highly leveraged company in an economic downturn, the number of times that earnings can cover interest charges will be very few. In the worst scenario, there is insufficient earnings to cover interest and there is the danger that the company will go into bankruptcy.

The following table shows interest cover for both companies in a good economic situation and when the economy is poor:

	Soprano		Alto	
	Calculation	Interest cover	Calculation	Interest cover
Good economy	$80,000 / $20,000	4 times	$80,000 / $40,000	2 times
Poor economy	$40,000 / $20,000	2 times	$40,000 / $40,000	1 time

When the economy is good, you can see that there is a danger in investing in a highly leveraged company. The interest cover of Alto is only twice compared to the four times of Soprano. When the economy is poor, then Alto can only cover the interest charge once and there is no profit left for the shareholders.

Earnings per share

We have already discussed earnings per share in Chapter 12 but we will refresh your memory of the main points in this chapter. As a shareholder in a company, you will be interested in the amount of dividend you receive. A company may pay out part of the earnings in dividends but retain some of the earnings in the company to fund growth. Although the retained earnings are kept in the company, they belong to the shareholders and are shown under the heading of Equity.

A shareholder can identify the total amount of earnings for the period but this is to be shared amongst all shareholders. The individual is interested in the amount that his or her own shares have earned.

IAS 33 Earnings per Share requires companies to calculate and to disclose the basic EPS on the face of their Income Statement. The information that a company must provide is:

- details of basic and diluted EPS on the face of the Income Statement;
- the amounts used as the profit or loss for ordinary shareholders in calculating basic and diluted EPS;
- the weighted average number of ordinary shares used in calculating basic and diluted EPS;
- a description of those ordinary share transactions or potential ordinary share transactions that occur after the balance sheet date and would have had a significant effect on the EPS.

The basic EPS is calculated by dividing the profit or loss attributable to ordinary equity holders of the parent entity (the numerator) by the weighted average number of ordinary shares outstanding (the denominator) during the period. This is all ordinary shares in issue during the year. If a company has not issued further shares during the year, the calculation is shown in the example below:

Example of basic EPS calculation

Profit for year ended 31 December 2010: $3,500,000
Weighted average number of shares in issue: 25,000,000

$$\text{Basic EPS} = \frac{\$3,500,000}{25,000,000} = 14 \text{ cents.}$$

As we explained in Chapter 12, you may have to make some adjustments to allow for new shares issued for cash during the year, bonus issues and rights issues to arrive at the basic EPS. The other disclosure is the diluted EPS. The diluted EPS is a warning to existing shareholders that there is the risk that more ordinary shares will be in issue in the future.

Dilution arises where some individuals have the right to receive ordinary shares in the future in exchange for another type of investment. For example, they may have preference shares or convertible debt they can convert into ordinary shares in the future. If they choose to do this, there will be more ordinary shares in issue, so the EPS will decline.

The number of ordinary shares is the weighted average number of ordinary shares outstanding, as calculated for basic earnings per share, plus the weighted average number of ordinary shares that would be issued on the conversion of all potential dilutive ordinary shares into ordinary shares. The calculations are:

- Start with the basic EPS.
- Increase the net profit by the amount of financing costs the company will save by not having convertible instruments in issue.

- To the weighted average number of shares, add the number of shares that would be issued if the convertible instruments were converted. Assume that conversion takes place at the beginning of the period.

Price/earnings ratio (P/E ratio)

Having calculated the earnings per share, we can use that figure to calculate another ratio which is of interest to investors. The P/E ratio reflects the stock market's opinion on the possible future earnings of the company. In the simplest terms, the question being answered is how much is it worthwhile paying for that share now based on the current level of earnings? The formula is:

$$\frac{\text{Current price of one share in the market.}}{\text{Earnings per share}}$$

We can take the calculation of the basic EPS in the previous example which was 14 cents. We will call the company Bright Futures plc and imagine that the current market price is $2.10. If we apply the above formula, the P/E ratio is:

$$\frac{\$2.10}{\$0.14} = 15.$$

Sometimes the answer is referred to in years, so in the above example the P/E ratio is 15 years. This means that at the current level of earnings per share, it would take 15 years before you managed to get back the $2.10 you have to pay for it currently.

As with most ratios, one figure is neither good nor bad and you need a comparison. Let us imagine that there is a competitor and at the current market price the P/E ratio would be 8 years. Although you may not find it immediately obvious, the best share to purchase would be the one in Bright Futures plc with the higher P/E ratio of 15 years.

Most students think that it would be preferable to get your investment back sooner, i.e., in 8 years in this case. But in pricing the share based on the current EPS and arriving at a P/E ratio of 15 years, the market is predicting that the company will increase its earnings in the future. So the higher the P/E ratio, the better, as it reflects the stock market's confidence in the company's financial prospects. The market is therefore willing to pay more for the share than the current level of earnings would justify.

If you believed that Bright Futures plc would not improve its earnings in the future and that the P/E ratio of its competitors is correct at 8 years, you can calculate how much you would be willing to pay for Bright Futures' shares. With an EPS of 14 cents per share and your predicted P/E of 8 years, you would be willing to pay $1.12.

Dividend per share

As mentioned earlier in this section, a successful company will be paying dividends to its shareholders. As we calculated earnings per share using the total earnings and dividing by the shares in issue, we can do the same calculation to arrive at dividend per share. We can calculate both the dividend net, which is the amount of dividend per share for the financial year, and also the dividend yield. This latter ratio measures the dividend yielded on a share in relation to the current market price. The calculation of these two ratios is shown in the following example:

Example of dividend per share

Blaze Company has 2,500 shares in issue and for 2009 it declares dividends of $500. Its current share price is $4.00 per share.

$$\text{Dividend net} = \frac{\text{Total dividends}}{\text{Number of ordinary shares}} = \frac{\$500}{2500} = 20 \text{ cents per share.}$$

So for each share they own, the shareholders are receiving a dividend of 20 cents per share. Once again, comparison with other companies or previous years will reveal whether this level of dividend is acceptable. However, the shareholder may have purchased the share several years ago at a much lower amount than the current market price. The dividend yield ratio reflects the dividend as a return on the current price of the share. The formula is:

$$\frac{\text{Dividend net}}{\text{Current share price}} \times 100 = 5\%.$$

The investor has the choice of retaining the share and receiving a return of 5% or selling the share and reinvesting the proceeds. If the investor believes that a higher return than 5% can be obtained and the P/E ratio does not indicate that the stock market believes that earnings will increase in future years, the investor may decide to place his money elsewhere.

14.8 Cash Flow Ratios

One of the problems of ratios calculated using the Statement of Income and the Statement of Financial Position is that they suffer from the same defect as the financial statements on which they are based. We have discussed above the issues surrounding historical accounting, the different treatment of some items, and the alternatives permitted by some standards.

The calculation of ratios using amounts taken from the Statement of Cash Flows attempts to remove some of the defects of the other financial statements. If you refer back to earlier chapters, you will see that it is possible for a company to make a profit but have a cash deficit. It is usual that for a financial period, a company will have a different profit figure from the cash figure because of the application of the accruals concept.

Important and valuable as the profit or earnings figure is, in the long run a company must generate positive cash flows. If a company becomes bankrupt, it is because it does not have sufficient cash. We will explain some of the main ratios and how they are calculated.

Cash flow from operations to current liabilities

The purpose of this ratio is to assess how much cash is available to pay the current liabilities. The net cash flow from operations is taken from the Statement of Cash Flows and the current liabilities from the Balance Sheet. It is preferable, where possible, to calculate the average liabilities by adding the figure from last year's balance sheet to this year and dividing by two. The formula is:

$$\frac{\text{Net cash flow from operating activities}}{\text{Average current liabilities}} \times 100.$$

Cash recovery rate

This ratio is used to assess the amount of cash generated by assets. A company invests in the assets and, in the long-term, those assets must generate more cash than they cost. The quicker the company can recover the cash that they invested in the assets, the lower the amount of risk. The cash flow figure is taken from that statement. Some people take the total assets and others only the non-current assets from the balance sheet. The formula is:

$$\frac{\text{Net cash flow from operations}}{\text{Average total assets}} \times 100.$$

Cash flow per share

In the previous section we calculated the earnings per share. The intention of this ratio is similar but it tries to ascertain the amount of cash each share earns. Some users will take the earnings before interest, tax, depreciation and amortisation (EBITDA) as the "Cash flow" amount. Others prefer to take the net cash flow from operating activities as shown on the Cash Flow Statement, but may adjust it by adding any cash received from the disposal of assets. The formula is:

$$\frac{\text{Cash flow}}{\text{Weighted number of ordinary shares in issue}}.$$

There are other cash flow ratios and many of them attempt to predict the future of a company. Cash generated by a company in successive financial periods is likely to be less variable than the profit figure. This consistency in the cash figures makes it easier to extrapolate to future periods. However, with all ratios, it is not their calculation that is important but their analysis and interpretation. In this chapter we have given you guidance on the procedures you should follow and the various sources of information.

14.9 Chapter Summary

☞ Ratio analysis is a technique for evaluating the financial performance and stability of an entity, with a view to making comparisons with previous periods, other entities and industry averages over a period of time.

☞ Accounting ratios are calculated from the financial statements to assess the performance of an entity, and investment ratios are used to assess the performance of the shares of that company.

☞ It is important that you understand the context in which a company is operating before you attempt to analyse and interpret ratios.

☞ Accounting ratios are used to assess the profitability, liquidity and working capital of a company.

☞ The leverage or gearing ratio of a company is used to examine the impact of the financial structure of a company and the potential impact on earnings.

☞ Investment ratios are mainly constructed from company information and the current share price.

☞ Cash flow ratios have been developed only in recent years and attempt to reduce the deficiencies of the main financial statements that are based on the accruals concept.

Progress Test

1. Net assets is calculated by:

   a) adding non-current assets and current assets
   b) deducting current liabilities from non-current assets
   c) adding non-current assets and current assets and deducting current liabilities
   d) adding non-current assets and current assets and deducting long-term liabilities

2. A company has accounts receivable of $40,000, cash of $12,000, inventory of $26,000, accounts payable of $14,000 and a bank overdraft of $12,000. The current test is:

   a) 2:1
   b) 3:1

c) 3.7:1
d) 2.86:1

3. A company has revenue of $160,000, purchases of $120,000 and a gross profit of $40,000. The gross profit mark-up is:

a) 33.3%
b) 25%
c) 18%
d) 20%

4. To calculate the return on net assets, you would:

a) divide earnings before interest and tax by the total assets
b) divide earnings after interest and tax by the total assets
c) divide earnings before interest and tax by the net assets
d) divide earnings after interest and tax by the net assets

5. The price/earnings ratio is calculated by:

a) dividing the share price of one share by the total earnings before interest
b) multiplying the share price of one share by the total earnings before interest
c) adding the share price of one share to the earnings per share
d) dividing the share price of one share by the earnings per share

6. A company has accounts receivable of $40,000, cash of $12,000, inventory of $26,000, accounts payable of $14,000 and a bank overdraft of $12,000. The acid test is:

a) 2:1
b) 3.7:1
c) 2.86:1
d) 2.5:1

7. The dividend yield ratio shows:

a) the return in dividend per share based on the current price per share
b) the return in dividend per share based on the price per share last year
c) the return in dividend per share based on the predicted future price per share
d) the return in predicted dividend per share based on the predicted future price per share

8. Shareholders in a highly leveraged company get a poor return when:

    a) the economy is very buoyant
    b) the economy is depressed
    c) all the loans are held by banks
    d) they never receive a poor return

9. Working capital is calculated by:

    a) adding current assets and current liabilities
    b) adding total assets and current liabilities
    c) deducting current liabilities from current assets
    d) deducting current assets from current liabilities

10. The leverage ratio compares the relative proportions of:

    a) total assets to current assets
    b) equity to total assets
    c) equity to debt
    d) debt to total assets

Appendix A

Double-Entry Bookkeeping

Introduction

Double-entry bookkeeping is that part of the accounting process concerned with record-keeping. It is an essential part of the process because it is from the records that you generate your financial statements. It tends to be a somewhat tedious subject, but if you want to be a qualified accountant you need to be good at it. Other students can please themselves, although some enjoy it because it is extremely logical, once you know the basic rules.

Double-entry bookkeeping has been in existence for about 500 years and this has proved that it is useful and it works. Originally, all accounting records were kept by hand, usually in big books called ledgers. Nowadays, even small businesses use standard accounting software or spreadsheets, and only a very small minority keep their records manually. Large organisations carry out thousands of transactions every day and need sophisticated, tailor-made computerised accounting systems.

Computerised systems manage the system of record-keeping very well and have the added advantages of being able to integrate several operations and produce more information much more rapidly than a manual system. However, the basic procedures of double-entry bookkeeping are more easily explained as if it is still a manual system and we still write the accounting entries into the ledgers.

In this appendix we will outline the main points of the manual system and the rules of double-entry bookkeeping. There are:

- Source documents
- The concepts of double-entry bookkeeping
- Recording assets and liabilities
- Recording revenue and expenses
- Drawing up a Trial Balance.

Source Documents

This is the start of the accounting system and it is from the source documents that we will record the transactions undertaken by the business. The main documents are:

- those documents concerned with the sale of goods such as orders, delivery notes, invoices sent to customers and credit notes issued for goods returned by customers;
- those documents concerned with the purchase of goods such as purchase orders, invoices received from suppliers and credit notes received for goods returned to suppliers;
- those documents concerned with the overall management of the business such as payroll records, stock records, banking records.

If you have not worked in a business environment, you would be amazed at the multitude of documents that are involved with every transaction. For example, if the company wishes to purchase some materials, the purchasing department will submit a purchase order to the supplier. When the supplier sends the materials, the warehouse will issue a Goods Received Note as evidence that the materials have been received. The supplier will send an invoice which has to be checked with the purchase order and the Goods Received Note as evidence that these were the materials ordered and that they were received. The rest of the procedure entails paying the invoice and ensuring that this is entered correctly into your banking records.

All of these source documents relating to the transactions that the business enters into have to be recorded in a systematic manner. This is where double-entry bookkeeping is applied.

The Concepts of Double-Entry Bookkeeping

Definition — double-entry bookkeeping

The method of recording the transactions of a business so that every transaction has a dual aspect and has to be recorded in two separate accounts.

This recording of every transaction twice is linked to the accounting equation which we encountered in Chapter 4. It is:

$$\text{Assets} = \text{Capital} + \text{Liabilities}.$$

You know from your earlier studies that the accounting equation always balances. If you are unsure about this, refer back to the example of Will Games in Chapter 4. The underlying reason it balances is because of the dual nature of transactions. We can explain this by taking the accounting equation and adding some figures.

Imagine that a new business is started by the owner investing $10,000. If you think of the accounting equation, then the Capital will have increased by $10,000 and the assets, most likely cash, by $10,000. With the cash, the business purchases equipment for $3,000. This means that our asset of cash will only be $7,000 but we have the asset of the machine. The accounting equation therefore looks like this:

	Assets	**=**	**Capital**	**+**	**Liabilities**
Machine	$3,000		$10,000		
Cash	$7,000				

We know from Chapter 4 that the balance sheet always balances and that is because of the dual nature of transactions. However, it is obvious that we cannot draw up a balance sheet every time we conduct a transaction and we therefore use double-entry bookkeeping.

Before we look at the actual recording of transactions, it will be useful to explain some of the terms used. Imagine that you have a piece of paper and you draw a vertical line from top to bottom. The half of the page on the left-hand side we will call the debit side. The half of the page on the right-hand side we will call the credit side. The piece of paper we will call an account.

The important things to remember are:

- Debit always means the left-hand side of the page. If we say that we need to debit an account, we mean that we need to put an entry on the left-hand side of the page. If we say that something is a debit entry, we mean that it is on the left-hand side of the page.
- Credit always means the right-hand side of the page. If we say that we need to credit an account, we mean that we need to put an entry on the right-hand side of the page. If we say that something is a credit entry, we mean that it is on the right-hand side of the page.

Having explained the terms, we can now look more closely at our piece of paper that we call an account. It will need a heading and for every item that we transact in, we need a new account. We are also going to record information on our account so we will need some columns.

A basic account can be drawn up as follows:

Name of the account

Date	Details of transaction	Amount	Date	Details of transaction	Amount

Going back to our example of the person investing $10,000 into a new company, we will need two accounts as follows:

Capital account

		$			$
			1 Jan	To Cash	10,000

Cash account

		$			$
1 Jan	From Capital	10,000			

If the owner decided to put in another $5,000 of capital on 2 January, then we would credit a further $5,000 in the Capital account and debit $5,000 in the Cash account. This means that the right-hand side of the Capital account balances with the left-hand side of the Cash account. In other words, the debits equal the credits.

Obviously, for this to work we need to know which entries go on the left-hand side (debit) of the account and which ones go on the right-hand side (credit).

Recording Assets and Liabilities

The rules for recording transactions concerning assets and liabilities are as follows:

- To show an increase in an asset account, debit the account.
- To show a decrease in an asset account, credit the account.
- To show an increase in a capital or liability account, credit the account.
- To show a decrease in a capital or liability account, debit the account.

To illustrate these rules, we will continue with the example we started above and add some more transactions:

> January 2 — a friend lends $5,000 to the business.
> January 2 — the business pays $3,000 for machinery.
> January 3 — the business pays $2,500 for materials for resale.
> January 3 — the business repays $2,500 of the loan.

The accounts will look as follows when we apply our rules for assets and liabilities:

Capital account

		$			$
			1 Jan	Cash	10,000

Cash account

		$			$
1 Jan	Capital	10,000	2 Jan	Machinery account	3,000
2 Jan	Loan account	5,000	3 Jan	Purchases	2,500
			3 Jan	Loan account	2,500

Loan account

		$			$
3 Jan	Cash account	2,500	2 Jan	Cash account	5,000

Machinery account

		$		$
2 Jan	Cash account	3,000		

Purchases account

		$		$
3 Jan	Cash account	2,500		

The above example can be continued until we have hundreds, if not thousands, of entries. With asset and liability accounts, it will always be the same system:

Asset account

Increase	Decrease

Liability account

Decrease	Increase

Recording Revenue and Expenses

The double-entry bookkeeping rules for recording transactions involving revenues and expenses are as follows:

- To show an increase in an expense account, debit the account.
- To show a decrease in an expense account, credit the account.
- To show an increase in a revenue account, credit the account.
- To show a decrease in a revenue account, debit the account.

As required in double-entry bookkeeping, every transaction will involve making a credit entry to one account and a debit entry to another account. An increase in a revenue account occurs when the company makes a sale which is a credit to the revenue account. An increase in an expense account occurs when a company incurs expenses.

We will take the Cash account from above and open a revenue account and an expense account for the two following entries:

January 4 — the company sells materials for $3,000 cash.
January 4 — rent is paid of $1,000.

Cash account

		$			$
1 Jan	Capital	10,000	2 Jan	Machinery account	3,000
2 Jan	Loan account	5,000	3 Jan	Purchases	2,500
4 Jan	Revenue account	3,000	3 Jan	Loan account	2,500
			4 Jan	Rent account	1,000

Revenue account

		$			$
			4 Jan	Cash account	3,000

Rent account

		$			$
4 Jan	Cash account	1,000			

Purchases, Sales and Inventory

Purchases are recorded as a debit entry in the Purchases account and a credit entry to the Cash account. When the business sells the goods, they are not shown as a credit entry in the Purchases account for two reasons. First, they will not be sold at the price for which they were purchased, as the business adds a mark-up in order to make a profit. The second reason is that at the end of a financial period, it is likely there will be some unsold goods remaining, i.e., closing inventory.

As this is a new business, we will not use an Inventory account until the end of the financial period. Instead, the purchases and sales of goods have been recorded in separate accounts, named the *Purchases account* and the *Sales account*, respectively.

If you refer back to Chapter 3 you will see that our cost of sales calculation is:

Sales		$xxx
Purchases	$xxx	
Less closing inventory	$xxx	$xxx
Gross profit		

To account for the closing inventory properly, the business must carry out a physical count and a valuation at the end of the financial period. We discussed the valuation of closing inventory and the requirements of IAS 2 in Chapter 3.

Some businesses use a manual count of closing inventory; others operate a computerised control system which allows up-to-date inventory figures to be read off at any time. If there is a considerable amount of inventory, it is normal to only count a part of it as evidence that the records are accurate.

We will come back to our inventory figure at the year end when we discuss the Trial Balance later in this appendix. You will appreciate that inventory is an asset and if we have some remaining at the year end, there must be a debit to the Inventory account.

Credit Transactions

All the transactions in the examples we have used so far have been for cash. If there are credit transactions, accounts must be opened in the name of the customer or the supplier. If a customer owes us money this is an asset account (accounts receivable), and if we owe a supplier money this will be a liability account (accounts payable).

At the end of the financial period, all the accounts of those customers still owing us money will be aggregated into one Accounts Receivable account. Similarly, all the accounts of the individual suppliers to which the business still owes money will be aggregated into one Accounts Payable account.

We will use the Purchases account and the Revenue account above to illustrate credit transactions, but credit transactions can apply to many transactions such as the acquisition of machinery. In our example, for simplicity, we will use accounts for Accounts Receivable and Accounts Payable and not open accounts in the name of individuals. The transactions are:

> January 5 — the business buys $4,000 of materials on credit.
> January 5 — the business sells $6,000 of materials on credit.

The entries are (remember a debit and credit for each transaction) as follows:

Revenue account

		$			$
			4 Jan	Cash account	3,000
			5 Jan	Accounts receivable	6,000

Purchases account

		$		$
3 Jan	Cash account	2,500		
5 Jan	Accounts payable	4,000		

Accounts receivable account

		$		$
5 Jan	Revenue account	6,000		

Accounts payable account

		$			$
			5 Jan	Purchases	4,000

In the next section we are going to explain how accounts are "balanced" or "closed". Before we end this section we will summarise the rules on double entry:

To show an increase in an account

Debit	Credit
Purchases	Revenue (Sales)
Assets	Liabilities
Expenses	Capital

To show a decrease in an account, the above columns are reversed.

Balancing Accounts

As you can imagine, with many transactions, an account comes to be very long. Periodically, and at least at the end of a financial period, a company closes or balances its accounts. The rules for this are straightforward and we will illustrate them by using some of the accounts above. The date we are closing the accounts is 6 January.

1. If the account contains entries on each side which are equal to one another, they can be double-underlined to close the account for that financial period. This means that there is no outstanding balance on this account at the end of the period.
2. If the account contains only one entry, insert the balancing figure on the opposite side and carry this down to the same side as the original entry to start the next period. The term "carried down" is often abbreviated to c/d; "brought down" is abbreviated to b/d. We will use the Accounts Receivable to show this transaction:

Accounts receivable account

		$			$
5 Jan	Revenue account	6,000	6 Jan Balance c/d		6,000
7 Jan	Balance b/d	6,000			

3. If the account contains a number of entries, add up both sides. If both sides are the same, insert the totals and double-underline them. This means that there is no outstanding balance on this account. This is the same action as number 1.
4. If both sides do not agree, first insert the balancing figure on the side with the lower amount and then insert the totals, which should now be equal, and double-underline them. Complete the entry by carrying down the balancing figure on the opposite side as the opening balance for the new financial period. We will use the Cash account to illustrate this action:

Cash account

		$			$
1 Jan	Capital	10,000	2 Jan	Machinery account	3,000
2 Jan	Loan account	5,000	3 Jan	Purchases	2,500
4 Jan	Revenue account	3,000	3 Jan	Loan account	2,500
			4 Jan	Rent account	1,000
			6 Jan	Balance c/d	9,000
		18,000			18,000
7 Jan	Balance b/d	9,000			

You will have realised that for every debit, we are making a credit and vice versa. Also, as long as we have been careful with our work, the list of debit balances and credit balances will equal. This process of adding and comparing the two lists of account balances is known as preparing a Trial Balance.

The Trial Balance

A trial balance is a list of all the balances on the accounts of an organisation with debit balances in one column and credit balances in another. If the double-entry book-keeping has been done properly, the two totals should agree. We have calculated the balances on the above accounts and drawn up the trial balance:

Trial Balance as at 7 January

	Debit $	Credit $
Capital		10,000
Revenue		9,000
Purchases	6,500	
Accounts receivable	6,000	
Accounts payable		4,000
Rent	1,000	
Loan		2,500
Machinery	3,000	
Cash	9,000	
	25,500	25,500

Looking at the two columns, you will see that the debit column is a list of all the expenses (for example, purchases) which will appear on the Income Statement, and assets (for example, machinery) which will appear on the Balance Sheet. The credit column is a list of the capital and the liabilities which will appear on the Balance Sheet, and the sales or revenues which will appear on the Income Statement.

The only figure still missing is the closing inventory. On 6 January the business counts and values its inventory and determines it is $1,000. As this is an asset, we would have to debit the Inventory account. The credit entry goes to the Income Statement as that is really a part of the double-entry system. The original title of the Income Statement, which is still used in some parts of the world, is the Profit and Loss Account.

We can now draw up our Income Statement, putting in our closing inventory amount. This is a credit amount, so we show it as a deduction from the purchases (to calculate our cost of sales as explained in Chapter 3). As the Income Statement is part of the double-entry bookkeeping system, we completely close the accounts involved (e.g., revenue, purchases, expenses) by either debiting them or crediting them. The corresponding debit or credit entry is to the Income Statement. In other words, those accounts that reflect the financial performance of the business over a period are closed completely when the period is ended.

When you are preparing the financial statements from the trial balance, it is helpful to tick every figure on the trial balance. Every amount should be ticked once and once only.

Income Statement for the period to 6 January

	$	$
Revenue		9,000
Purchases	6,500	
Less closing inventory	1,000	5,500
Gross profit		3,500
Rent		1,000
Net profit		2,500

We can now prepare the Balance Sheet, ticking the remaining amounts on the trial balance. There are three things to bear in mind:

1. The Income Statement is really an account and part of the double entry. It has a net profit and this amount is a credit balance and will be shown on the Balance Sheet as retained profit.
2. The closing inventory was not on the Trial Balance but was an additional note. You have ticked the figure once when it was used on the Income Statement, but you can tick it again as it will be used on the Balance Sheet.
3. The Balance Sheet is not part of the double-entry bookkeeping system. It is a list of the "balances" at the end of the financial period, and those balances will be carried forward to the start of the next financial period.

Balance Sheet as at 6 January

	$	$
Non-current assets		
Machinery		3,000
Current assets		
Inventory	1,000	
Accounts receivable	6,000	
Cash	9,000	16,000
Total assets		**19,000**

Capital	10,000
Retained profit	2,500
Loan	2,500
Accounts payable	4,000
Capital and liabilities	**19,000**

This is only a simple example, but you can appreciate how the recording of transactions by using double entry has advantages. It is a logical system and for every debit there must be a credit and vice versa. A full record of all transactions is maintained. The Trial Balance demonstrates that you have maintained the system properly, although there are errors that can arise that are not shown by the Trial Balance. If the Trial Balance does not balance, you know you have made a mistake in your original double-entry bookkeeping.

The final advantage of the Trial Balance is that it allows you to draw up the Income Statement and the Balance Sheet.

Appendix B

Answers to Chapter Questions

Chapter 1

1. a
2. a
3. c
4. d
5. a, b, and c
6. b
7. a
8. c
9. a
10. d

Chapter 2

1. b and d
2. d
3. a and b
4. a and c
5. a
6. d
7. b

8. All
9. a and c
10. d

Chapter 3

1. c
2. c and d
3. a and d

4. Opening inventory 1,000
   Purchases 4,000
   5,000
   Closing inventory 500
   Cost of sales 4,500

5. Opening inventory 100
   Purchases 400
   500
   Closing inventory 50
   Cost of sales 450

6. Opening inventory 50
   Purchases 680
   730
   Closing inventory 210
   Cost of sales 520

7. Opening inventory 1,020
   Purchases 10,210
   11,230
   Closing inventory 1,550
   Cost of sales 9,680

8. Sales 600
   Cost of sales 450
   Gross profit 150

9. Sales 17,000
   Cost of sales 13,500
   Gross profit 3,500
   Total expenses 3,250
   Net profit 250

10. Opening inventory 14,960
    Purchases 163,570
    178,530

Closing inventory	18,815
Cost of sales	159,715

Chapter 4

1. c
2. a
3. $15,000 and $105,000. Annual depreciation charge for five years = $21,000
4. b
5. d
6. a and c
7. c
8. b
9. c
10. c

Chapter 5

1. b and d
2. a
3. b
4. a and c
5. a and c
6. a
7. a
8. a
9. d
10. b

Chapter 6

1. c
2. No, because value in use is higher than carrying amount
3. The value in use is approximately $546,000, so the machine is impaired
4. a
5. d
6. a and b
7. c
8. b
9. c
10. b and d

Chapter 7

1. b
2. d
3. All
4. a
5. a
6. c
7. All
8. a
9. a
10. b

Chapter 8

1. a
2. a
3. c
4. b
5. c
6. d
7. a
8. a
9. b
10. b

Chapter 9

1. c
2. d
3. d
4. a
5. b
6. c
7. b
8. c
9. c
10. b

Chapter 10

1. a
2. d
3. c
4. b
5. a
6. c
7. a
8. c
9. a
10. c

Chapter 11

1. c
2. c
3. c
4. d
5. a
6. a and d
7. c
8. d
9. b and d
10. c

Chapter 12

1. d
2. b
3. a and c
4. b
5. a
6. b and c
7. c
8. b
9. b
10. c

Chapter 13

1. a
2. c
3. b
4. b
5. d
6. c
7. c
8. c
9. b
10. d

Chapter 14

1. c
2. b
3. a
4. c
5. d
6. a
7. a
8. b
9. c
10. c

Index

accounting
 concepts 9
 definition 2
 equation 86
 regulations 7
accounting estimates 48, 161, 162,
 165–167, 171, 177, 179, 254
accounting policies 5, 44, 46, 48, 49,
 161–163, 165–167, 177, 179, 254, 266,
 275, 276, 290, 292, 294, 296, 335
accounting standard
 definition 2
 structure 43
accruals assumption 12, 57, 60, 62, 76,
 87
acid test 330, 331, 334, 348
acquired intangible assets 143
acquisition and mergers 228
active market 144, 214–217, 224
adjusting events 161, 168–170, 177, 178
agriculture 48, 254, 261, 269
Aluminium Corporation of China 46,
 47

amortised cost 213, 215, 216, 219
asset
 change in useful life 102
 definition 90
 revaluation 47, 97, 102
associate company 244, 251
AstraZeneca 56, 231
available-for-sale financial assets 47, 213,
 215, 216, 224, 278, 280

bad and doubtful debts 81, 123
balance sheet, *see* Statement of Financial
 Position
BHP Billiton 267
biological assets 44, 140, 253, 261, 262,
 269, 271, 277
bonus issue of shares 285
bonus payments 298
books of account 4
borrowing costs 48, 85, 104–107, 110
brands 140, 142, 143, 146
British Airways 189, 227
business acquisition 231, 314